AF228285

ON RETIREMENT

On Retirement

How Aging Is Transforming American Lives

Daniel Horowitz

New York University Press

New York

NEW YORK UNIVERSITY PRESS
New York
www.nyupress.org

Library of Congress Cataloging-in-Publication Data
Names: Horowitz, Daniel, 1938– author
Title: On retirement : how aging is transforming American lives / Daniel Horowitz.
Description: New York : New York University Press, [2026] |
Includes bibliographical references and index.
Identifiers: LCCN 2025024119 (print) | LCCN 2025024120 (ebook) |
ISBN 9781479841219 hardback | ISBN 9781479841233 ebook |
ISBN 9781479841240 ebook other
Subjects: LCSH: Aging—Social aspects—United States | Older people—United States—
Social conditions | Retirement—United States
Classification: LCC HQ1064.U5 H66 2026 (print) | LCC HQ1064.U5 (ebook) |
DDC 305.260973—dc23/eng/20250615
LC record available at https://lccn.loc.gov/2025024119
LC ebook record available at https://lccn.loc.gov/2025024120

This book is printed on acid-free paper, and its binding materials are chosen for strength and durability. We strive to use environmentally responsible suppliers and materials to the greatest extent possible in publishing our books.

The manufacturer's authorized representative in the EU for product safety is Mare Nostrum Group B.V., Mauritskade 21D, 1091 GC Amsterdam, The Netherlands. Email: gpsr@mare-nostrum.co.uk.

Manufactured in the United States of America

10 9 8 7 6 5 4 3 2 1

Also available as an ebook

To members of the two groups that have sustained me as we all age:

The Boston-Cambridge Bookies and The Huntington Library Snowbirds Seminar

CONTENTS

When in 1998 I published *Betty Friedan and the Making of "The Feminine Mystique": The American Left, the Cold War, and Modern Feminism*, I devoted only one paragraph to her book *The Fountain of Age* (1993).[1] I was focusing principally on the first half of her life, and as I approached my sixtieth birthday, I had little interest in old age. As I grew older, aging and longevity increasingly captured my interest. In the fall of 2022, I began to think about a book on retirement, aging, and longevity—already retired for ten years, six months before my eighty-fifth birthday, and less than a year before I would celebrate my sixtieth wedding anniversary with my wife, the historian Helen L. Horowitz.

As I researched and wrote, my own situation and those of friends and family members close to me were continually on my mind. To be sure, for the time being, I could keep worries about myself at bay. For more than a dozen years, I had seen my primary care physician mainly for routine health matters and had published a book every two years. I was on the verge of outliving my parents—my father died at eighty-six and my mother on her eighty-seventh birthday—and after all, I told myself, what ended their lives were conditions I did not have. I am a very present-minded and emotionally optimistic (and/or well-defended) person, and dying and death were almost never on my mind (an afterlife never), though on occasion I feared a medicalized existence.

Of course, there were moments when what I was researching deeply moved and on occasion frightened me. At a time when Helen and I were thinking of no longer aging in place, I read a book that managers of retirement communities rely on to handle people like us. I noted that the author, without mentioning how Elisabeth Kübler-Ross described five stages of grief in her 1969 book *On Death and Dying*, applied that model to what happened to people after they entered Continuing Care Retirement Communities (CCRCs). When I encountered what Erik H. Erikson and Joan M. Erikson said about disease and death as they themselves aged or the story about the end of Nora Ephron's life, I felt painfully moved. More recently, in December 2024, I watched on Netflix episode 5 of *A Man on the Inside*, which focuses on how the retired professor Charles (played by Ten Danson) becomes a resident of a San Francisco retirement community on a gig to solve a case of stolen jewelry. He encounters Elliott Haverhil (John Getz), who bristles at his doctor's "positivity" when he confirms a diagnosis of prostate cancer. And, remembering how he could not protect his late wife from dementia, Charles tries (largely unsuccessfully) to help Gladys Montrose (Susan Rutman) with her serious cognitive problems before, we learn, she disappears into the dreaded memory care facility. As time went on, I increasingly confronted similar challenges of aging among dear friends and family members. As one observer noted, retirement has three phases: "go go, slow go, and no go."[2] In the years I researched and wrote this book, I painfully confronted the deaths of dear friends and family members—especially a member of the Huntington Library Snowbirds Seminar, Barbara Oberg; one of the Boston-Cambridge Bookies, Fred Goldberg; my beloved brother-in-law Len Katz; and my wonderful Smith College colleague Louis Wilson.

As I look back on an early draft of the preface, I am struck by how I insisted that there was little personal about my engagement with the subjects I was focusing on. "I am sure that many readers will suspect this book was a highly personal undertaking," I had written. "Mostly not," I continued as I seem to have reassured myself. "What drove me was much more my work as a professional researcher and writer than as someone worried about my own situation and prospects. After all, when I began to work on this project, I was more worried about climate change, the war in Ukraine, and the rise of authoritarianism than about my own situation. Healthy and financially secure so far, I had achieved more than modest success in replacing the pleasures of sociability of college life with those possible in retirement."

To the rescue came folks who wanted something more honest, genuine, and personal. One reader whom New York University Press's editor Clara Platter secured urged me to pay more attention to something I largely avoided discussing precisely at a time when I was talking to friends about what they encountered: "the specific challenges of mental health and cognitive decline, which are crucial aspects of aging that affect quality of life and independence."[3] Another reader, noting my insistence that my interest in these topics was not personal, nonetheless "found the moments where Horowitz speaks from a personal voice to be some of the most compelling. To my mind—and Horowitz may well disagree— what sets this book apart from others is the standpoint from which it is written, coming as it does from a professional historian with expertise in the cultural history of the twentieth-century United States and a retired person sifting through this culture of old age and contemplating how his own experience is changing over time. It is the sense of skin in the game that underlays some of the most insightful analysis. Bringing forward more of the personal voice would be worth considering."[4]

Stephen Katz, a distinguished Canadian social scientist whose work focuses on aging, urged me on along similar lines. "One of the mainstays of critical gerontological literature," he wrote as he helped provide arguments that easily enabled me to overcome any reluctance to break with the accepted scholarly detachment, "is highlighting the voices of older people, which are too often muted, even in their own works. And there's a difference between the personal being a narrative of self-identification, and the personal being a contextualizing and reflexive exercise of situating the writer in their own time and place, how their words and ideas are living testaments to a particular set of issues." After all, he noted perceptively, "why would somebody write about a subject like aging with scant reference to their own aging and its challenges?"[5]

Inevitably, as I carried out research, I quickly realized how issues of aging seemed omnipresent well beyond my life and the lives of the people I know and love. A cover of *The New Yorker* in early October 2023 featured a drawing of Donald Trump, Mitch McConnell, Nancy Pelosi, and Joe Biden uneasily navigating with walkers. In a little over a year, Trump was headed back to the White House, McConnell and Pelosi had given up their leadership positions in the Senate and House, and following a problematic performance in a debate, Biden relinquished his quest for a second presidential term. Four weeks later, the magazine printed two protesting letters. In one of them, Jerrold Hirsch, writing from Kirksville, Missouri, criticized Barry Blitt's image of four "enfeebled" political figures as "an example of both ableism and ageism." Emphasizing "the assumption that those who use assistive technology to walk are no longer competent," and then, referring to Franklin Delano Roosevelt,

Hirsch noted that "a very famous President used a wheelchair to accomplish the things that he did."[6]

Once Google's algorithm coordinated searches on my computer and postings on my iPhone, other references to the challenges of aging flooded my way. For example, were I to subscribe to *The Economist*, I could read Geoffrey Carr's September 25, 2023, article titled "Slowing Human Ageing Is Now the Subject of Serious Research." I read the Editorial Board's September 10, 2023, opinion piece in *The New York Times* asking, "Can Americans Age Gracefully?" It focused on how "an aging America needs . . . an honest conversation about growing old. Safer streets. Sustainable caregiving. Flexible housing. Entrepreneurs pay attention. To see and be seen."[7] As friends and family members heard what I was doing, they too weighed in. My son Ben, a computer scientist, coached me on how to use ChatGPT to get a list of popular and scientific books on longevity. Having read my chapter "A Short History of Longevity," Susan Matt, a historian of emotions, appreciated my "observation about the shift in the longevity studies from descriptive to prescriptive." And another historian, John Demos, recommended that I read his 1978 essay "Old Age in Early New England." There, he noted, "for historians, among others, old age is a time whose idea has come."[8]

I finished drafting the introduction of this book in early March 2023. That coincided with fierce battles in France as millions around the nation took to the streets to protest the attempt by Emmanuel Macron to force the raising of the retirement age from sixty-two to sixty-four. Macron and his allies pointed to the fact life expectancy and the cost of funding retirement had increased dramatically since the present system was put in place soon after the end of World War II, "part of a series of celebrated social measures intended to help bind the fractured country together," wrote the *New York Times* reporter Catherine Porter. The fact that people were living longer bumped up against the declining number of working-age citizens, something that threatened the passionately embraced generational interdependence. Yet resistance to change, Porter reported, "springs from a deep sense of what defines France." Those who took to the streets or put pen to paper (or the online equivalent) celebrated "a society that cherishes retirement and reveres a generous balance between work and leisure perhaps more than any other Western industrial country." In the United States, Social Security underwrote economically insecure retirements. In contrast, "the average French pensioner," Porter noted, "is richer than the general population, accessing roughly 75 percent of their previous earnings with fewer expenses." What was at stake was the liberty to enjoy life, the equality of social conditions, and the fraternity that the social contract underwrote. "Life is not just about working," remarked a fifty-eight-year-old money manager who was participating in his fifth protest in Paris, "dressed in a striped prisoner's uniform, carrying a ball and chain, and wearing a sign that said, 'Prisoner of Work.'"[9]

At the same time, retirement, longevity, and aging reverberated across the Atlantic in much different ways. Movies offered varied and mostly optimistic renditions. Social scientists and scientists amassed data from which they drew conclusions and then made recommendations. People snapped up books on how to retire and how to live longer lives. Scholars developed theories to understand longevity. Researchers at institutions—including the American Association of Retired Persons (AARP), the National Institute on Aging, and university and corporate think tanks—studied the implications of public policies and private decisions. Elderly people and their family members wrestled with the choice between retirement communities and aging in place, if, as was often the case, health and financial challenges prevailed. Gradually I realized how much work there was to do as I aged, no longer gainfully employed as a professor but not yet retired as a scholar.

So here I was reading advice books, not to figure out how to retire successfully but how to write successfully about retirement itself. Among them was Michelle Pannor Silver's 2018 *Retirement and Its Discontents: Why We Won't Stop Working, Even If We Can*. A sociologist, Silver focused on how five groups—medical doctors, CEOs, professors, elite athletes, and homemakers—experienced retirement. As a cultural historian, I focused attention on all five, but as an emeritus professor, I paid attention to my own tribe of people, who, Silver reveals, had an easier time of it than the others. "In academia," she notes, "the boundaries between work and nonwork are particularly blurred." Although some professors resisted retirement, many of them went on with their lives much as before. As was true for those who worked in place, "retirement represents not a departure but a continuation of their life's work."[10] That described me, and here I was scribbling away.

Introduction

The History, Political Economy, and Demography of Aging

In 1980, the scholar William Graebner published *A History of Retirement: The Meaning and Function of an American Institution, 1885–1978*, which was then the best book on the subject's history. In 2023, forty-five years later, his son Bennett S. Graebner was one of the show runners and the executive producer of ABC's *The Golden Bachelor*. The first season featured seventy-two-year-old Gerry Turner. Six years a widow, fit, handsome, and reliant on a hearing aid, he was the central feature in the drama involving the prolonged process of his choosing a wife from among several dozen women. Writing in *The New York Times Magazine*, Mireille Silcoff described them as "typically lithe, sexy, and hyperactive; some wear stilettos to breakfast, along with tube tops and hot pants and all manner of plunging décolletage; there are boobs everywhere, often huge ones." Two months and two days after the show premiered, Turner decided to propose to Theresa Nist, who had worked for twenty years as a financial services executive and had six grandchildren, triple the number of Turner's. *The Golden Wedding* followed on January 4, 2024, and a divorce ensued three months after, following their April 12 announcement, on television of course, on their impending split.[1]

Much changed from what William the father reported on in his book to when Bennett the son helped produce the episodes. To begin with, as Silcoff notes, "older women are not what they used to be." Instead of highlighting the golden years as distinctive, the episodes provide opportunities for the contestants to participate in a "tight-and-toned show in which success involves being able to repeat Chapter 3 for as long as possible," emphasizing as it does that the focus is on "working extremely hard to remain the same as you were when you were younger (or maybe even more fabulously youthy)."[2] Other things have changed over the long historical run, not the least of which is that great numbers of people are living longer and more healthily. This is so even though the story immediately following Silcoff's was titled "Hadley Vlahos Wants Us to Try to Make Peace with Death, Not to Extend Life." Vlahos, who has 1.7 million TikTok followers, wrote a best-selling book about her "tragic, graceful, earthy, and at times apparently supernatural" time as a hospice nurse. A footnote to the story noted a breakthrough that might enable people to live to 120 by drinking "drug cocktails that get rid of senescent cells." When asked about such extensions of life, Vlahos responded that she had no desire to live that long and had "never met someone 100 or older who still wants to be alive." The rest of the magazine's features focused on the dangers of climate change.[3]

Historians have focused on race, class, and gender as analytic categories. However, age also matters; as Corrine T. Field and Nicolas L. Syrett note, it is "both a biological reality and a social construction," compelling our attention as scholars and citizens.[4] In a nation that has often celebrated youth, the lives of seniors have not always been a matter of public and scholarly interest, whether defined as a problem to be solved or an opportunity to be celebrated.[5] In the United States in recent years, retirement and longevity have increasingly captured considerable interest. At various moments, I use these terms (as well as "the aged," "seniors," "senior citizens," "older people," "olders," "the elderly," or "the elders") interchangeably because as phenomena experienced and portrayed, they are so closely related.[6] It is not hard to figure out why the related issues command such attention from varied sources. As the 2024 election approached, voters initially faced a choice between candidates who were well past the widely accepted retirement age of sixty-five. Every day approximately ten thousand baby boomers retire. Publishers, authors, filmmakers, and scientists rush to take advantage of opportunities that this demographic transformation provides. Ordinary citizens and their political representatives worry whether Social Security, Medicare, and Medicaid are adequately funded. Movie makers, government officials, people involved in think tanks and interest groups, activists, real estate developers, entrepreneurs, motivational speakers, and scholars enter the fray with their robust and varied interventions. Seniors, their friends, and family members worry about what the future holds with regard to finances and health. People also wonder whether it will be possible to age in place or must move into housing provided for seniors. For me and others, aging raises profound issues: fear of cognitive and physical decline, disease, and death in a nation that often celebrates youthfulness and progress. Alzheimer's will inflict about a third of those eighty-five and older.[7]

This book offers multifaceted examinations of what creates such intense interest. I explore how and why retirement and longevity—driven by prosperity that has opened opportunities for millions of seniors, by government programs, and by people living longer, some sick and others healthy—have emerged as prominent issues. If for previous generations, illnesses dominated old age, the fortunate many can experience years of creativity and purpose. This is so even though the benefits of healthy and extended lives are far from evenly distributed in a US society where the luckiest, healthiest, and wealthiest have the respect and resources to thrive. For so many, getting older ain't easy, filled as the supposedly golden years are for many with challenges that require adaptability, support from friends and family members, resilience, and often scarce public and private resources. In important and pervasive ways, chronological age has grown less relevant in the lives of elders, while gender, class, and race have become more significant. The ever-increasing importance of science, medicine, and pharmaceuticals has enhanced the power of biomedicalization of aging. And over time, responsibility for caring for older folks has shifted from the family to two opposing locations and in between: the often lonely individual and the larger society as shaped by public policy.

Indeed, many popular films depict the affluent, and virtually all popular advice books have them as their intended audience. Many discussions of longevity—by activists, social scientists, and policy wonks—underscore problems with the many socioeconomic and existential challenges that people encounter as they age. The fact that more people are living longer and remain active and healthy is among the factors that underscore how often arbitrary age is as a category. Gerontologists, public policy specialists, and others insist that, as W. Andrew Achenbaum reports, "In the wake of the Longevity Revolution," they "question the utility of *chronological age* in categorizing the potentials and needs that accompany advancing age."[8] The wide range of places where seniors live—from prisons, the streets, and nursing homes to often luxurious 55+ communities, Continuing Care Retirement Communities (CCRCs), and Naturally Occurring Retirement Communities (NORCs)—reveal how social class and ethnic identity powerfully shape choices. Many Americans can aspire to and achieve active and fulfilling lives as they age, but for others, such prospects remain out of reach given racism, inequalities of wealth and income, and physical and cognitive challenges. Sales of advice books and movie viewership reveal a voracious hunger for, if not happy endings, then at least postretirement beginnings—again more available to some than to others. This is also true of the scientific work whose aim is to extend how long many of us can live. Underwritten by government agencies and venture capitalists and carried out in university and corporate labs, this rapidly emerging field promises that, before long, millions of Americans will live, if not as long as Methuselah's nine hundred years, then well past one hundred. But only if they take advantage of time-consuming and expensive medical interventions.

In addition to using a critical eye to explore all the ways retirement and longevity command so much attention today in the United States, this book offers an examination of the ways the emphasis on self-governance rather than reliance on government or communal support results in dramatic inequalities in how Americans experience retirement and long lives. "Welcome to the do-it-yourself system of retirement planning in America!" the economist Teresa Ghilarducci writes at the very beginning of *How to Retire with Enough Money and How to Know What Is Enough* (2015), before going on to document how so many Americans face precarious situations in retirement. "Forty-nine percent of middle-class Americans," she notes as she draws on statistical evidence, "are on track to be living in or near poverty after they quit working. They'll have a food budget of about $5 a day." Though "bookstore shelves are all but collapsing under the weight of financial-planning books," she correctly points out that the crisis is a problem not only for individuals but for society. After all, she observes with clever exaggeration, with the shift from defined benefit pensions to defined contribution plans, Americans are now in a "Wild West" like what you could "expect if we were all asked to cut our own hair, install our own toilets, and do our own electrical wiring," as a result of which "there'd be an awful lot of bowl haircuts, flooded bathrooms, and smoldering houses out there."[9]

Several factors have helped make retirement and longevity such prominent issues in the United States since 1945, as seen so abundantly in newspaper coverage, movies, institutional lives, and discussions of public policy. The first is the aging of baby boomers, who now constitute one-fifth of the population, with significant numbers of them retiring daily. This silver tsunami has tremendous implications for the housing and job markets, to say nothing of its impact on the federal budget. Also powerfully in play are dramatic increases in life expectancy that have enabled tens of millions of Americans to live not only longer but more healthily. A related issue is that for many seniors, the long and sustained prosperity of the post–World War II United States has greatly expanded options of where and how to live. Finally, the role of the federal government and, to a lesser extent, state and local ones has shaped lives, often in ways that enhance opportunities for how elders live. To be sure, and not surprisingly, not all Americans have reaped the benefits of longer and healthier lives, prosperity, and government policies.[10]

Only after World War II did widespread life expectancy begin to surpass age sixty-five. In 1950, about 7 percent of Americans reached that marker, a figure that now stands at about three times that percentage. Discussing life expectancy historically is tricky, principally because throughout the nineteenth century so many women died giving birth to children and newborns perished as a result of childhood illnesses. If we do not count these threats to the lives of mothers and young children, then on the surface not much has changed since the mid-nineteenth century. From then to recently, the average life expectancy of those who survived early dangers hovered in the mid- to high seventies. Yet, calculated from birth, change is dramatic, rising from thirty-five in 1865 to just short of eighty recently, which along with other factors has resulted in a greater number of older people in the US.[11] The US Census Bureau predicts that by 2060, the figure will increase to eighty-six, albeit there are chronological bumps and demographic variations along the way. Already, as Jonathan Rauch writes, "the average American 65-five-year old can expect to live another 18.5 years. . . . The mortality rate of 80-year-old women in 2019 was the same as that of 68-year-old women in 1933. An American child born today has a better-than-even chance of living to age 95."[12]

Several factors account for these changes. First came elemental advances in sanitation, especially the disposition of bodily waste and the provision of clean water. Next were immunizations for diseases such as scarlet fever and typhoid, followed by the development of antibiotics. Over time, to this were added the success of programs for other vaccinations, stopping smoking, and reducing obesity as well as the spreading adoption of exercise programs. And, of course, medical advances lowered the rate of death from cancer and heart disease, the most common and lethal threats to life.

The growth in the US economy has also been a powerful force. The Great Depression lasted for a decade beginning in 1929. That changed with mobilization for World War II, which preceded a formal declaration of war and then intensified with the nation's entry into war in Europe and Asia. Although postwar affluence spread unevenly throughout the nation, its impact on the lives of many seniors was nonetheless profound. Adjusted for inflation in 2017 dollars, the gross domestic product (GDP), the widely accept measurement of the size of the US economy, stood at $1,191 billion in 1929 and grew to $22,375 billion in 2023. Adjusted for inflation and with dividends reinvested, $1,000 placed in stocks in the Standard and Poor Index in 1939 by 2024 would be worth almost a third of a million dollars, a factor that enabled many people to enjoy financial security as they aged. Someone born in 1942 who purchased a typical house in 1967 at age twenty-five for $24,000 and then retired at age sixty-five in 2007 would have a residence worth $310,000—adjusted for inflation, at a still impressive figure just above half that amount. If amply employed with robust benefits, such a retiree might well have significant income from a retirement account and Social Security as well as health care expenses covered by Medicare. What such figures about the growth of GDP, the prices of stocks and houses, and federal programs (as well as dramatic improvements in medical care) only partially hide is the impact of prosperity on retirees. These changes provided elders with medical advances that extend life, larger residences with improved climate control and more conveniences, safer automobiles, the possibility of living in a variety of retirement communities, enhanced ways of interacting with friends and family members, and more varied recreational opportunities.

Institutional imperatives and public policies have played increasingly powerful roles in shaping how Americans live as they retire and age. As William Graebner notes, in the twenty-five years after 1940, "the leading advocates and beneficiaries of retirement—corporations, labor unions, and insurance companies—became increasingly aggressive in marketing retirement as a consumable commodity."[13] Well into the nation's history, county and town governments shaped the conditions under which the indigent among the elderly lived. They resided, along with other destitute people, in workhouses or poorhouses, punitive institutions that the historically informed journalist Erin Blakemore has described as "bare bones facilities designed to make poverty seem even less attractive."[14] Before the Great Depression of the 1930s, on the federal level, the most important relevant government activity involved providing pensions for government employees and their widows and children. Earlier, several colonies offered pensions to soldiers disabled in battles against Indigenous peoples. What followed were provisions by both the colonies and the Continental Congress covering those who fought in the American Revolution and then throughout the nineteenth century funding for those injured in battle and facing retirement. Toward the end of the nineteenth century, the federal government and some states began to offer pensions for some civilian employees as well. In 1910, the administration of President William Howard Taft promoted private pension systems, which by 1920, though relatively rare, had begun to spread. Especially after 1920, those for federal employees and many state ones were systematized on solid ground.[15]

The year 1935 marks a major, formative turning point in the role of the US government in the lives of retirees. At the time, the United States was the only industrialized country without systematic, government provisions for social welfare, something that Germany had pioneered in the 1880s. In 1933, responding to the dire conditions of the Great Depression, Dr. Francis Townsend had proposed what became the wildly popular Townsend Plan, which, funded by a sales tax, would provide every citizen over sixty with $200 a month, about $4,700 in today's dollars. In response to many factors, FDR proposed and Congress passed the Older Workers Pension Act, soon retitled the Social Security Act of 1935, legislation that disadvantaged women and African Americans. If Townsend had linked provisions to citizenship, the legislation connected benefits to employment, funded as they were by a payroll tax to which employers and employees contributed equally. However limited and imperfect initially, over time Social Security transformed how scores of millions of Americans experienced old age. It made that period of life, traditionally personal and familial, increasingly social. For decades beginning in the mid-1930s, it enabled many older men to leave the paid workforce in great numbers. Its Old-Age Assistance provision was a means-tested welfare system. In contrast, its Old-Age Insurance provision, what we know today as Social Security, made it possible for many elders to live in one-generation households, freed from reliance on their children. As the historian Brian Gratton remarks in his history of the elderly in Boston, which focuses not on attitudes but on lived experiences, Social Security brought about "an unprecedented reconstruction of the relationship between the state and its citizens and the relationship between young and old." Eventually, federal legislation concerning retirement and aging made setting "generations against each other" more likely and made "older people vulnerable to the complaints of taxpayers," one of many factors that fed the flames of ageism.[16]

Though the 1935 act extended coverage to widows and children, in other ways it was notably restricted, a condition that post–World War II legislation rectified to some extent. Among the groups not originally covered were all agricultural laborers and domestics as well as some professionals such as librarians, social workers, teachers, and nurses. This meant that slightly more than one in four white employees had no coverage along with almost two-thirds of African Americans, who were not covered because so many of them worked on farms or in private homes. Notably, when the 1935 legislation established sixty-five as the retirement age, the average life expectancy for Americans was sixty for men and sixty-three for women. Although many people who survived the health dangers of childbirth or childhood lived much longer, relatively few retirees collected benefits, and when they did, they earned little more than the minimum amount needed to live on.

Federal legislation established precedents that have shaped US public policy since then. With funding coming from employees and employers, Social Security legislation focused on retirees as workers and not citizens. More specifically, because so many of the workers in question had been those employed in large industrial organizations, they were mainly urban, white, and male. In addition, with future benefits based on past incomes, the persistence of historically embedded financial advantages was built into the economics of retirement. Moreover, as the historian James Chappel writes, federal programs "were designed to pay for the lives of healthy people with short-term hospital needs, and not people with chronic disabilities, many of whom require expensive long-term care." Without public provisions for long-term care, care for the old and frail required labor of "women who are either unpaid, as family members, or poorly paid as home health aides or nursing home employees."[17] The long-term results of these patterns were mixed. On the one hand, white able-bodied men who had steady employment in large organizations benefited more than did people of color, older women, the disabled, and those who were sporadically employed. On the other hand, especially in the postwar world, the approximately one-third of the federal budget dedicated to protecting the income and health of elders dramatically and substantially improved the economic and psychological well-being of older Americans. This was so even though beginning in the 1970s, slower and uneven economic growth, political divisiveness, and the rightward shift in US politics meant the erosion of some of the dramatic, life-enhancing economic gains for older Americans that occurred in the third of a century beginning in the mid-1930s.[18]

Indeed, as Chappel has so compellingly shown in his unendingly thoughtful *Golden Years*, there were alternatives to the systems of provisions for older Americans. His book, which offers complementary and helpful treatments of many but not all of the issues that I cover, appeared when I had a reasonably complete book manuscript, However, with one issue, he compelled me to significantly rethink what I had originally written: the paths not taken that might have structured public policy more robustly, especially from the New Deal forward.[19]

Relying on *My Face Is Black Is True: Callie House and the Struggle for Ex-Slave Reparations* by Mary Frances Berry, Chappel recovers an alternative to provisions for retirement that was more expansive and inclusive than the one that legislation from Social Security in 1935 to Medicare thirty years later represented.[20] The formerly enslaved woman Callie House led the Ex-Slave Mutual Relief, Bounty, and Pension Association, founded in 1896 and, at its height, a mass movement with hundreds of thousands of members. Although the association did not claim to provide a model for universal old-age pensions, it nonetheless represented an alternative that would have fundamentally reshaped the lives of older Americans. As Chappel notes, the association advocated "a model of old-age policy that would not discriminate between men and women, and that was designed specifically to reward unwaged labor." Callie House and her associates insisted "that there was no important difference between work in the fields, oriented toward the market, and work in the home, oriented toward familial care and domestic work." One's status as a citizen, rather than as an employee, would reign.[21] Tragically House was imprisoned for mail fraud by a jury composed of white men, and her movement was suppressed; although, given the forces at work in the US in the very late nineteenth century and the early twentieth, the association and its model had no chance of significantly impacting public policy.

Chappel suggestively credits an organization very different from the association with providing the model for retirement policy: the Fraternal Order of Eagles, which counted many US presidents, including FDR, among its members. It was founded in 1898 as many Civil War veterans were approaching their sixties, and its members were white, nativist, and politically conservative or, as its constitution noted, "male members of the Caucasian race."[22] Chappel acknowledges the importance of the Townsend Plan and notes that unlike the industrial employment-based provisions of Social Security, it connected retirement funding to citizenship and promised pensions to all regardless of gender, race, or the kind of pre-retirement work performed. Much was at stake because, as Chappel notes, "Townsend and his movement were the first group in American history to conceive of a vision for modern aging—one that sought to fundamentally rethink the place of the elderly in an industrial society." Yet it was the vision of the Fraternal Order of Eagles, he writes, with its origins in advocacy for pensions for Civil War veterans, that "put old-age poverty and old age-pensions onto the political map" and over time placed "the issue of old-age pensions" on "the political mainstream." And it did so by celebrating "white and virtuous" men, most of whom had worked tirelessly in industrial jobs in urban areas. Though its vision initially had little impact on legislation, it significantly helped "define the problem of 'the aged' for American policymakers, politicians, scholars, and experts."[23] This meant the sidelining, if not exclusion, from public provisions of retirement of women (except for those who might garner benefits via their husbands), people of color, and in general those who labored outside wage-based systems of employment.

The path taken, inspired by the Fraternal Order Eagles and then built into federal legislation beginning in 1935, endured. And in the postwar world, several other, often related changes transformed what retirement and aging meant. Beginning in the 1950s, mandatory retirement became increasingly common, although it came under attack beginning in the 1970s as part of a reconsideration of what retirement meant and involved. The practice became illegal with the passage in 1986 of the Age Discrimination in Employment Act. What postemployment years meant also shifted, a phenomenon promoted by vested interests, with insurance companies in the lead, soon joined by other corporations, some labor unions, and organizations catering to present or future retirees. As Graebner has written, "as work morality yielded to fun morality, as the Protestant ethic lost meaning in a society of consumption rather than production, so would retirement cease to be a wrenching, uprooting experience. . . . In the postindustrial society, retirement was not only natural but welcome." With the AARP leading the way, evocations of individual responsibility came to the fore. In 1965, President Lyndon Johnson signed into law the Social Security Amendments of 1965, which launched the health insurance programs Medicare for seniors and Medicaid for people with limited incomes, including seniors and many others. All this helped transform the meaning of retirement as a key issue in the relationships between workers and employers. Increasingly after 1950, there emerged a vision of that period of people's lives to be savored. As Graebner has written, it replaced disengagement from work with time for the pursuit of leisure. This was a period "to be welcomed and even celebrated," as over time, this stage of life "had become a state of being, apparently benign, classless, and apolitical."[24]

Beginning in the 1930s, federal housing policy also profoundly affected the lives of seniors, although in many cases what it covered was usually not age specific. Bankruptcies, foreclosures, and more generally the collapse of the financial system adversely affected existing and prospective home owners. In response, the Banking Act of 1933, which created the Federal Deposit Insurance Corporation (FDIC), and the National Housing Act of 1944, which established the Federal Housing Administration (FHA), over time helped underwrite markets for private housing for seniors but not just for them. The Hill-Burton Act of 1946 helped finance nursing homes in which some elderly people lived and in ensuing decades provided precedents for financing a variety of retirement communities. Then the 1965 Housing and Urban Development Act, which created the Department of Housing and Urban Development (HUD), contained a series of programs that over time impacted housing for seniors, including rent subsidies for the elderly, provisions for affordable housing, and long-term care residences for seniors. Later came a series of Older Americans Reauthorization Acts, which contained several provisions that enabled the elderly to reside more independently in a variety of settings, including their own homes and long-term care institutions.[25]

Long life expectations, prosperity, and the impact of the federal government—all of these are important. Yet all is not so well in retirementland. There is a considerable contrast between the often pessimistic socioeconomic and health data about retirement, on the one hand, and on the other, how so many of the popular how-to books and media portray aging. To begin with, there is uncertainty about life expectancy, something experienced not only on the individual level but also nationally. Indeed, COVID-19 lowered that figure, especially for African American and Latino citizens.[26] One study, published in 2021, revealed that both groups experienced reductions in life expectancy at rates three to four times greater than for whites. This meant, its authors noted, that COVID "is expected to reverse over 10 years of progress made in closing the Black-White gap in life expectancy and reduce the previous Latino mortality advantage by over 70%."[27] Similarly, although all seniors face the possibility of having serious illnesses that adversely impact their lives as they age, the risk is greater for those living in poverty and for members of some minority groups.[28]

Then there are the connected issues of loneliness and the fraying of social connections. That families are becoming smaller is among the factors that strain intergenerational connections. Children move to places distant from their parents. Rates of divorce and single-family parenthood rise. Many factors undermine the power of local communities to provide connective tissues among their residents. Online shopping, lowered attendance at religious institutions, and declining membership in labor unions diminish opportunities to see old friends and meet new ones. Two books explore the impacts of these changes: Robert D. Putman's *Bowling Alone: The Collapse and Revival of American Community*

(2000) and Marc J. Dunkleman's *The Vanishing Neighbor: The Transformation of American Community* (2014).

Historically and comparatively, the United States has been and remains an incredibly prosperous nation. Yet, in addition to how unevenly the benefits of affluence are spread, there are ominous signs that all either is not or will not be well. Between 1950 and 1978, there were at least twelve years when GDP raced ahead by 5 percent or more, and in 1950, that figure was 8.7 percent. Since then, the nation achieved the growth rate of 5 percent only twice, in 1984 and 2021, in the latter case because of the significant easing of the consequences of the COVID shutdown.[29] The United States has had an annual budget deficit every year for a decade, a figure that reached $1.7 trillion in 2023. The nation's debt now exceeds $37 trillion, interest on which accounts for 17 percent, or $357 billion, annually in federal spending. Both any slowdown in the economy's growth and the burden of the national debt may adversely impact the ability of the federal government to protect seniors in their retirement.

I cannot remember when I first encountered the word "precarity" and why it is preferable, if it actually is, to the word "precariousness," but precarity certainly describes the conditions that many seniors encounter.[30] All face the existential uncertainties of their futures, and many will encounter more mundane challenges than death and dying. The socioeconomic data for the United States is quite clear. Substantial numbers of Americans, a figure perhaps in the range of 60 to 70 percent, encounter financial precarity as they age. This means that though for now I have the luxury of writing about aging, many of my fellow citizens do not have the luxury of celebrating longevity when daily life is a struggle, often marked by precarious finances and health.

Let me count the ways. Significant financial uncertainty plagues tens of millions in retirement. Having spent decades without socking away enough money while in the workforce, many retirees face uncertainty driven by inflation, turmoil in financial markets, and uncertain public policies. COVID increased threats to the lives and health of millions and both exposed and intensified problems that imperiled the well-being and availability of health care workers. Those who rent their domiciles or seek to buy a home run into a tough housing market. As people age, they encounter threats to their ability to protect their health and health care. Medicare and Medicaid do not cover everything, including some wildly expensive prescription drugs. A recent study by the Bureau of Labor Statistics revealed that in addition to almost $5,000 that the average household headed by people sixty-five and older spent on health insurance, they paid almost $1,000 for drugs and medical supplies. Then there is the problem that the nation has no adequate system that covers long-term care for elders.[31] More generally, the future of government provisions for the health care system is far from certain. Unless Congress more adequately funds Medicare, before long there will not be sufficient money for full benefits. Recently, many states began to make significant numbers of people ineligible for Medicaid benefits, and as I write, federal legislation threatens more cuts to Medicaid. A crucial turning point in the history of federal programs for elders came in the 1980s, in the transition from what Robert H. Binstock (a cousin of my wife and our dear friend who died at age seventy-six a year after these words were published) called "compassionate ageism" to "intergenerational conflict" driven by the rightward shift in US politics during the presidency of the Ronald Reagan, the rising costs of Social Security and Medicare, and the image of the "greedy geezer."[32]

Consequently, tens of millions of retirees experience grave uncertainty about whether they will have enough money to live decent lives. Pensions provided by employers that promised a defined benefit and that usually included inflation protection were once a principal bedrock for those who were no longer gainfully employed. In the 1980s, increasing numbers of these plans shifted from defined benefit to defined contribution arrangements, such as 401(k) and 403(b) plans, resulting in greater numbers of retires facing increasing financial uncertainty. For folks approaching retirement and actually retired, according to Vanguard, the figures are sobering. For those age fifty-five to sixty-four, $207,874 is the average savings for individuals, with a much lower median figure at $71,168. For those in the next age cohort, sixty-five to seventy-four, the numbers are $232,710 and $70,620.[33] In late 2023, the average monthly Social Security payment was $1,767. According to the Census Burean in 2022, the median household income for seniors was just over $50,000.[34]

Scholars and journalists have explored what such figures mean. Writing in *Harper's Magazine* in August 2014, Jessica Bruder offered a picture not unlike what we see in *Nomadland*, her 2017 book that was made into a movie in 2020. Under the title "The End of Retirement: When You Can't Afford to Stop Working," she insisted that "in an era of disappearing pensions, wage stagnation, and widespread foreclosures, Americans are working longer and leaning more heavily than ever on Social Security." For some, this meant that "surviving the golden years now requires creative lifestyle adjustments"; for "those riding the economy's outermost edge, adaptation may now mean giving up what full-time RV dwellers call 'stick houses' to hit the road and seek work."[35] In December 2023, the *New York Times* reporter Miriam Jordan wrote of how American farmworkers who had neither Social Security nor Medicare faced "retirement without a net."[36] Nor would many of those who were more fortunate have smooth sailing, something highlighted by the title of a Goldman Sachs report on retirement for 2022: "Navigating the Financial Vortex."[37]

Then there were urgent and unaddressed policy issues. Social Security provides modest monthly income to tens of millions of people who are largely dependent on it. The seemingly untouchable third rail of US politics, it is nonetheless something whose future is uncertain. Unless Congress acts decisively, by 2033 Social Security benefits for sixty-six million Americans will be reduced by a figure estimated to range between 23 and 25 percent. Politicians, activists, and scholars have proposed many solutions, but an intriguing one focused on generational dynamics. In the fall of 2023, C. Eugene Steurle of the Brookings Institution and Glenn Kramon of Stanford proposed that funding for both Medicare and Social Security could be placed on more secure bases (and protect the futures of younger citizens) by having seniors work longer, since they were living longer and more healthily than in 1935, when Social Security established the retirement age at sixty-five.[38] In early 2024, the reporter Paula Span focused on a class rather than a generational divide as she highlighted a relatively recent and growing division within the middle class. Members of the more fortunate upper middle class anticipated retirement with reasonable confidence about their financial futures. On the other hand, those in the lower middle class, people with incomes averaging just above $30,000, were not so fortunate. As Span wrote, such a figure may well "portend insecure retirement" and has "disturbing implications for both health and life expectancy." She noted that the Older Workers Retirement Security Task Force had proposed remedies, including ones that would expand and strengthen Social Security.[39]

In late 2023, *The New York Times* devoted considerable editorial and reportorial space in a six-part series titled "Can America Age Gracefully?" It included an editorial, "An Aging America Needs an Honest Conversation About Growing Old," and a photo section titled "An Aging America Needs to See and Be Seen." Members of the Editorial Board insisted that demographic changes contradicted how the United States continued to think of itself as a young country. In less than a dozen years, the aging of the baby boomers would mean the nation would have more citizens over sixty-five than children. This statistic underscored the potential downside of extended longevity. Among the consequences were the exploding costs of funding programs for the elderly, shortages of workers that would result in weaker economic growth, problems businesses would have in adapting, and highly personal challenges to elders and their children regarding living and dying. The piece ended by insisting that "Americans of every generation owe it to themselves and their families to begin asking the question: Is this a challenge we want to handle on our own? Or is it something that we as a society should confront together?"[40]

Popular how-to books, studies of longevity, and media including long books and short TikToks often celebrate the opportunities that long lives in retirement make possible. However, critical assessments serve as counters to such hosannas. Prominent among them is what the anthropologist Sarah Lamb and her colleagues described in her 2017 edited book, *Successful Aging as a Contemporary Obsession*. "This is not another book on how to age successfully," she announces at the very beginning. With historical precedents, the concept of successful aging emerged in the 1980s in the research, writing, and advocacy of government agencies, gerontologists, and popularizers, but it has had an often implicit whiff of revulsion against aging, "resting on a deep North American cultural discomfort with aging, old age, and being old," Lamb writes. It also has reflected a readily apparent set of assumptions about retirement as a masculine project and even more emphatically one shaped by class and race. Above all, Lamb acknowledges that successful aging is part of the neoliberal project that elevates self-governance over the importance of society and government. Thus, what suffuses the successful aging compulsion is "certain understanding of individualist, autonomous personhood, featuring a sense of individual control over one's self and life, as well as the values of agelessness and avoiding oldness."[41] Somewhat parallel is the emergence in the 1980s of critical gerontology. Among others, Carroll L. Estes, Meredith Minkler, and Stephen Katz have questioned how some gerontologists see older people as problematic and as a result have done their best to control them; have minimized how varied the lives of seniors are, shaped as they are by race, class, and gender; and have paid minimal attention to aging as a social construction. Instead, they call for an emphasis on positive intergenerational relationships and a vision of longevity that for all involves complication and for some liberation.[42]

* * *

Here is the road map to what lies ahead. In chapter 1, I explore popular advice books on retirement, ones that, given market conditions, are aimed at those who are sufficiently affluent to have choices about how and where to live. As befits a US political economy that increasingly emphasizes self-government rather than support from the federal government or community, advice literature typically envisions retirement as relying on individual responsibility and is amply confident about how retirees can easily manage their lives once they are no longer working for a living.

With chapter 2, I turn to how scholars have studied the lives of elders as marking a specific phase of life. I focus especially the work of Joan M. Erikson and Erik H. Erikson and a series of studies that collected data and then analyzed the lives of Americans over many decades, into their old age. These include the Genetic Study of Genius (later known as the Terman Study of the Gifted), developed by Lewis Terman at Stanford; the Intergenerational Studies at Berkeley's Institute for Human Development, on which the Eriksons worked, both early on and late in their lives; *Unravelling Juvenile Delinquency* (1950), by the husband-and-wife team of Sheldon and Eleanor Glueck; and by far the most influential and robust longitudinal study of longevity, the Harvard Study of Adult Development, which began in 1937 and continues to this day.

Chapter 3 focuses on a different genre, best-selling books on longevity and its future. They come from authors with varied credentials, from a Nobel laureate to motivational speakers who have moved from one topic to another. These books about living longer range from the research-based analytical to the practical, with stops along the way. With the books significantly based on serious science, I cannot easily judge the legitimacy of their findings. Treating them and others as a cultural historian, I ask why there is such an immense audience that so often reminds us of the long-standing popularity of books, even those informed by science, that rely on hucksterism and positive thinking. Moreover, these publications, along with related materials, provide windows into the intertwined and complicated relationships between science, medicine, venture capitalism, and mass media. There is an incredibly robust market now for these books and the robust protocols they recommend— seen notably in the popularity of the best seller *Outlive: The Science and Art of Longevity*, by Peter Attia.

Chapter 4 examines key institutions relevant to elders, among them the AARP, the Gerontological Society of America, the Gray Panthers, the National Institute on Aging, enterprises that help corporations market to elders, and a variety of centers whose work focuses on retirement and longevity. Here and in so many other considerations of aging, gender plays a prominent and often transformative role.

Chapter 5 focuses on many options for senior housing. Over the course of US history and continuing to this day, most senior citizens have remained in their own homes or resided with younger members of their families. Increasingly since the end of World War II, other options have proliferated, especially for those who are able to afford choices. Driven by government policies, affluence, and greater longevity, they could remain in place and benefit from a wider range of local services or choose from among a variety of recently developed communities, ranging from trailer parks for seniors to luxurious accommodations in communities that offer a wide range of amenities and options. And the less fortunate might end up in custodial care or among the unhoused on the street.

Less institutional and more personal in focus is chapter 6, an examination of how creators of cultural documents present the experiences of living long in and out of retirement. Many texts I examine rely on bromides found so commonly elsewhere. But some—for example, writings by Nora Ephron, May Sarton, and Roz Chast, as well as the Tik-Tok production "Retirement House"—break fresh ground, sometimes painfully and often inventively. Yet, in the end, most examples explore individualistic solutions.

Chapter 7 focuses on how at least since the 1970s, scores, if not hundreds, of films (and many TV shows) have dramatized major issues that people face in retirement. There is one important precursor to these relatively recent onscreen shows, the 1936 movie *Dodsworth*. Some of its major themes reverberated in more recent cinematic renditions, painting as they do often complicated pictures of retirement in the US. In the process, they emphasize the importance of social class and highlight gendered dynamics. Recent films explore other issues, including the attractiveness and problems with retirement communities, as well as the prospect for happiness in retirement, even at death's door. Above all, what dominates Hollywood's vision of what we face is the importance of reconciliation and remembrance.

In the coda, I wonder about the perils and prospects of retirement, aging, and longevity in the US as the twenty-first century advances.

1

Here's How to Retire and Live a Long and Happy Life

There is a seemingly unending number of books advising readers about retirement. I should know. I have read almost two score of them that I bought inexpensively online or took out from a local public library because no respectable university library was likely to have many, if any, of them on its shelves. Even though they offered information that might be useful to me as a retiree, I looked at them principally as a cultural historian. In selecting from a vastly greater number, I relied on lists to which Google led me when I asked for the best or most popular ones.[1] Although popular retirement advice books share much in common, it is useful to think about them along several continuums. One stretches from the almost purely financial to the mostly inspirational. A second travels from the naïve and celebratory at one end to those that recognize constraints retirees face. Then there are the differences between how-to books that draw principally on personal beliefs and experiences and those that rely on data-driven scholarship. Sometimes they refer to economic or health challenges, even though by and large, best-selling how-to books celebrate successful aging. Most authors embrace retirement by emphasizing how exciting it can be. They may well do so because, aware that readers know the challenges that lie ahead, books are trying to inspire readers by emphasizing an abundance of positive possibilities. In addition, as is true in so many other instances, how-to books reflect a shift in the view of old age from a period of rest and deterioration to one of active engagement and possibilities for personal development.

Regardless of genre, it is critically important to remember that in these books the concept of retirement normally involves a transition from a time when one worked for a living, being amply rewarded for many years. Such conditions leave out millions of people. Historically and to a significant extent today, the structural conditions of employment have made retirement profoundly shaped by masculinity, especially that of privileged white men. In so much of US history, as William Graebner and others show, because women worked inside the home or in poorly paid jobs, they could not take advantage of government or corporate provisions for retirement.[2] Historically and even today, women's roles as caregivers and as employees who do not earn as much as their male counterparts significantly shape the conditions under which they live when they leave the paid workforce. As Amber Christ and Tracey Gronniger remark in their 2018 report *Older Women and Poverty*, "Women are the primary caregivers in the United States, both of children and of adults who require caregiving services later in life. As such, women are more likely to take significant time out of the workforce, lowering their ability to both make ends meet and save for retirement."[3] Even if considerable numbers of women can now retire supported by Social Security and pensions, there remain lingering effects that have influenced retirement as a series of conditions shaped by abilities, race, class, and gender.

When, many decades ago, normal retirement age at sixty-five was just shy of normal life expectancy at birth, there was not much of a market for books aimed at retirees. Now, with people working longer and living longer lives and with ten thousand baby boomers retiring daily, authors and publishers hope to attract a robust readership. However, their aim is quite specific—not so much explicitly with regard to gender or race and even more rarely sexual orientation but with socioeconomic class. Because people who struggle economically are unlikely to buy books, especially ones celebrating the choices people will encounter after they stop working for a living, it is hard to find any aimed at people who will battle poverty in retirement or even aimed at members of the struggling lower and middle classes. After all, although the average life expectancy of those who have reached age sixty-five is twenty years, a tremendous number of people thinking about no longer working full-time do not have enough funding to contemplate the presumably ample set of choices they might enjoy. About two-thirds of Americans from their mid-fifties to mid-sixties have retirement accounts with a median value of $134,000.[4] How-to books aim at buyers with much more ample resources, but not at the very wealthy, who do not need inexpensive guidance on planning for retirement or presumably on how to choose among less tangible options. Yet, between the socioeconomic highs and lows, there are enough potential book buyers to stoke the ambitions of authors, literary agents, and publishers. The market for such books is enormous. Joseph F. Coughlin, the director of the Massachusetts Institute of Technology's AgeLab and the author of *The Longevity Economy: Unlocking the World's Fastest Growing, Most Misunderstood Market* (2017), writes about opportunities businesses face worldwide. They are "so enormous," he asserts, that "it's as though a new *continent* were rising out of the sea, filled with more than a billion air-breathing consumers just begging for products that fulfill their demands."[5]

Jane Bryant Quinn's *How to Make Your Money Last: The Indispensable Retirement Guide* (2016) stands out among the books whose focus is mostly on financial issues retirees face. It does so in good measure because of the clarity and authority its author brings to the task, based on her more than forty years as a prominent financial writer who has offered her advice to tens of millions of people through newspapers, magazines, books, television, radio, online venues, and social media. Her book, now in its second edition, covers a wide range of topics—among them Social Security, health insurance, pensions, savings, spending down, investing, housing, life insurance, annuities, and reverse mortgages. Yet, like so many other advice books, it implicitly assumes that those who are reading it have homes, Social Security, investments, and good health—and freedom to choose how to live. It provides more reassurances than warning signs, especially given that it pays little attention to exogenous personal, political, or economic forces that might disrupt or complicate retirement's idyll. As is true for other authors, she often shifts from "we," which includes herself, to "you," members of her intended audience—making clear that she (who was in her late seventies when the first edition of this book appeared), like some but not all of her fellow authors, might gain credibility because she writes as part of the audience she is addressing.[6]

Although Quinn offers sophisticated but accessible financial advice, she could hardly restrain herself from framing what she writes in rhetorically aspirational and naïve terms. As others would do, she remarks that "no sane human being can watch that much television or play that much golf." After all, "A 3G retirement (golf, gossip, and grandchildren)" is insufficient. Initially, she predicts, we would "fling ourselves into leisure as if a great vacation lay ahead. But permanent vacations can get pretty boring." Then, having come to think of retirement "as perhaps the most creative period of your life," you would develop a sense of "social worth" by discovering "new interests, new places, and new friends." In the end, what mattered most, she insists, is that "we need to find a new way of being—a fresh identity, different passions and pastimes, and a deeper involvement with family, community, and friends." She acknowledges that some of her readers would face retirement with difficulty because their health has deteriorated or their marriages have broken up. Yet she more persistently emphasizes what strikes me as an unduly simplistic sense that this phase of life involves bold acts of self-creation and re-birth. Leaving the past behind, you would embark on an "adventure, demanding all of your creativity and force." She ends the final paragraph, which she titles "Your New Life," by insisting that "we let go of who we were and discover who we've become."[7]

Suze Orman's 2020 *The Ultimate Retirement Guide for 50+: Winning Strategies to Make Your Money Last a Lifetime* resembles Quinn's book in important ways. It also comes from someone whose financial advice seems everywhere, including in many widely read books and on PBS stations. Like Quinn, Orman focuses principally on money matters, but at the book's beginning and end, she frames her wisdom with rhetorical inspiration. Yet, if Quinn emphasizes both social relationships and re-birth by leaving the past behind, Orman offers up a highly individualistic version of positive psychology that would enable people to overcome obstacles. Mentioning the possibility of a tragic or painful event such as spouse dying or the stock market crashing, Orman acknowledges that many of her readers experience frustration, fear, and anger. Yet she insists on the importance of "a positive, can-do attitude" that will enable you "to face the future with the strength and conviction that you can handle whatever comes your way," thus making "the so-called golden years truly golden." By teaching lessons that enable us to draw on "our inner strength," adversity could "deliver spiritual riches you never imagined." She calls on readers, whom she identifies as her "warriors," not to "forget that with faith, integrity, and courage, everything is possible." You should live your life, she implores as she nears the book's end with syrupy positivity, not with backward-looking regret but with a forward-looking commitment to "make the most of every day of this precious life" by living "with joy and not fear."[8]

In addition to books like those of Quinn and Orman whose focus is mostly financial, others occupy positions ranging from ones that balance the financial and inspirational to a handful that minimize the importance of planning for retirement and instead celebrate what lies ahead. The title and cover of Ernie J. Zelinski's *How to Retire Happy, Wild, and Free: Retirement Wisdom That You Won't Get from Your Financial Advisor* (2017) capture the spirit of such an extreme. The cover depicts a man holding a book in one hand and a drink in another as he sits on a bike driven by a horse. Inside, Zelinski tells us that his is the number-one best-selling retirement advice book among the twelve thousand written on the subject. And the book amply delivers on what the title and cover promise, in the process making what Quinn and Orman mention briefly the book's prevalent note. Deploying the language of happiness, self-fulfillment, reinvention, letting go of the past, and embracing freedom, Zelinski implores readers to realize "it's up to you to design a lifestyle that is as relaxing and invigorating as you want it to be. . . . Recreating yourself as a person can be challenging, but through patience and positive thinking you can do it." As he approaches the book's ending but the beginning of your new life, he urges you "to make your stay on Earth as close to a heavenly experience as can be. Indeed, Zen masters tell us that there is no sense to waiting for Heaven. Zen says that life lived today is Heaven."[9]

Despite differences along the spectrum from mainly practical to principally hortatory, almost all these books have much in common. Writers claim expertise that ranges from what they learned from their work on their doctorates to insights gleaned from their practical experiences and mundane observations. But they typically describe themselves in terms not unlike what Zelinski offers up, that he is "a best-selling author, prosperity life coach, innovator, professional speaker, and unconventional career expert."[10] Authors rely on stories, aphorisms from famous writers and anonymous sources, scholarly and folk wisdom, and to-do lists, while often leaving space for readers to jot down their reactions and plans.[11] Usually without acknowledging the composition of their target audience, they reach out to people with wealth and income above the US median but below the top 1 or 2 percent. They pay relatively little attention to gender and religion but even less to disabilities, sexuality, race, and ethnicity. They wrestle with the importance of work pre- and post-retirement. Although they write of the importance of social connections and giving back, they more typically celebrate individualism, freedom, and reinvention. The pursuit of meaning and purpose remains uppermost in their recommendations.

The target audience for books offering advice for retirees is different from others in the how-to genre, principally with regard to age. Yet, to a very considerable extent, they offer strikingly familiar bromides in abundance, among them positive thinking, optimism, self-governance, and reassuring strategies. In addition to the familiar deployment of stories, aphorisms, quotes from famous people, and to-do lists, clever turns of phrase and metaphors suffuse these texts. In *Keys to a Successful Retirement: Staying Happy, Active, and Productive in Your Retirement Years* (2020), Fritz Gilbert observes that his "brain somehow grasps onto concepts when they are presented through a metaphor." And the one he relies on is that "Retirement Is Like Baking a Cake." When he left his job in his mid-fifties, after having worked for more than thirty years in the corporate world, he writes, he had already put into practice what he was now preaching—that "just as in baking a cake, retirement requires detailed planning, careful selection of what to include and what to omit, and a process to combine the elements into an end product you can enjoy for as long as it lasts."[12]

Aside from the mundane but important ingredients that enabled Gilbert and his wife to live in a cabin in a small Appalachian town in northern Georgia and drive across the country in their RV to visit family in the Pacific Northwest, as an author he offers other strategies, including twenty-four retirement tips such as "If something interests you, pursue it." He sprinkles his book with aphorisms such as this one from "Author Unknown": "Retirement is wonderful if you have two essentials— much to live on and much to live for."[13] He also points readers to more nourishing ingredients, including books of general interest whose wisdom might well enrich your years in retirement. Among them are *The Second Mountain: The Quest for a Moral Life* (2019) by David Brooks, which urges its readers to move beyond the self-interested careerism of the first mountain in order the climb the second, more moral one, where relationships that transcend selfishness matter. He also recommends *Man's Search for Meaning* (1959), in which Viktor Frankl insisted that what he learned from his years in Nazi concentration camps was the importance of art, beauty, and humor in thriving amid the harshest of circumstances.

Gilbert offers many tricks of the how-to trade but stops short of leaving space for readers to develop their own to-do lists, which other authors do not hesitate to do. An example comes from Patrice Jenkins, who earned a PhD in industrial and organizational psychology from Capella University. At the end of her chapter "Discover What's Missing," in her brief and privately published *What Will I Do All Day? Wisdom to Get You Over Retirement and On with Living!* (2011), she provides space for her readers to "make a list of the nonfinancial benefits of work (ex. Socialization, structure, purpose, a sense of belonging, community, challenges, etc.)."[14]

Obviously, the target audiences for these books do not include poor people and even those precariously in the middle class who are likely to scrape by or are already doing so on modest incomes from Social Security and inadequately funded retirement accounts. Most of them pay little or no attention to those, especially women, who work in low-paid jobs, sometimes compensated off the books. Nor is attention paid to the armies of contingent workers in the contemporary US. Ditto those at the other end of the socioeconomic spectrum, who have carefully planned and benefited from decades of high incomes and ample wealth building as well as the advice of experts they hire rather than read. Nor, I suspect, would an emphasis on freedom and unlimited possibilities appeal to those who are facing disabilities or serious medical challenges (including cognitive decline) or even those who have strong and deeply held political or religious commitments. Nonetheless, judging by the proliferation of how-to-retire books, including some with more than ample sales, there is nonetheless a robust market out there.

Many authors sprinkle stories of the pleasure-filled experiences of retirees throughout their books to illustrate a point and appeal to the desired readership. Take two tales in Harriet Edleson's *12 Ways to Retire on Less: Planning an Affordable Future* (2021). "An expert on baby boomer retirement strategies," she has written for the AARP, *Kiplinger's Retirement Report*, and *The New York Times*. Although she acknowledges how little so many people have saved, the interviews she relies on and the tales she tells concern those in the upper middle class. One story focuses on a retail executive in her mid-sixties who, facing retirement with her husband, had stopped working for a living after consulting with several advisers. Now settled into new routines, she was thinking about adding an art studio to their home. Then there is Bob McDonald, once secretary of veterans affairs in the Obama administration after he retired as president, CEO, and chair of the board of Procter and Gamble. He was, Edleson notes, "busy, even in retirement," serving as he was on corporate and civic boards. Of more modest but nonetheless ample means are Kathi and Patrick, who "know what they like: entertaining, gardening, traveling, and spending time with their children and grandchildren." Now retired, they "wanted to keep the family home and find a second one" in Florida that family members could easily visit.[15] Thus, even though the book's title emphasizes how to retire on less, it features someone thinking about building an art studio, another who had left an exalted position at a major corporation, and a third planning to buy a second home. But to most Americans, these choices are not among the "12 Ways to Retire on Less."

Social class remains the principal, almost exclusive category on which authors of retirement books focus. Race commands surprisingly little attention in such books. To be sure, Chris Hogan is an African American and author of *Retire Inspired: It's Not an Age, It's a Financial Number* (2016). However, he focuses not at all on African Americans or the distinctive issues they surely face, especially how adverse historical forces have placed them in disadvantageous positions.[16] He began his career as a debt collector, but his book features no stories of the struggles to which that experience exposed him. Indeed, he followed *Retire Inspired* three years later with *Everyday Millionaires: How Ordinary People Built Extraordinary Wealth—and How You Can Too*. Like so many others, in his 2016 book, Hogan offers a familiar mixture of financial planning and inspiration. More distinctly, of all the books I have read, this is the most Christian one in its emphasis. This is not surprising given that Hogan was part of the sprawling Ramsey Solutions empire, which promises to provide "biblically based, commonsense education and empowerment that give HOPE to everyone in every walk of life."[17] David Ramsey is an evangelical Christian, someone conservative both politically and financially, who offers tough-love advice in books and on his radio shows, including those I follow on Facebook. As if to underscore the choices Hogan made, Ramsey insists in his own best-selling financial advice book that he stands for biblical wisdom and "spiritual" values and against political correctness.[18]

Gender and sexuality command slightly more explicit and extensive attention than race in these books, albeit not in very probing or significant ways. There is less-than-equal attention to women because long-held attitudes and some socioeconomic conditions have often made discussions of retirement a masculine project. *The New Senior Man: Exploring New Horizons, New Opportunities* (2017), by Thelma Reese and Barbara M. Fleisher, is a prime example. Aside from references to "manning up," little in the book is gender specific. The authors do make several claims about distinctively gendered experiences. One is that if women enter retirement enmeshed in networks, men do so largely alone. A second is that this generation of men experiences retirement differently from how their fathers did, provided as they were "with the proverbial gold watch and the gift of a new set of golf clubs." In many but hardly in all cases, unlike their wives, husbands making the transition from full-time employment have been the man of the house, the protector and provider. Otherwise, to a fault, Reese and Fleisher offer up familiar nongendered nostrums. Their stories and invocations belie their claims that they are speaking to "men of all walks of life," a statement undermined by their talk of reinvention, adventure, and freedom, more easily available to the well-to-do than to those who are less financially fortunate.[19]

Two notable books focus on women: Anne C. Coon and Judith Ann Feuerherm's *Thriving in Retirement: Lessons from Baby Boomer Women* (2017) and Fleisher and Reese's *The New Senior Woman: Reinventing the Years Beyond Mid-Life* (2013). The first made a somewhat convincing case for gendered distinctiveness by acknowledging that female baby boomers in or facing retirement deserve special consideration because they would carry over their pioneering efforts in the workplace into their retirement. As Coon and Feuerherm write, "this representative group of First Wave Baby Boomer women was not finished." Just as they were change agents when they followed "career paths that had often been closed to women," so now "they were prepared to make changes again." Yet the authors quickly slip into familiar rhetorical territory when they talk of energizing "popular thinking about the postcareer years, focusing on the future and celebrating what they were capable of, what they were interested in, and how much they had to give back and pass on to others." Indeed, in part because of the focus on financial information, the middle class and above, and exciting possibilities, their analysis is not more than superficially gendered and in other ways treads conventional territory, focusing as it does on professional women and invoking the promise of a new stage of life that "encourages you to move into a new, positive identity."[20]

In contrast, *The New Senior Woman* places women's generational experiences front and center, often in a way influenced by feminism. Referring to the book's readers, the authors insist, "our world is light-years distant from our mothers' and grandmothers', whose roles in life were much more predictable and circumscribed than ours." Invoking the importance of "this new empowerment," they write of "the need to draw together to find sisterhood and fellowship within this wider world," because, since women rely on the importance of female friendships, they "yearn to speak to, understand, and support one another." Yet sometimes, they trip on their generation's feminism. Their mothers, they remark in a way that relies on one-dimensional and overly simplified treatments of the experiences of the women who came before, were "seldom seen and *never* heard." Their roles, they continue in historically inaccurate ways, were "to be as invisible as possible, sitting quietly by while younger generations marched ahead. . . . We ElderChicks are doing what has never been done before, breaking new barriers every day." Yet they nonetheless credit foremothers of their mothers' generation with leading the way. "Women have experienced a profound role change following the 1960s," they note, "as a result of the work of Betty Friedan, Gloria Steinem, and other doyens of the women's movement. Many women were transformed: their expectations, their reach, their influence, their empowerment became the genesis of today's senior women."[21]

There is only one widely available book that pays more than minimal attention to a broader range of people than usually covered. Part of the AARP's Real Possibilities series, Carol Levine's *Navigating Your Later Years for Dummies* (2018) discusses the unique challenges that older LGBTQ people and veterans face. It does so even though, like so many others, its more general appeal is to people who have financial resources, choices, and the ability to navigate complex situations. With the former group, Levine explores the consequences not only of specific health issues but also of persistent patterns of "stigma and discrimination" when it comes to health and long-term care, including visitation rights and the necessity of identifying sympathetic facilities and providers. When she turns her attention to vets, Levine explores the challenges and opportunities of accessing care from the Veterans Health Administration.[22]

Like those who focus on gender, generational change is one issue that many authors use to connect past and present. Quinn, Fleisher, and Reese are among the several writers who deploy a familiar straw horse. Nancy Collamer, a "career coach, author, and speaker who is an expert at helping people create lifestyle-friendly careers," colorfully captures the shift. "For many people," insists the writer of the jacket copy for her book, "retirement is no longer a trifecta of gold, grandkids, and gardening—it's an opportunity for new pursuits that involve both earning income and exploring personal passions."[23]

The title of Collamer's 2013 book, *Second-Act Careers: 50+ Ways to Profit from Your Passions During Semi-Retirement*, underscores the important role of remunerative work to people who have left full-time careers behind. For some people, she notes, working after leaving full-time employment is a choice freely and positively made. Other baby boomers, faced with insufficient savings bumping up against unrelenting expenses, are "struggling with the reality that they *need* to work." To both groups, she offers advice on how to find alternatives to nine-to-five jobs. New patterns of flexible employment, technological changes, lowered costs in starting and running a small business, and the proliferation of freelance opportunities are all inspired by "Your Personal Motivators." At the very end of the book, she deploys language that has suffused so many competing ones, as she speaks of "reinvention" and mentions, "your second act is about to begin. Godspeed, and enjoy the journey."[24] The labor economist Teresa Ghilarducci explores the issue of working after supposedly retiring, and does so evoking more realism and less joy, in her 2024 *Work, Retire, Repeat: The Uncertainty of Retirement in the New Economy*. This is a how-to book that melds the political and personal, one based on a careful analysis of the failures in the current system and how to provide alternatives to a situation that is harmful socially and economically across generational lines.[25]

In contrast to the optimism of most advice books stands the data of what Americans actually face in retirement. A December 2022 report by the financial services company Transamerica paints a sobering picture, undercutting the celebratory tone that Collamer and so many others offer. The report, influenced by both long-term trends and experiences with the COVID-19 pandemic, relies on a survey of more than ten thousand respondents. Some of its findings are reassuring: 70 percent of those questioned, it reports, were "confident they will be able to fully retire with a comfortable lifestyle, including 24 percent saying they are 'very confident' and 46 percent saying they are 'somewhat confident.'" Yet other data underscore the problems that tens of millions of Americans face. More than one-third of the respondents had experiences as caregivers that complicated their personal and work lives. Most workers were struggling to pay off debt while adding to their retirement savings. The report notes that "a concerning percentage of workers are dipping into their retirement savings before they retire," with more than one in three taking out loans or making withdrawals from what they were putting away. Many worried that they would outlive the funds they had accumulated and that health issues would necessitate long-term care that they could hardly afford. An ample percentage of respondents, slightly over 70 percent, worried that Social Security would be reduced or eliminated. At the end of 2021, the median household savings for retirement was $67,000, with one in every five workers having accumulated less than $10,000. "I Don't Have Enough Income to Save for Retirement" reported slightly more than half of the respondents.[26]

Less tangibly financial were reports of fears and dreams. On the one hand, well over half of the sample mentioned concerns about their physical and mental health, with worries about memory loss, diminished independence, and isolation prominently emphasized. On the other hand, many workers had high hopes for their retirement years. They dreamed of active retirements, with travel, time with family and friends, and hobbies prominently anticipated. Over half of the respondents expected to have paid or unpaid work later on—ranging from continuing in their current careers to pursuing a new one, launching a new business, volunteering, or taking care of grandchildren. The reasons for continuing to work varied, with substantial percentages emphasizing that they wanted to stay active or needed to earn money.[27]

The Transamerica study also drills down on the distinctive experiences of different groups. Part-time workers faced more uncertainty because of the episodic nature of their employment and the likelihood that their employers did not fund retirement plans. Rural workers were less confident and faced more precarious futures than did urban or suburban ones. On some important metrics, there were no substantial differences between LGBTQ+ workers and others. Yet LGBTQ+ workers articulated worrisome responses, for which the report offered no explanations. They were less likely to feel positively about their circumstances—experiencing as they did a greater sense of distress, concerns about mental health, problems in their relationships with friends and family members, and difficulty making ends meet. With regard to finances, they were less confident that they were accumulating a sufficient nest egg. Indeed LGBTQ+ workers had "saved dramatically less in total retirement accounts compared with non-LGBTQ+ workers, with the median figure of $31,000 about half of that of their peers ($31,000, $70,000, respectively)."[28]

When the report turns to race and ethnicity, it uses white, Black/African Americans, Hispanic, Asian Americans/Pacific Islanders (AAPI) as its categories, but it includes no Native Americans in its sample. The most striking finding involves the disjuncture between the median amounts each group had saved for retirement and their judgments of their futures. AAPI workers had socked away the most, $105,000. In contrast, African Americans had set aside $34,000, or about one-third of that higher figure. Yet, on another metric, whether "they will be able to fully retire with a comfortable lifestyle," African Americans were the most confident—78 percent for them, compared with 68 percent for whites. Similarly, more than members of any other group, African Americans had the most positive view of aging.[29] As is true with so many other issues, what is notable is that the authors make no attempt to explain their findings, something especially striking because there was for African Americans such a contrast between financial data and expectations about the future. In light of what we know from other studies about comparative wealth among various groups, what African Americans reported on their retirement savings is not surprising. What did call out for explanation is why they were so confident about the financial conditions they would face in retirement.

More generally striking is the contrast between the sobering conclusions the Transamerica report offers and the paeans to retirement that dominate advice books. Many authors, especially those on the nonfinancial end of the practicality–inspirational spectrum, insist that when facing retirement, money is not as important as meaning, purpose, and passion. Take, for example, *The New Retirementality: Planning Yor Life and Living Your Dreams . . . at Any Age You Want* (2020), by Mitch Anthony, described on the book's cover as "bestselling author, financial philosopher," well known to audiences from what he has said on over a thousand radio stations and has written in *The Wall Street Journal* and *Kiplinger's Magazine*. Money, he writes confidentially to readers who are likely to have, or aspire for, more than adequate financial resources, is "not the primary component" of retirement, because "what needs to be planned for is much bigger than the accumulation and distribution of your means." Rather, what demands attention is "meaning." If readers explore what he has written with an open mind, he is confident that they will "cross the bridge toward the most meaningful stage of life yet."[30]

The title and content of Robin Ryan's 2018 *Retirement Reinvention: May Your Next Act Be Your Best Act* also capture an ample sense of new possibilities. "This book is a symbol of my recovery" from breast cancer, she writes, as she conveys a sense of rejuvenation that others echo less dramatically. "And," she continues, "I want you to benefit from what I learned: *live for now*."[31] She describes herself as the author of "eight best-selling career books" who has "appeared on 3500 TV and radio shows, including Oprah and Dr Phil," someone "known as America's Top Career Expert," ready to help you improve your résumé or interviewing skills.[32] Drawing on stories of well-to-do and wealthy people, she minimizes the importance of relying on work for income in retirement. Instead, deploying the usual range of clichés, she focuses on pursuing your passion in the "*happy years* of retirement" by doing "the things on your bucket list as soon as possible, . . . the fun and meaningful things that make you truly happy, satisfied, and fulfilled."[33]

Even more exuberant about reinvention is David C. Borchard's 2008 *The Joy of Retirement: Finding Happiness, Freedom, and the Life You've Always Wanted*. Borchard, someone who counsels people on work–life balance, here serves as the author, assisted by Patricia Donahue, a Presbyterian minister. The biggest challenge "that stands in the way of self-realization" is not problems with money or health but clarifying "your deepest aspirations, your strongest interests, and your most energizing talents." Suffusing the book are words or phrases like "reinvention," "self-liberation," "fulfillment," "self-realization," "sustaining vitality," and "authoring your life." The book, Borchard insists, "presents mind- and vision-expanding perspectives for creating a lifestyle for your senior years that is meaningful, enjoyable, and rejuvenating."[34]

Like Borchard, numerous authors of books on how to retire successfully psychologize the challenges of retirement. Among them is Kenneth S. Shultz's 2015 *Happy Retirement: The Psychology of Reinvention.* Schulz is a professor of psychology at California State University–San Bernadino, where he serves on the Executive Board of its Center on Aging. The publisher of *Happy Retirement* is the media company DK, whose books rely not on traditional paragraphs but on dazzling visuals to drive home their points. Like others, Schulz draws on the findings of positive psychology, developed and popularized by Martin Seligman. He endorses Seligman's approach to well-being, which relied on PERMA, or the value of **p**ositive **e**motion, **e**ngagement, **r**elationships, **m**eaning, and **a**ccomplishment.[35] Other writers rely on the findings of positive psychology. This is true of *What Color Is Your Parachute?*, by Richard N. Bolles and John E. Nelson, the authors of the immensely successful book on how to parachute into the job market. They insists that Seligman's "clear-thinking, hard-nosed, let's measure-it-and-see-if-it-stands-up approach to the study of human strengths [and] positive emotions" is "not just a variation on 'positive thinking'" developed by Norman Vincent Peale. Bolles and Nelson hail Seligman's emphases as transcending the isolated self by connecting people with God, family, the environment, a political party, "your ethnic culture, the free enterprise system, your community."[36] Others use a key concept of positive psychology when they urge readers to get off the "hedonic treadmill." Stop chasing after never-to-be-attained worldly pleasures, they advise, and embrace the importance of nonmonetary goals.[37] When advice givers insist that giving back during retirement benefits both the giver and the recipient of aid, they underscore the benefits of the "helper's high," also a key concept in the field of positive psychology, one that points to the pleasure people experience when they help others rather than the positivity that the recipient feels.

The fact that Bolles is an Episcopal minister should remind us that religion and spirituality as well as psychology undergird the advice many writers offer, often in a particular genre of how-to-retire books. In the 2019 *Getting Good at Getting Older*, Rabbi Laura Geller and her late husband, Richard Siegel, offer a mixture of practicality, spirituality, and scattered references to Jewish traditions such as *tikkun olam*, Hebrew for "repairing the world."[38] In the early 1970s, Ken Dychtwald, one of the authors of *A New Purpose: Redefining Money, Family, Work, Retirement, and Success* (2009), spent time at Esalen Institute, a key launching pad for the Human Potential Movement. Now, more than a third of a century later, he and coauthor Daniel J. Kadlec speak of retirement as "an exciting and liberating time as you begin to think about your life not as a mission accomplished—but as a time for finding a new purpose that will give your life meaning and just might become your most joyous and nourishing time on earth."[39] In the foreword to *Retire Inspired*, the evangelical Christian and finance entrepreneur David Ramsey introduces Chris Hogan, noting that "once in a generation, God sends a fresh, loud voice into the area of personal finance."[40] Gilbert offers "a special thanks to God," for "there's nothing more important than the assurance of an eternal life—without God's sacrifice, it's a gift none of us would know." Yet it is hard to avoid the conclusion that his advice on how to bake a cake is more indebted to the Mammon he experienced during his more than thirty years with a multinational aluminum corporation than to his religious commitments.[41]

In popular advice books, there is remarkably little attention to religious themes such as the importance of the contemplative life or of meeting one's maker. Indeed, there is an often-unresolved disjuncture between heavenly longings, earthly finance, and the possibilities of personhood. Other problematic and usually unacknowledged issues call for attention. The first is the tension between obligations to the self and society. Many authors celebrate individualism and pay minimal attention to social obligations. Thus, Zelinski insists that "it's up to you to design a lifestyle that is as relaxing and invigorating as you want it to be. . . . Recreating yourself as a person can be challenging, but through patience and positive thinking you can do it."[42] In *Don't Retire, Rewire! 5 Steps to Fulfilling Work That Fuels Your Passion, Suits Your Personality, and Fills Your Pocket*, the husband-and-wife team of Jeri Sedlar and Rick Miners, with "over 25 years of experience in executive talent search, transition coaching, and personal development mentorship," strike similar notes.

Invoking words and phrases like "Pro-You," "Independent Minded," and "Unique" and preferring "rewirement" to "retirement," they celebrate those "who live by the motto: 'If it is to be, it is up to me'": "Your tomorrow is in front of you. All you have to do is go for it."[43]

Many how-to books emphasize staying active by giving back in retirement. The most extensive such focus comes in the 2020 *How Seniors Are Saving the World: Retirement Activism to the Rescue!*, by Thelma Reese and B. J. Kittredge. Like others, they work to avoid the word "retirement" because it suggests turning away rather than turning toward—preferring instead "*unretirement*." They rely on interviews with well-to-do but culturally diverse "fixers": a Japanese-born Quaker who discovered feminism in 1960s California, a Jew practicing Tzedakah, an African American and a Native American experiencing racism, and a Madison, Wisconsin, radical committed to fighting against wars and imperialism. Without mentioning the power of the Helper's High, they emphasize the importance of a win-win situation. "While you are saving the world or saving someone else," they note, "you're saving yourself or discovering yourself" by alleviating "anxiety, depression, and awareness of physical pain" and even "making them actually go away."[44]

Work is also an issue that elicits complex reactions. Some books reveal a real revulsion to it, as if retirees had to reject something that in their earlier years was necessary but is now either meaningless or painful. In contrast, many writers underscore the capacious celebration of nonremunerative retirement activities such as volunteering, traveling, or pursuing a hobby. The statistics on working for pay are striking. In the early twenty-first century, more than three out of every four Americans said that they planned to do so in retirement, supposedly mostly out of desire, not necessity. At any given time, however, only 12 percent actually did so.[45] Yet the authors of most books seem to align themselves closer to the former than the latter figure, as they emphasize the benefits to the self and to society of work late in life and celebrate retirees as entrepreneurs.[46] Sedlar and Miners highlight the contrast between before and after when they speak of rewirement as a time "to reroute the personal energy you spent on full-time work into deeply satisfying, personally customized work activities . . . that can transform your next act into the most rewarding time of your life."[47] Moreover, many books treat paid work as a glorious adventure and not what it is for so many people, a grinding necessity. Like others, Ryan, after discussing how many retirees would work because they fear the consequences of living longer and running out of money, quickly turns to how "Boomers seek greater purpose, stimulation, and fulfillment in retirement."[48]

Tensions between heaven and earth, individualism and society, paid work and its alternatives are reason enough for cautioning against joyful celebration. Ageism, financial difficulties, disabilities, illness, and death also loom—remarkably more so in people's lives than in the advice books they read. Like so many books in the genre, Hyrum W. Smith's 2019 *Purposeful Retirement: How to Bring Happiness and Meaning to Your Retirement* avoids mentioning any obstacles to the joy and happiness in making sure "the rest of your life can be the best of your life."[49] Others acknowledge obstacles, mostly in passing, and blithely assume they can be easily overcome. A few discuss lonely isolation and disruptive dislocation, issues that I worry about. Writers mention ageism, a prejudice that can adversely affect people seeking work and friendship, but quickly move on to other, more promising topics.[50]

A similar optimistic sleight of hand occurs when it comes to the possibility of financial difficulties. Referring to money troubles, Farrell remarks, "the 'crisis' [*sic*, as if to say there really isn't one] involves segments of society that are highly vulnerable to falling living standards in their elder years, including the disabled, widows, and people with careers that didn't come with retirement benefits," but he quickly moves on to claim inaccurately that "a large majority of Americans are on track to support a reasonably comfortable retirement."[51] Bolles and Nelson mention how stock market gyrations, the shift from defined benefits to defined contributions, and the precarious future of Social Security threaten dreams of smooth sailing. But in the end, they remark, it is "your call" as to whether "the Fourth Movement of our lives, the final movement be *pathetique* or *eroica*—pathetic or heroic?"[52]

Then there are the issues of the likelihood of serious illnesses and the inevitably of death. Oh, sure, there is plenty of discussion of downsizing, moving into a new home or retirement community, having life insurance and Medicare (less so Medicaid), but what they are buffering against rarely receives attention. This is understandable given the way publishers are aware that potential readers are more interested in hearing about the joys of retirement than the traumas of diseases and death. You can see this in the responses of readers to Zelinski's book on Amazon's website. One buyer makes clear the intended audience by remarking that this is "not a book for those who have not saved enough for retirement and are looking for someone to rescue them from their financial dilemma" but is "for those who are comfortable that they have sufficient money in their retirement accounts." Also astute, though obvious, is the comment that his book is "a refreshing change amidst a sea of staunchy [*sic*] retirement planning books." Others make clear that readers want upbeat books that avoid the trials of disease and death and instead celebrate the pleasures of life in retirement. One reader calls it "inspirational," another applauds it for being "full of ideas to help you transition into a happy retirement," and a third calls it "life-changing." The author, someone else notes, "paints a picture of retirement so enticing that you may want to retire early even if you are in your fourties [*sic*] or fifties." Finally, there are expressions of gratitude: "Thank you Mr. Zelinski for opening our eyes to the art of living our lives in the mature phases of our lives!" and "Thanks Ernie for your friendship and inspiration! :)."[53]

How most advice books minimize frailty, illness, and death reminds us of the consequences of the distinction that the British scholars Paul Higgs and Chris Gilleard make between an active old age and an "inactive, unhealthy, unproductive, and ultimately unsuccessful ageing." Moreover, the fragmentation of old age, along with the commercialization of aging successfully, which we have seen so often in how-to books and elsewhere, is significant. It has "had the effect of pushing to the margin those aspects of later life that are most discomforting, distressing and, indeed, disgusting and that have long defined old age."[54]

The exception to the numerous hosannah-filled books comes in Borchard's *The Joy of Retirement*, in which joy is the culmination of the anticipation of death. As he nears the end of his book, he adds a chapter titled "Transcending Fears of Death." He writes of how therapy taught him "not to see death as an eternal black void but simply as a transition to another realm." Reading Brian L. Weiss's *Many Lives, Many Masters: The True Story of a Prominent Psychiatrist, His Young Patient, and the Past-Life Therapy That Changed Both Their Lives* (1988) taught him about the experience of "regression into past lives," which inspired him to no longer fear death as he once had. Moreover, he reports, "my friends who work with the dying tell me they can become so free of fear that our final transition becomes one of peaceful joy."[55]

Finally, I want to focus on two books by scholars who break the mold of jaunty how-to offerings. These authors offer powerful correctives to the frequent emphasis on reinvention that is prominent in so many popular how-to books. They also stand in contrast to books by many of the authors already discussed who hold doctorates, even though you might not necessarily know that from what and how they write.[56]

In the 2018 *Retirement and Its Discontents: Why We Won't Stop Working, Even If We Can*, published by a university press, the Canadian sociologist Michelle Pannor Silver relies on research to reveal what varied groups face in retirement. Although she hopes her book inspires "readers to question the social construct of retirement and to create a retirement strategy that avoids some of the discontentment shared throughout this book," she provides no roadmap lined with practical advice. Though Sigmund Freud in *Civilization and Its Discontents* (1930) focused "on the contrast between an individual's quest for freedom and societal norms that restrict primitive instincts," she observes, she would explore "a fundamental tension between the freedom and autonomy associated with retirement and the need to maintain structure, a sense of social connectedness, and personal fulfillment." She concentrates on how retirees could "struggle with feelings of discontent in their retirement because" of how their "personal and work identities are intertwined." In some cases, this could lead to "a situation whereby relatively no moral guidance is provided," with people losing a "sense of identity."[57]

Silver looks at the lives of medical doctors, CEOs, professors, elite athletes, and homemakers. They are groups of "highly privileged individuals," but she wonders that if they suffer, how could less privileged folks "be expected to make a seamless transition to retirement"? Some in her samples struggled in retirement more than others. Though many professors resisted retirement, they continued to "work in place," as is true of me as I work on this book. Several of them, she notes, "saw the work they were doing in retirement as the most gratifying and meaningful work of their career." She included homemakers without really grappling with what it means to retire from unpaid work. She writes of how by and large they continued doing what they had previously done; for them, retirement involved what their spouses and peers only started doing. Now able to "embrace a new title and a socially preferable status," at last they could "square their roles with those of their peers," something that revealed "how the constraints of social norms around retirement can be rewoven to achieve greater contentment in later stages of the life course."[58]

Retired CEOs found retirement more challenging. Abandoning "a consistent, career-focused life" revealed that "they were not as competent at developing a life distinct from their work identity." Now sharing "a common sense of discontentment and ennui" underscored "that media depictions oversimplify this important life transition," a perceptive judgment that is more widely applicable. Doctors who stopped practicing faced a different and even more problematic situation. When still taking care of patients, they had set aside too little time for other pursuits. Now they often felt like they were both "deserting their life's work" and figuring out how to engage with spheres, familial and other ones, they had often neglected. Their earlier "total commitment" to their professions was now a "key barrier to finding contentment in retirement." Aging out early on, elite athletes struggled more than people in any other group. No longer able to compete, "they felt like foreigners in their bodies and minds. Their ability to focus on an adrenaline-fueled goal served them well as Olympians, but it created discontent as they struggled to find a new purpose in life as retired athletes."[59]

In contrast to almost all how-to books is Teresa Ghilarducci's 2015 *How to Retire with Enough Money and How to Know What Is Enough*, a conventional enough title that little prepares readers for how this how-to book differs from almost all others. This is a work by a professional economist and expert on pension plans, published by Workman, an imprint with numerous best-selling advice books to its credit, many of them with edginess of one kind or another. Her book, conventional in its commonplace advice, came as a surprise to me for its progressive politics, unconventional merely in its presence.

Much of the book's focus—on Social Security, Medicare and Medicaid, planning, investing—is familiar enough. Where Ghilarducci differs from others is in her addition of the political to what more commonly is individualistically apolitical. "We can't get out of this mess one by one," she insists. Relying on what supporters of the Townsend Plan had done in the 1930s in a way that helped build support for Social Security legislation and what the Gray Panthers were doing more recently, unlike most how-to books, she calls on her fellow citizens to get involved, advocating for more robust support of the federal government's role in supporting retirement by voting and mobilizing others to do so, "to support the government programs that ensure a baseline of income and health-care security"—and not only to protect and improve Social Security, Medicare, and Medicaid but to support "Guaranteed Retirement Accounts." This is "a national pension system that would remedy failures" of existing programs. All employees would contribute 2.5 percent of their pay to a fund that employers would match. Professionals would manage the account, with the government guaranteeing a 3 percent rate of return above inflation.[60]

So, here we have a book with the usual financial advice but with progressive politics added. More so than in lives as lived, advice books generally keep illness, death, and dying under wraps. How-to books discuss the importance of sociability and connecting with others, yet more prominent are emphases on freedom, the individual's search for meaning, and the reinvention of the self in what often appears as a lonely crowd. Ghilarducci's stance in *How to Retire* reminds us that most of the others treat retirement as an issue of individual rather than familial or communal responsibility, are overly confident about people's ability to manage this phase of their lives, and are aimed at the affluent.

2

A Short History of Longevity

When I pick up *The New York Times* at our front door, I almost always turn first to the obituaries. I am not sure for how long I have done so or why I persist, but I tell myself that as a historian, I love to figure out the logic and trajectory of people's lives. On very rare occasions, this ritual dovetails with my work on a current project. This was strikingly true on July 27, 2023, when I read the obituary of Louise Levy, whom the headline writer told me had died at 112 and "was studied for her very long life." She had only recently moved from independent living in a retirement community to its assisted living facility, and she was, wrote the obit writer, Richard Sandomir, one of more than seven hundred Ashkenazi Jews studied by researchers at the Albert Einstein School of Medicine's Longevity Genes Project. They had "discovered gene mutations that are believed to be responsible for slowing the impact of aging on people like Mrs. Levy," he wrote, "and protecting them against high cholesterol, heart disease, diabetes and Alzheimer's disease." In contrast, Levy "credited her longevity in part to her low-cholesterol diet, positive attitude and a daily glass of red wine." Yet the researchers revealed that a considerable percentage of people whose lives they tracked smoked, were obese or overweight, and rarely exercised.[1]

The story of Louise Levy comes from an eons-long line of philosophers and scholars who have studied why some people live so long and what longevity involves for them, many of the considerations not as scientifically exacting as this one but often more interesting.[2] Among the many evocations of longevity, few are as memorable as the monologue by Jaques in William Shakespeare's *As You Like It*. Here "All the world's a stage, . . . And one man in his time plays many parts. His acts being seven stages." The first is "the infant, mewling and puking in the nurse's arms." After "the whining schoolboy" comes the lover, the soldier, and the justice. The sixth is "the lean and slippered pantaloon, with spectacles on nose and pouch on side; his youthful hose, well saved, a world too wide for his shrunk shank, and his big manly voice, turning again toward childish treble pipes and whistles in his sound." Finally, the "last scene of all, that ends this strange and eventful history, . . . the second childness and mere oblivion, sans teeth, sans eyes, sans taste, sans everything." On the American scene, few references are as memorable as what Sportin' Life evokes in the song "It Ain't Necessarily So" in *Porgy and Bess* (1935): "Methuselah lived 900 years / Who calls that livin' / When no gal will give in / To no man what's 900 years."

Yet longevity as a subject of scholarly inquiry, especially among psychologists, could only emerge with scientific advances and when considerable numbers of people lived long lives, including those who did so while remaining healthy. In the postwar US, Erik H. Erikson and Joan M. Erikson offered one of the most interesting explorations of what life in old age meant in ways that reflect advances in and limitations to life expectancy. What they wrote was important both because of the audiences they had commanded with their earlier work and because as elderly people writing about aging, they stood in contrast to so many younger authors who wrote as outsiders to the experiences of getting older. Erik, born in 1902 and pursuing psychoanalysis in the world of Sigmund Freud and especially Anna Freud in Vienna from 1927 to 1933, stayed one step ahead of the Nazis when he migrated to the United States with his Canadian-born wife, Joan. There he began a long and distinguished career as a clinician and writer, teaching at Yale, Berkeley, Harvard, and the Austin Riggs Center in Stockbridge, Massachusetts. Starting in the mid-1930s, he built on but broke with or expanded on Sigmund Freud's emphasis on formative experiences in very early childhood that linked sexuality to psychosocial events, something that Erikson's work as a child analyst and father underwrote. He was one of the prominent developers of ego psychology, the coiner of the phrase "identity crisis," and an author whose elegant explorations of lives—from Martin Luther to the Lower Brule Sioux Native Americans—reached a broad public, especially in the 1960s, when he emerged as a major celebrity author who spoke so profoundly to many Americans.[3]

In the mid-1940s, Erikson developed fresh approaches to understanding the broad sweep of lives. On this topic and others, as a thinker and writer, Joan always played a major role in her husband's career, a situation that intensified beginning in the mid-1970s as her husband's health began to deteriorate. What shaped Erik Erikson's writings was his command of theory, his experiences as a therapist, and his and Joan's experiences, including with their children. Especially formative was what they encountered with Neil, born in 1944 with Down syndrome. It was in *Childhood and Society* (1950) that Erik Erikson first brought together for lay and professional readers a capacious and richly suggestive theory of human development.[4]

If Shakespeare wrote that life began with a "puking" child and ended with an individual "sans everything," Erikson's formulation was both more optimistic and more abstract. He focused on "Eight Stages of Man," from "Basic Trust vs. Basic Mistrust" with infants to "Ego Integrity vs. Despair" in "Maturity."[5] His choice of a gendered term, like the Bard's, was common for contemporary writers, even if at key moments Erikson both evoked gendered assumptions he shared with most Freudians and yet offered probing explorations of gendered distinctions.[6] With each phase, he linked past and present, with early experiences and recent ones interacting with each other in reciprocal ways. At every stage, people encountered the challenge of how to wrestle with a set of opposing tensions. They would ponder what it meant to have successfully resolved the momentous choices they encountered—in the case of older folks, a tension between facing regret or moving forward by embracing cautious but hopeful optimism. Because he still drew on the deep well of Freudianism and was himself in midlife and focused on people younger than he was, he initially placed major emphasis on a person's early stages. Consequently, his section on the eighth and final stage was brief, only three paragraphs in which he assigned no specific age for maturity and never mentioned retirement.

Erikson acknowledged that people in every culture experienced the challenges of ego versus despair in distinctive ways, shaped by specific social and historical conditions. Yet there were certain constants. On the one hand, despair captured those who had not "accrued ego integration," unable to resolve the challenges of tensions in life's earlier stages. Consequently, such people feared death, feeling that "time is now short, too short for the attempt to start another life and to try out alternate roads to integrity." On the other hand, someone who successfully achieved Ego Integrity was able to "ripen the fruit" of earlier stages, "ready to defend the dignity of his own life style against all physical and economic threats." A person who avoided despair "has taken care of things and people and has adapted himself to the triumphs and disappointments adherent to being, the originator of others or the generator of products and ideas." Erikson insisted that Ego Integrity involved "a post-narcissistic love" and an acceptance of the choices that made life turn out as it "had to be." Consequently, "death loses its sting." In all this, the relationship between generations was crucial. "An emotional integration" facilitated "participation by followership as well as acceptance of the responsibility of leadership." Parents had the capacity to foster a relationship characterized by generativity with their children. And "healthy children," he noted at the section's conclusion, "will not fear life if their elders have integrity enough not to fear death."[7]

In 1968, Erikson published *Identity: Youth and Crisis*, in which he devoted only a few pages to aging and death. Once again, he honored the importance of integrity and wisdom as people faced the end of their lives. He defined the former as "the ego's accrued proclivity for order and meaning," which involved being at peace with the choices an individual had made and the commitment to be "ready to defend the dignity of his own life style against all physical and economic threats." Without integrity, disgust and despair would reign. On the other hand, wisdom, when faced with "a possible terminal senility, . . . serves the need for that integrated heritage which gives indispensable perspective to the life cycle," which took "the form of that detached yet active concern with life bounded by death, which we call *wisdom* in its many connotations." For most people, he continued, "a living *tradition* provides the essence of" wisdom. He ended this nuanced and profound assessment by insisting that "to whatever abyss ultimate concerns may lead individual men, man as a psychosocial creature will face, toward the end of his life, a new edition of an identity crisis," in which "I am what survives me" is crucial.[8]

The implications of Erikson's theory of longevity were clear. People struggled with the choice of looking backward with regret or being satisfied, one leading to despair and the other to wisdom. "There may have been a modicum of glibness," Erikson's biographer Lawrence Friedman accurately writes of what Erikson offered in 1950, "as Erikson elevated integrity over the constant and realistic apprehension of a great many people toward the finality of death."[9] Yet Erikson's statement about the meaning of wisdom that he offered a little over a quarter of a century later, when at age seventy-four his health problems began to take hold and death seemed closer, strikes me as profound but vague. Wisdom, he noted, "is the detached and yet active concern with life itself in the face of death itself," maintaining as it does "the integrity of experience, in spite of the decline of bodily and mental functions."[10] Moreover, as the psychoanalyst Daniel Jacobs notes, "Erikson's subsequent cognitive decline was not a subject of conversation. Instead, there is a focus on gero-transcendence, a helpful look at aging though it skirts around the growing sense of shame or despair that many elders feel as their minds and bodies weaken."[11]

Childhood and Society appeared in 1950 and *Identity: Youth in Crisis* in 1968, when Erikson was forty-eight and sixty-six, respectively, and when, especially in the first instance, old age and death seemed far off. As the years passed, he and Joan paid more attention to aging and death, something surely driven by mounting health problems. These began in the mid-1970s, when Erik was in his early seventies and intensified in the 1980s and early 1990s, before he died on May 12, 1994. Among them were impaired vision and hearing, prostate cancer, adverse reactions to prescription drugs, and eventually diminished cognitive abilities and mobility.

As Friedman notes about the years beginning in the late 1970s, the conflict between integrity and despair was one Erikson "was on intimate terms with, for there was no getting around the fact that he was negotiating the last stage in his life cycle model."[12] As Erikson himself remarked to friends in 1976, "Without a bit of despair (quite a bit) there can't be any integrity. That's what I said long ago, and (dammit) it is even true." For him, despair originated in "a sense of being lost on the periphery," along with "the stigma of chronic impairment and the sentence of inactivation."[13] The clinical psychologist Daniel Benveniste recalled seeing Erikson in 1987 as "a great oak swaying in the wind with roots losing their hold on the ground below."[14] Yet, at best, Erikson found solace in the pursuit of wisdom, which for him involved the ability to integrate impulses and experiences.

In one of Erikson's last books, *The Life Cycle Completed: A Review*, published in 1982 when he was eighty years old, he grappled with issues that his conditions raised but to which he had paid little attention in 1950.[15] To begin with, he acknowledged how much had changed in how he and Joan understood aging, since it was in their "middle years" that they formulated it: "at a time when we certainly had no intention of (or capacity for) imagining ourselves as really old." Back then, "elders" still seemed like "the few wise men and women who quietly lived up to their stage-appropriate assignment and knew how to die with some dignity in cultures where long survival appeared to be a divine gift to and a special obligation for a few." Now, in contrast, old age involved "a quite numerous, fast-increasing, and reasonably well-preserved group of mere 'elderlies,'" despite "the distilled knowledge that has survived in folk wit as well as in folk wisdom." Having pondered historical relativity, he proceeded to describe, at length, the ravages of old age that marked "the total end (unpredictable in time and kind) of this our one given course of life." He explored the many trials that aging involved, including the "increasing state of being finished, confused, helpless." Referring to patients seeking psychotherapy, perhaps at some level to himself, he mentioned the "mourning not only for the time forfeited and space depleted but also . . . for autonomy weakened, initiative lost, intimacy missed, generativity neglected—not to speak of identity potentially bypassed or, indeed, an all too limiting identity lived." Even though the "last stage finds" people who are "relatively freer of neurotic anxiety," that did not mean "one is absolved from the *dread* of life-and-death."[16]

Yet, in the end, Erikson held out hope in his formulation and for the lives of the aged. Ever the modern Freudian, he pointed to the "final psychosexual state . . . for (pre-senile) old age," when what he called "a *generalization of sensual modes* that can foster an enriched bodily and mental experience even as part functions weaken and genital energy diminishes." As he had done earlier, he evoked the power of connections across time with friends and family. Central to that temporary victory was "a human being's potential capacity," he asserted, "under favorable conditions, more or less actively to let the integrative experience of earlier stages come to fruition" with the embrace of "a childlikeness seasoned with wisdom." He evoked "viable reritualizations, which must provide a meaningful interplay between beginning and ending" of life. Perhaps thinking of Joan, his three children other than Neil but especially Kai, to whom he had drawn close personally and professionally, and his favorites among the many professional comrades with whom he had worked, he spoke at the end of this section of "a timeless love for those few 'Others,' who have become the main counterplayers in life's most significant contexts. For individual life is the coincidence of but one life cycle with but one segment of history; and that for him all human integrity stands or falls with the one style of integrity of which one partakes."[17]

Although Erikson's name was on the title page along with Joan's, my best judgment is that some of what appeared in *Vital Involvement in Old Age* (1986) was the work of Helen Q. Kivnick, who was listed as the third author. Kivnick was a psychologist and social worker then in her mid-forties, and her professional work continued to focus on what she called "Vital Involvement Practice."[18] In a key chapter of the book, titled "Old Age in Our Society," the authors (as I will call them) addressed end-of-life issues. I am pretty sure Erik did not write this section because in it, there is little evidence of his subtle psychological analysis and elegant prose. Instead, the authors focused on programmatic suggestions, subjects that Erik rarely, if ever, wrote about. In a section titled "Retirement," they lamented that for so many people, "retirement is required too early" and suddenly because of rigid policies. This left them in a society that had "no place for these elders," relegated "to the onlooker bleachers of our society," classified "as unproductive, inadequate, and inferior," and to be entertained with "bingo games and concerts" that only served to patronize them. For those "whose identity is largely derived from" paid work, the end of employment brought on "a bitter and deprived feeling of being expelled and depreciated." Calling for better housing for the elderly, the authors spoke of "their real horror of 'those homes for the elderly,'" which "are too often run solely as business ventures, and expenditures are minimized for the sake of profit." More generally, the truly aged were "forced into the position of supplicants at a point in history when their role identities as storytellers, historians, counselors, and arbiters of disputes have all but disappeared and when their sense of personal dignity is threatened by those who have the power and means to alleviate their needs."[19]

The authors focused on alternatives, ideally activities that crossed generational lines and available as long retirees remained in good health. They honored the formation of meetings of fellow retirees drawn from the cohort of those with whom they had once worked, the application of their work skills in new ways, the development of creative activities like gardening, and engagement with the arts that countered the tendency to have "nothing to think about except their own deterioration." They also celebrated the experience of being grandparents and of programs for lifelong learning. Given the cultural power of youthfulness and of poverty in old age, especially among women, efforts to "incorporate them into the social fabric" were important, something made more difficult by the expensiveness of Medicare and the failure of efforts to staff relevant agencies with elders, as mandated by the Older Americans Act of 1973. A hopeful sign was the political activism of older folks who are "indignant about their enforced powerlessness." The authors ended on a positive note, hoping that "our society confronts the challenge of drawing a large population of elders into the social order in a way that productively uses their capacities."[20]

At one point in this book, the authors asserted that many elders "demonstrate a tolerance and capacity for weighing more than one side of a question that is an attribute of the possible wisdom of aging."[21] Inevitably, of course, though wisdom might conquer despair, Erik Erikson's life ended. Joan, capturing the gravity of his final years but also some of the issues she faced before she too passed away, wrote about "The Ninth Stage," a subject she had discussed with her late husband. She did so in an "Extended Version" of *The Life Cycle Completed*, published in 1997, the year she died.[22] Although Joan's prose lacked the elegant subtlety and often elusive abstraction that marked what Erik offered, her essays evidenced a blunt frankness that captured what it meant to experience the travails of old age in anticipation of death. As people aged, she noted, they "began to face unavoidable—and certainly not amusing—realities," and "Death's door, which we always knew was expectable but had taken in stride, now seemed just down the block" as their nineties arrived.[23] If her husband had avoided linking the eighth stage to a specific age, she focused on seeing the ninth and final one "through late-eighty- and ninety-year-old eyes." Now, she wrote, "even the best cared-for bodies begin to weaken," losing their "autonomy." Despair intensified, weakening "self-esteem and confidence." With "hope and trust" no longer powerful enough "to face down despair," she insisted, "faith and appropriate humility" were "perhaps the wisest course." Yet her use of the word "perhaps" qualified what she wrote. If her late husband had typically placed the positive response before the negative one, as in "Basic Trust" before "Basic Mistrust," she insisted on reversing the order because that is what old age demanded. When it was "a serious challenge at ninety just to locate misplaced eyeglasses," it is difficult to have the capacity that "wisdom demands." Moreover, she observed that elders, now "often ostracized, neglected, and overlooked," were "seen no longer as bearers of wisdom but as embodiments of shame."[24]

As counters to these ravages of old age, Joan Erikson offered two alternatives. One was the development of communities that provided vital support and connections to counter "a totally playless second childhood" en route to "the last long trek to death's door." Placing "inmates" and "retired" in quotation marks, she criticized retirement communities as too costly for many, subject to "unexpected breakdowns in the systemic 'machinery.'" Instead, she advocated fostering situations where elders remained enmeshed in dense communities where they would be venerated and benefit from sustained relationships across generations.[25] She then ended the book with her second recommendation, an embrace of "gerotranscendence." Faced with constricting encounters with time and space, elders could embrace alternatives to "enforced withdrawals." Then, using otherworldly language that I doubt Erik Erikson would have deployed and that as an earth-bound Jew I find less than useful, they could "rise above, exceed, outdo, go beyond, independent of the universe and time," an option that "provides an opening forward into the unknown with a trusting leap."[26] Notably, what the Eriksons offered tended to be more analytic and descriptive than prescriptive. This is true even though it was possible to read what they wrote and know what to do: become self-aware of your life's trajectory and strengthen your commitments to wisdom, hope, and other people.

Important and richly suggestive as was what the Eriksons wrote, also influential is a series of studies that collected data on and then analyzed the lives of Americans over many decades, into their old age. One of the most important was the Genetic Study of Genius (later known as the Terman Study of the Gifted), developed by Lewis Terman at Stanford beginning in 1921, when the typical age of its subjects was eleven. World War I had revealed, the study's authors insisted, how many Americans lacked the intelligence needed to operate complex military equipment. And yet many military experts and policy makers also worried that intellectually gifted recruits or potential recruits might lack the ability and the characterological or physical abilities to provide much-needed leadership.[27] Consequently, at the outset, Terman's project was less interested in emotional and physical well-being, or longevity, than in a eugenics-inflected version of intelligence designed to prove that exceptionally intelligent people, rather than being maladjusted, were normal and effective. As Terman insisted in 1926, an examination of the lives of people who evidenced "precocious indications of superior mental ability" proved "the essential falsity of certain traditional opinions regarding the childhood of genius."[28] With his associates, he identified 1,528 high-IQ children and young adults in California, born between 1900 and 1925, virtually all of them white, mostly from middle-class families and above, with northern European ancestry, and more male than female. What plagues the study's reliability and reputation were problematic approaches, not only its commitment to eugenics and less-than-scientific methods but also Terman's interventions into the lives of its subjects.

Over the ensuing years, Terman (who died in 1956) and his colleagues followed the lives of those who were sometimes called the Termites, gathering and then analyzing a wide range of data.[29] Beginning in 1926, six books emerged directly from the project, the first five with Terman's involvement and the sixth, Carole K. Holahan and Robert R. Sears's (himself a Termite) *The Gifted Group in Later Maturity* (1995), a title that avoided words like "aging" and "old age." What began in early volumes as books overwhelmed with data over time emerged as treatments that more successfully balanced data and conclusions. And then in 2011, the psychologists Howard S. Friedman and Leslie R. Martin reported on fresh analysis of the data in *The Longevity Project: Surprising Discoveries for Health and Long Life from the Landmark Eight-Decade Study*, a book that ventured into elements of the how-to genre.

The Gifted Group in Later Maturity focuses on the children now grown up, "on average in their mid-70's" in 1986, when the data were last collected for "psychology's longest lifecycle study."[30] The authors devote a good deal of attention to correlation rather than causation and to a range of outcomes, of which emotional well-being was one of many. Consequently, their work is not centrally focused on what predicted and promoted happiness. The book lacks the subtlety and profundity that Erik Erikson offered and pays remarkably little attention to issues of illness and death. Compared with the Harvard Study of Adult Development, discussed extensively shortly, it relies on a narrowed range of rigorous methods and pays no attention to data from a more socially diverse and multigenerational sample. What remains largely implicit is any advice on how to live a long and good life. Nonetheless, Holahan and Sears draw on longitudinal data to reveal what happened to the gifted children when they grew up.

The authors offer generally optimistic assessments, concluding that the subjects of Terman's study, compared with those in a wider sample, "approached aging with continuing mastery and competence." Blessed by historical circumstances and favorable family backgrounds, most of them, with ample financial resources and "sufficient social resources," revealed "the potential for continuing achievement of meaning in later years." In a section on retirement, they conclude that the men they studied were able to make that transition gradually, with "their continued work and creative endeavors" affirming the productiveness of these "precocious individuals." As for the women, their retirements were also successful, although they worked less for income and engaged more in volunteer activities. By and large able to live independently, the men and women self-reported "favorable overall levels of psychological well-being" that "were moderately positively related to self-appraisals of physical health," with Holahan and Sears also deploying the word "happiness" to describe their emotional conditions.[31]

When the authors turn to causal factors that explained these positive conclusions, they emphasize both "previous health and well-being" and positive expectations about the later years. More "modestly related" was the power of "ambition and involvement in work in early years of later maturity," with ambition early on a "negative predictor of men's psychological well-being in aging." Notably important was "an easygoing disposition (happiness of temperament and being easy to get along with) as measured by self-ratings in young adulthood." Among other factors related to psychological well-being were "involvement and participation in life at many levels," especially in social networks (including as volunteers and citizens), "positive and hopeful approaches to life," "the ability to cope with and create meaning from the challenges they faced," and, especially with women, "satisfaction in relationships." All these conclusions reinforced the emphasis that had early on driven Terman's study and now persisted in this study of longevity: that exceptionally gifted people could lead happy and productive lives that undermined wonkish stereotypes.[32]

Never explicit in the book's body is there any suggestions as to how readers could benefit from its findings. However, in the final paragraph, where the authors look forward to future studies, they present hints. "These remarkable individuals," they insist, offered the possibility of providing "us with a model of optimal approaches to one of the greatest challenges that human beings face—bringing meaning and integrity to the final years of later maturity," a phrase they persist in using instead of a less hopeful phrase that might remind readers of death's inevitability, even though Sears had died six years before the book's publication, something mentioned in the foreword. Then, in the book's final sentence, presumably written by Holahan, the book notes that a study of the lives of the gifted Termites would provide "continuing insights into the possibilities for enabling persons to live enriched and fuller lives in these later years."[33]

Sixteen years later came *The Longevity Project*, by the psychologists Friedman and Martin. Any of Terman's subjects still alive when the book appeared would have ranged in age from the mid-eighties to just over one hundred. For twenty years, Friedman and Martin, supported by the National Institute on Aging, relied principally on the extensive self-reports and interviews by the cohort of 1,528 Termites, which they and colleagues (whom they called Termanators) went over imaginatively as they relied on a varied range of methodological approaches, principally analyzing material from self-reports and interviews. The authors combined storytelling, data analysis, and practical advice. Evoking the power of genetics, health psychology, medical sociology, and epidemiology, they cast skeptical eyes on commonly accepted explanations of longevity, such as getting married, eating well, being religious, exercising vigorously, taking happiness courses, or even the benefits of modern medicine.

Their exploration of the relationships between longevity and happiness underscores how they approached the question of coincidence and causation. Exercise of a virtuous skill could backfire and endanger longevity. "Healthy people," they concluded from data, "are happy but happy people are not necessarily healthy." Part of the problem was that sometimes optimism and cheerfulness had their "downsides" because "too much optimism can leave you surprised, disappointed, and seriously frustrated with any unexpected long-term hardships." In contrast, they state, "worrying is sometimes a *good* thing." The people in the Terman sample "did not pursue happiness. They were happy and laughed *because* they were healthy, wealthy, and wise—their happiness was a by-product of their pathways to a long life."[34]

What predicted or caused longevity were "sociability" and "conscientiousness and social dependability," a range of commitments that included activity as volunteers and citizens, they wrote, that "on average . . . account for five or more years of life." For Friedman and Martin, "the lives of Terman participants showed that taking time to cultivate social networks is important not just to the quality of life but also to its quantity," with social relationships as "the first place to look for improving health and longevity." Social relationships represented "an important—perhaps the most important—way to change one's life pathway," making these participants "much more likely to live into their seventies, eighties, and nineties, while their fellow participants (who were equally healthy and intelligent as children, but didn't travel such healthy pathways) often succumbed before age sixty-five." Pathways, a key concept on which the authors relied, involved the trajectory of people's lives, which Terman's subjects had been able to change, "albeit slowly and with substantial effort," as readers of their book could as well. The book's extensive emphasis on gender involves an insistence on its connections to social relations. "It is an especially good idea to nurture one particular feminine quality: social connectedness," the data reveal, because it helped "buffer against life's hardships."[35]

Social relationships were probably the most significant factor in predicting and promoting longevity. "An often-complex pattern of persistence, prudence, hard work, and close involvement with friends and communities," they emphasize, enabled people to pursue "interesting life paths" and to find "their way back to these healthy paths each time they were pushed off the road." Helping others, "having a large social network, engaging in physical activities that naturally draw you in, giving back to your community, enjoying and thriving in your career, and nurturing a healthy marriage or close friendships can do more than add many years to your life. Together, they represent the living with purpose that comes from working hard, reaching out to others, and bouncing back from difficult times."[36]

If most studies of longevity paid little or no attention to public policy, Friedman and Martin weighed in, in their final chapter, having earlier remarked that "individual health depends on social health." Pointing to escalating costs of health care, they note that "traditional approaches to health care and health promotion have some disquieting deficiencies." Without offering any specific policy recommendation and neglecting the connections between psychological determinants and sociocultural causes, they call for more attention to the importance of "unconscientious personalities, marital instability, exposure to traumatizing stress, social isolation, workplace failures, and social-psychological anomie and estrangement."[37] Like so any others who study longevity, they were stronger on psychological analysis than on social and political solutions. As psychologists, Friedman and Martin focused significantly on private, individualistic virtues, with minimal attention to public policy or communitarian virtues in any specific or extensive ways.

Above all, what differentiated the work of Friedman and Martin from that of earlier studies that relied on Terman's data is their emphasis on how you too, as readers, can apply and benefit from their findings. In many sections, along with a summary of "what it means for you: guideposts to health and long life," they offer a questionnaire for "self-assessment." For example, to enable readers to evaluate their "neuroticism," defined as "the relationship between moody worrying and longevity," they present ten questions to which a reader can respond with a yes, no, or question mark. Among the questions are "Do you often feel miserable?" and "Do you worry long over one humiliating experience?" Then readers could add up their scores, which would enable them to decide if they were "a relaxed, laid-back kind of person" or, at the other end, "something of a neurotic," a word the authors were not using clinically since they believed all people to some extent had these traits. Those whose scores place them in the middle are "probably rather high-strung at times and appear a bit neurotic, but at other times" are calmer and more serious. With this issue and others, the authors advise readers, "fill out the scales, gather up the scores, and create a view of the key contours of your life."[38]

Other work in the Bay Area explored changes that people experience over the course of their lives: the Intergenerational Studies and the Berkeley and Oakland Growth Studies, carried out at University of California–Berkeley's Institute of Human Development. Researchers gathered data from slightly over five hundred subjects born in the Bay Area from 1920 to 1932, ranging from infants to adolescents.[39] For the most part, their discussions of the data stopped before those in the sample who were still living were past their sixties.[40] As luck would have it, the one exception was what appeared in *Vital Involvement in Old Age*, in a 184-page section titled "The Voices of Our Informants." The Eriksons and Helen Kivnick stated that in 1981 they had interviewed twenty-nine of the children's parents from Berkeley's Guidance Studies, then ranging in age from seventy-five to ninety-five. Five of them, they reported, were living in the Bay Area "in retirement communities" that were "fairly luxurious developments." Notably, Erik had been on the staff of the original study in the 1940s when he played with, studied, and wrote about the children. Now the authors spoke of carrying out their more recent studies in order to explore what the data collected in the 1940s could predict "about the life course of the children and, by implication, about the old age of the parents." When they carried out interviews, the authors remarked, Erik and Joan "found it natural to share 'dated' expressions, to joke about their Victorian backgrounds, and to draw out early memories by offering an occasional one of their own. Gestures, laughter, and tone of voice," they continued, "in many cases triggered a feeling of warm empathy."[41]

What the interviews reported on in *Vital Involvement in Old Age* revealed was how people in old age struggled to resolve a series of tensions as they drew on and sometimes consolidated what had shaped them earlier in their lives. The three authors adopted Erik's lingo and his preference to place the positive before the negative—"integrity" before "despair," for example. They did their best to embrace "caring" to reconcile the tension between "generativity" and "stagnation." They also embraced "love" to strike a better balance between "intimacy" and "isolation." At their best, they mobilized "fidelity" to place "identity" above "identity confusion." Some of those among their sample were able to deploy "competence" to place "industry" above "inferiority." Similarly, they could mobilize "purpose" to locate "initiative" over "guilt." They also relied on "will" to help make "autonomy" win against "shame/doubt." And finally, the authors explored how "hope" could help "trust" win the battle against its opposite.[42]

Their descriptions of aging were often frank, even brutal, even as they offered readers (and perhaps themselves) reassurances. Again and again, they reiterated confident conclusions. "It is precisely this process of reconciling the past and the present that remains the essence of living with the tensions and challenges of a lifetime." In contrast stood their compelling descriptions of what people faced in old age. "Burdened by physical limitations and confronting a personal future that may seem more inescapably finite than ever before," they noted, "those nearing the end of the life cycle find themselves struggling to accept the inalterability of the past and the unknowability of the future, to acknowledge possible mistakes and omissions, and to balance consequent despair with the sense of overall integrity that is essential to carrying on" as they, for the first time, "find themselves recognizing that death may well come sooner rather than later." While some were more successful than others in integrating or reconciling past and present, the authors concluded, perhaps too optimistically, that all were "involved in the process of trying" an "effort that is the basis for growth at all stages of the life cycle."[43]

A relative latecomer to longitudinal studies and one that was more focused than others was *Unravelling Juvenile Delinquency* (1950), by the husband-and-wife team of Sheldon and Eleanor Glueck. Respectively a law professor and social worker, over a long career they sustained an interest in how to predict the effectiveness of the punishment of criminals. From 1940 to 1948, they collected data on 456 white, nondelinquent inner-city boys in Boston, most who had at least one parent who had migrated to the US and all of them who grew up under adverse socio-economic conditions in what the Gluecks called "underprivileged" or "unwholesome neighborhoods." Comparing them with a control group whose members did become delinquents and tracking the lives of both groups from first grade on, the Gluecks were interested in developing metrics that would help them understand why some became juvenile delinquents while others did not. Members of the multidisciplinary team gathered and analyzed a robust variety of data—social, physical, and psychological. In the Gluecks' data-driven and methodologically sophisticated book, which has long remained an influential classic in criminology, they displayed no interest in the lives of their samples beyond their teen years—certainly not their old age.[44]

By far the most influential and robust longitudinal discussion of longevity (and one that eventually incorporated data from the Gluecks' sample) is the Harvard Study of Adult Development. It began in 1937 as the Grant Study because the foundation started by the department-store magnate William Thomas Grant provided the initial seed money, with abundant future funding across the ensuing decades coming from private foundations and the National Institutes of Health. Initially concerned with normality rather than well-being, early on the study of longevity was not among its concerns.[45] Although eventually influenced what by what Erik Erikson had written, this famous and pathbreaking longitudinal examination of longevity began descriptively but over time drew on psychological portraits to offer advice about how its subjects achieved well-being and, by implication (or eventually more explicitly), how you might also. Begun in the Depression, shaped by World War II, and anticipating troubled transitions to peacetime, the Grant Study focused on "the 'normal' individual, . . . whose combination of traits of all sorts allows him to function effectively in a variety of ways." This seemed especially urgent in 1945, as expressed in the first of many books on the study, one titled *What People Are: A Study of the Normal Young Man*. "Peacetime societies have an overabundance of frustration, of disharmony, of unqualified leadership," wrote the book's principal author and lead investigator, Clark W. Heath. "Yet the great body of social planning which is today current proceeds in ignorance and unconcern about the material that must compose and sustain this structure: the nature of normal human beings."[46]

The unexamined assumption of who would provide such leadership inevitably led to a focus on males—not Radcliffe College women but men who attended Harvard College and, more specifically, men carefully selected by psychiatrists and deans in their sophomore years, because they were "normal," talented, and stable. Researchers tracked the lives of these 268 Harvard graduates from the classes of 1939–44, one of them John Fitzgerald Kennedy, all of them white and native born, most of them from the Northeast and Midwest, most of them Protestants, some of them from modest socioeconomic backgrounds, others from prominent and wealthy families, and most of them in between. Every two years, and sometimes more frequently, social scientists, social workers, medical doctors, and psychiatrists secured information about them from questionnaires, examinations, and interviews. Eventually focusing on understanding what characterized long-term well-being, they collected data on the subjects' physical and mental health, their careers and marriages, and eventually their experiences with retirement and aging.

George E. Vaillant, a Harvard-trained psychiatrist and professor at its medical school, directed the study for thirty years beginning in 1973. Born in 1934 and perhaps influenced by his father's suicide in 1945, Vaillant was centrally interested in what made people thrive over the long haul. From *Adaptation to Life* (1977) to *Aging Well* (2002) and then to *The Triumphs of Experience* (2012), in three books he offered what he had learned from the lives of these men. As he did so, he remained a Freudian, albeit he eventually came to rely on other perspectives, notably what the neo-Freudian Erik Erikson offered. Over time, Vaillant more fully acknowledged and then remedied his sample's demographic biases. As he focused more and more on longevity, he became increasingly convinced that sustaining a sense of well-being was possible even to the end of life. And he added to description and analysis an emphasis on how to mature successfully—or as the subtitle of *Aging Well* heralded, he offered "Surprising Guidelines to a Happier Life from the Landmark Study of Adult Development."[47]

In *Adaptation to Life*, written when Vaillant was in his early forties and his subjects in their early to mid-fifties, Vaillant acknowledged the biases with the Grant Study's emphasis on an elaborate selection process to weed out troubled students and then focus on what psychiatrists and deans saw as "sound," "social" young men who would eventually be successful. "The absence of women in the Grant Study," he now realized, was an "unforgiveable omission." He made clear his indebtedness to Freud, offered little advice that was explicit, and evidenced only briefly any attention to the years ahead. His principal reliance on Freud came in his emphasis on adaptive styles that his subjects relied on, such as fantasy, altruism, sublimation, dissociation, passive aggression, and displacement. Now focused minimally on leadership by "normal" men, he was principally interested in what "healthy" means as well as whether and how his subjects thrived. His conclusion was that they "did not live happily ever after, but their experiences have meaning for us all," advice that he did not explicitly explore. There were, he continued, "no especially blessed individual turned up in this assessment; the luckiest of the lives here studied had its full share of difficulty and private despair," which led him to conclude "that psychopathology is always with us and soundness is a way of reacting to problems, not an absence of them." Though they had adapted to life, often successfully with regard to family and career, he insisted, *there is not one of the men who has had only smooth sailing,*" with all of them revealing "what Freud called the psychopathology of life."[48]

Though Vaillant rarely offered advice to his readers, there were moments when what he discussed might help them. "It is not the isolated traumas of childhood that shape our future," he concluded from a close examination of the lives of a select group of men, "but the quality of sustained relationships with important people." In addition, in a remark that also underscored the possibility of overcoming disadvantages, he noted that over time, socioeconomic factors mattered less and that "isolated traumatic events rarely mold individual lives." With a taste of what he would emphasize in later books, he extolled the importance of emotional attachments and social connections as people developed more "adaptive styles." He celebrated how well the men in his sample had overcome obstacles "with healthy stoicism, suppression and energy" and observed that good adaptation involves "unusually warm human relationships." "Whether a man can love friends, his wife, his parents, and his children," he had learned, "proved a far better predictor of his mental health and his generativity than whether at fifty he found bliss in a marital or extramarital bed." Also important was men's capacity to give "of themselves back to the world," in ways he did not explore.[49]

If researchers originally involved in the Grant Study believed adolescence marked the end of maturation, the lives of the Harvard graduates revealed that adults matured and changed. In a rare but extensive passage, Vaillant even looked beyond midlife. "From forty to senescence," he concluded, people had lost mastery over the bodies and emotions. "Thus, if the forty-year-old struggles with feelings, the fifty-five-year-old struggles once more with reality. If bitterness is to be avoided the promises and dreams of the thirties must be reviewed as nostalgia. Reality must replace the ideal and we must accept that life's seesaw has tipped; there are now more yesterdays than tomorrows." Some men by their mid-fifties had to "replace the indignities of physical decay with a sense of unshakeable self-worth. Worry over their own death is still of little significance, but for some, worry over or even rehearsal for the death of one's spouse has emerged as a major concern." Though they might worry whether they would make it successfully emotionally and financially to retirement, their more pressing concern lay elsewhere: "Deterioration, not death, is the enemy."[50]

When Vaillant published *Aging Well* in 2002, he was sixty-eight, and the subjects of the Grant Study were close to either side of eighty. Much remained the same in what he wrote compared with *Adaptation to Life* a quarter of a century earlier, especially his commitment to "stand on the shoulders of Sigmund Freud and chart the maturation of involuntary coping mechanisms (a.k.a. defense mechanisms)" in order "to explain emotional development." Yet to this he added standing also on the shoulders "of that wise artist-anthropologist-psychoanalyst Erik Erikson" so he could "explain social development." Erikson, he insisted, was "the first social scientist to conceptualize clearly adult development as progress not decline."[51] In addition, *Aging Well* revealed three major differences from *Adaptation to Life*: an emphasis on how to age well, albeit hardly in the manner of popular how-to books; robust optimism about how many of the people studied had done so, reflected in the shift in titles from *Adaptation* to *Aging Well*; and the incorporation of data and stories from investigations (the Gluecks' and Terman's especially and the Berkeley cohort less so) that compensated for the class and gender biases of the Grant Study.

"How can we control our last years?" Vaillant asked at the outset, and the answer came from the biographies that the Grant Study and other investigations offered, which "will reveal ingredients essential to successful aging," even as he unintentionally invoked a concept that others have subjected to criticism. And the conclusions he drew were both abundant and helpful. Primary among them was the importance of social relationships, something that reflected what Robert D. Putnam echoes in his widely read *Bowling Alone: The Collapse and Revival of American Community* (2000). "A good marriage at age 50 predicted positive aging at 80," while alcoholism foretold "unsuccessful" aging, damaging as it did so many kinds of relationships. "A capacity for gratitude, for forgiveness," "becoming eternally enriched by loving a particular person," and the ability "to love and to hold the other empathetically—but loosely"— mattered, as did how "learning to gain younger friends as we lost older ones" contributed "more to life's enjoyment than retirement income."[52] To remain healthy in retirement (a phase of life that he called "highly overrated as a major life problem") and into one's eighties, Vaillant emphasized the importance of not only social connections but also "learning how to maintain self-respect while letting go of self-importance." Play was also essential, with "mindless bowling on the green, atrocious golf, and amateurish watercolors" providing "great pleasure, and, equally important, freedom and meaning." More serious, reflecting class-based activities, was creativity that involved "committed talent" and lifelong learning. All this sustained well-being in old age "even if you are no longer 'important,' even if your joints ache, and even if you no longer enjoy free access to the office Xerox machine," a reference older readers will understand better than younger ones. As for spirituality and religion as we age, Vaillant concluded that "the jury is still out as to whether" they "really deepen in old age."[53]

When facing the inevitability of disease and death, following Erikson, Vaillant insisted on the importance of integrity, "the task of achieving some peace and unity with respect both to one's own life and to the whole world." Related to integrity was an embrace of "wisdom, detached concern with life itself," in the face of "the decline of bodily and mental function" and "of death itself." This involved, he wrote, "an almost Buddhist acceptance" of the inevitable. Again relying on Erikson, Vaillant insisted that "the task of longevity forces us to reflect upon human dignity in the face of" disability and death. Yet and strikingly, in *Aging Well*, Vaillant exuded abundant confidence that people do indeed age well. "Successful aging," he concluded, "is not an oxymoron," and as the members of the Harvard cohort surmounted "the inevitable crises of aging," they "seem constantly to be reinventing themselves." The "exceptional longevity and the prolonged retirement" that the Grant Study members evidenced, he predicted, "will become the rule for American children born in the year 2000."[54]

The most notable change from *Adaptation to Life* concerned inclusivity. In the earlier book, Vaillant had focused exclusively on the Harvard sample and barely mentioned what we could know from other studies. In contrast, in *Aging Well* and his next book, *Triumphs of Experience: The Men of the Harvard Grant Study* (2012), he acknowledges the importance of and draws lessons from two other major studies: the lives among the academically talented women from California cities that Lewis Terman and his colleagues had collected beginning in 1921 and of 456 disadvantaged, inner-city Boston nondelinquent youths, over half of whom had at least one immigrant parent, that Sheldon and Eleanor Glueck began to study in 1939.

The Triumphs of Experience completes the shift from adaptation to aging well and now to triumphs. With members of the Harvard sample who were still alive hovering around ninety and Vaillant at age seventy-eight, he mainly reiterated what he reported earlier. He honors Freud's emphasis on involuntary coping mechanisms and Erikson's on generativity and integrity. Above all, again, affectionate social connections and love mattered tremendously. They help people replace "narcissism with empathy, a progressive amalgam of love and social intelligence that is essential to the development of mature defense mechanisms and optimum adaptation skills." Underscoring the "difference between facile optimism . . . and the lifelong faith in the universe," he generally left usable how-to advice less explicit than he had in *Aging Well,* even as he underscored what he saw as the triumphs experienced in old age, including first or succeeding marriages, a judgment that reflected data of the Grant Study and his own experience with four marriages.[55]

Since the publication of Vaillant's third book in 2012, others have followed, often in ways that move well beyond what Vaillant offered in both expressions of optimism and proffering of advice. This is so of the work of Robert Waldinger, the current director of the Harvard Study of Adult Development. A psychoanalyst and Zen priest (and, along with Jon Kabat-Zinn and Richard Davidson, a prominent JewBu), with his collaborator the professor of psychology at Bryn Mawr College Marc Schulz, he extends the Grant Study into second and third generations. More extensively than Vaillant did, Waldinger and Schulz meld the study of Harvard men and Boston inner-city nondelinquent boys; include the wives from both studies, LGBQT+ folks, and others to make the longitudinal study more inclusive; and rely on data from new sources such as genetic testing, brain scans, and social media. They have also explored the impact of COVID-19 and social media. As Waldinger recommends in his TEDx Talk, "replace screen time with people time," and as he and Schulz advise in their book, "DON'T SCROLL, ENGAGE."[56]

Through many media, Waldinger spreads the word about what more than eight decades of research can teach us, including in a 2015 TEDx Talk that reached more than forty-four million viewers; through his role as founding director of the Lifespan Research Foundation; with interviews and articles; and in a 2023 book, *The Good Life: Lessons from the World's Longest Scientific Study of Happiness*, coauthored with Schulz.[57]

In their book, Schulz and Waldinger paint a vivid and largely optimistic picture of how many people thrive, some of them despite adverse circumstances. Their "findings," they insist, "reveal one of the most essential and hopeful truths about human beings: we are adaptable. We are resilient, industrious, and creative creatures who can survive incredible hardship, laugh our way through tough times, and come out stronger and come out on the other end."[58] They draw on the wisdom of poets, playwriters, philosophers, and others, including Seneca, Confucius, Shakespeare, Ben Franklin, Reinhold Niebuhr, and Maya Angelou. They also rely on the results of intensive investigations of studies carried out elsewhere but especially the lives of the Harvard and inner-city Boston subjects and their families, which they often dramatize with stories of individual lives. If the Grant Study had begun with a focus on normality and then shifted to attention to well-being, they hop on the crowded bandwagon of those who focused on happiness, a world I explored in *Happier? The History of a Cultural Movement That Aspired to Transform America* (2018). In pre-MAGA days, the celebration of positivity went hand in hand with a neoliberal emphasis on self-governance. Waldinger and Schulz use the words "happy" and "happiness" in their book, even though in a podcast issued two days after *The Good Life*'s publication, Waldinger insists that "well-being" is their book's focus because happiness is "a momentary thing."[59] Of course, Waldinger and Schulz are careful to distinguish between hedonic, short-term spurts of pleasure and more meaningful eudemonic ones that Aristotle had defined and celebrated—what they call "a state of deep well-being in which a person feels that their life has *meaning and purpose*."[60] In so many of their endeavors, they neglect to acknowledge the importance of Martin Seligman, the key figure in the field of positive psychology whose work had innumerable parallels to their own study of happiness. As Seligman did in his classes at the University of Pennsylvania, they urge members of their audience to see the positive effect of reaching out to a mentor or a stranger.[61] And if Seligman emphasizes five things that foster flourishing (**p**ositive emotion, **e**ngagement, **r**elationships, **m**eaning, and **a**ccomplishment, or PERMA), Waldinger and Schulz offer their own, but somewhat more circumscribed, acronym—to improve relationships, they advise to follow WISER: watch, interpret, select, engage, reflect.[62]

"If you had to make *one* life choice, right now to set yourself on the path to future health and happiness," Waldinger and Schulz ask on the book's first page, "what would it be?" Their most important conclusions are two, highlighted in italics. The first involved an insight Vaillant had not significantly emphasized twenty-one years before by presenting hard data drawn from medical and scientific studies. Over the past thirty years, they now emphasized, researchers involved in the Harvard Study of Adult Development had discovered that being happy enhanced not only people's sense of well-being but also their physical health—"living in the midst of warm relationships is protective of both mind and body," lessening the impact of the "slings and arrows" of difficult situations and measurably adverse indications of health problems ahead. Second is a conclusion they highlight in so many ways. It is not wealth or fame that matter, but *"good relationships keep us healthier and happier. Period,"* which, they acknowledge, is not always easy to achieve. Yet multiple studies, including the Harvard ones, they write, following up on what Vaillant had recently noted, "show that people who are more connected to family, to friends, and to community, are happier and physically healthier than people who are less well connected."[63]

Other conclusions followed from these insights. Waldinger and Schulz reiterate that being sustained by good relationships in one's fifties significantly predicted flourishing in one's eighties. It is not the number but the quality of what they, like Vaillant, call "warm relationships" with friends, family, and community members that matter most. In contrast, loneliness (a word that did not appear in the index of Vaillant's most recent book) adversely and significantly impacts people's emotional and physical well-being, increasing "a person's odds of death in any given year by 26 percent." Tracking the lives of over two thousand people, including those in the original Harvard and Boston inner-city studies (a handful of them still alive), they answer the question *"Is it too late for me?"* with "a definitive NO": late-in-life transformations are possible.[64]

Also striking is what a comparison with earlier examinations of the same data involved. Though Waldinger and Schulz often cite what Vaillant had written, there are significant differences between his emphases and theirs. Strikingly, they do not mention Sigmund Freud, even though at several points they refer to coping mechanisms, without, however, as Freud, Vaillant, and the Eriksons did, elaborating on their variety. Freud emphasized the importance of love *and* work, and though love occupied a central position in Waldinger and Schulz's analysis and advice, work was important not because it fostered meaning but because the workplace provided one of many locales of social interaction. They briefly mention how the Eriksons had offered a theory of life's stages and sparingly reference generativity. Yet, compared to what the Eriksons and Vaillant had discussed at length, there are in *The Good Life* remarkably rare discussions of how at the end of life, diseases take over lives or what it means for people to confront death, their own and that of their loved ones. Indeed, when they come to discuss what they call "late life," their treatment lacks the pain and profundity the Eriksons had movingly conveyed.[65]

If earlier books drew on much of the same data, the Gluecks and Vaillant had almost always refrained from offering personal, how-to-achieve-well-being advice. In contrast, Schulz and Waldinger fully embrace the commitment to proffer advice on how to achieve happiness. Abundantly threaded throughout their book are explicit appeals to readers, identified as "you," and what one can learn from the book. "The good life," they remark early on, "is right in front of you, sometimes only at arm's length away. And it starts now." "From Data to Your Daily Life," reads the title of one section of a chapter. "As we proceed," they continue, "we'll focus on identifying what you can do, regardless of the society you live in, or the color of your skin." Drawing on the university's evocative power, they encourage readers to think of the book as providing access to "your own mini-Harvard study." So, you should "jot down a few notes" as you examine a photograph of a much younger you, and "be as detailed as you like." This and other exercises develop a sense of your "social fitness" and gain from "the benefit of self-reflection that [the] Study members received throughout their lives." Moreover, like popular how-to books, *The Good Life* provides space for a reader to enter their responses to prompts, for example, by providing a list of "who are my closest friends and relatives" and then analyzing the data they enter. Again and again, they encourage readers to connect what their research discovered with their own lives, in the process enabling them to enhance the power of their social relationships. Exemplary of this emphasis is what they write at the book's end. "How do you move further along on your own path toward a good life?" they ask rhetorically. In the book's final three lines, they provide an answer. "Think about someone, just one person, who is important to you." Then "think about what you would thank them for if you thought you would never see them again. And at this moment—right now—turn to them. Call them. Tell them."[66]

In addition, there soon appeared *Interactive Workbook: The Good Life by Robert Waldinger and Marc Schulz: Lessons from the World's Longest Scientific Study of Happiness*, its author identified as "Study Genius," apparently the "author" of other workbooks connected to actual books. The Amazon website adds this "Important Note to Readers: This is an unofficial companion workbook based on" the book by Waldinger and Schulz, one "meant to enhance your original reading experience, not supplement it." What follows is a series of rhetorical questions. Some are consonant with the original book. "How to exercise your 'social fitness' to keep your mind sharp, mood stable, and connections strong" and "Would you like to develop healthier, more positive relationships?" are two examples. Yet some offer a level of hype I assume Waldinger and Schulz would find problematic. For example, there is the shout-out about "the shocking Harvard University secret to happiness that is revolutionizing what we know about life" and, of course, the inevitable end to the pitch: "If you're looking for the ultimate Harvard University life hack to happiness, and want to implement into your life immediately, then scroll to the top of this page and click Add To Cart now!"[67]

Though Waldinger and Schulz use the words "community" and "reciprocity" and emphasize the importance of mentorship, they offer remarkably few examples of people achieving happiness in the world beyond those encompassed by friends, family, and less often fellow workers or citizens. Focusing on lives enhanced by connections to friends and family members, except for the workplace, they pay no attention to how people might enhance their well-being by connecting with people in religious, community, or political organizations or even those inhabited by more than a few people in the nation's extensive range of less structured voluntary associations. Successfully adding women to their sample and acknowledging the impact of inequalities of wealth and income, the ways they draw on their samples prevent them from exploring the lives of African Americans and Latinos. A more ample social lens might have challenged their confidence that "nothing that has happened in your life precludes you . . . from thriving, or being happy," that there are few exogenous impediments on the road to flourishing. All this means that their evocation of "*social fitness*" has limited resonance or relevance.[68] Unlike the Eriksons, they evidence too little interest in the trials of people facing cognitive and physical challenges as well as death. Which is to say that though what the Eriksons wrote in their old age attracted little attention from readers, what Waldinger and Schulz offered did. In short, there is a more significant market for comforting reassurances than painful realities and for a focus on small social circles than for explorations of the importance of broader public engagement or public policy.

More generally, this short history of longevity reveals how so many writers avoid confronting the prospects of both serious illness and death as they seemed to become increasingly optimistic about the lives elders could live. The Eriksons provide moving and compelling exceptions, focusing as they did in their later work on illness and death. Related to this is that from Terman's studies in the 1920s to what Waldinger and Schulz offered a century later, the hold of Freud's emphasis on life's early stages diminished. Moreover, in ways the Eriksons usually did not, others who wrote about life's stages (Vaillant increasingly and Waldinger more significantly) added forward-looking practical advice to retrospective scholarly analysis. Publishers and the readers they attract want reassurance and encouraging advice, not sober truths such as what the Eriksons offered. Positivity and social privilege go hand in hand in ways that also keep socioeconomic inequalities and racism at a safe distance. Drawing on the genre of how-to books means that so often there are limits to how wide the circle of "we" is, with writers often offering a less than fully expansive sense of social obligations and connections. This is so even though over time, studies have reflected the dangers of a social world where, with lonely people increasingly living and bowling alone, social connections are urgently needed.

3

The Longevity Commercial Complex

Over time, discussions of longevity—especially by people involved in Harvard's Study of Adult Development—added advice to analysis. And with *The Good Life*, we have a full-blown how-to book. Then there is a different genre: best-selling books on longevity and its future. They come from authors with varied credentials, from a Nobel laureate who made important discoveries and commanded scientific knowledge to motivational speakers who have moved from one topic to another, alighting on aging along the way. They range from the research-based analytic to the practical, with stops in between.[1] Recent popular books written by well-credentialed professionals carefully balance analysis with advice.[2] In celebrating immortality, they are significantly optimistic about the possibilities of living long and healthy lives. In their embrace of the wonders of science, they displace religion, even as they offer visions of new heavens on earth. Nonetheless, despite their optimism, they often unintentionally reveal that all is not well in a United States threatened by climate change, inequalities, authoritarianism, and political dysfunction.

With the books significantly based on serious science, I cannot easily judge the legitimacy of their findings. Instead, I treat the material as a cultural historian, asking why there is such an immense audience that so often reminds us of earlier nostrums offered to those who were gullible to the appeals of hucksters. These publications, along with related materials, provide windows into the intertwined and complicated relationships between science, medicine, venture capitalism, and mass media. They reveal how in a world made frightening by climate change, authoritarian leaders, inequalities of wealth and income, polarized politics, and disastrous wars, people seek relief in what they can believe they can control. Focusing on their bodies offers the potential to postpone illness and death. In a United States that seems dangerous and fragmented, small communities, including far-off ones, also offer hope.[3]

Written with the help of the science researcher and writer Michael Rae, whose work linked calorie restriction to longevity, Aubrey de Grey's *Ending Aging: The Rejuvenation Breakthroughs That Could Reverse Human Aging in Our Lifetime* (2007) is the oldest of the five books under consideration here and among the most optimistic ones, arguing as it does that advances in biomedical technology can enable people to overcome the ravages of age-related illnesses and even the inevitability of death from health-related causes. A Brit, de Grey earned his PhD from Cambridge University for work reflected in his book *The Mitochondrial Free Radical Theory of Aging* (1999). Over time, he used the megaphone of British and US media, including the BBC, *Playboy*, *Popular Science Monthly*, and *The Colbert Report*, to promote his theories. Cofounder in 2003 of Methuselah Foundation, named after the biblical figure who reportedly lived to be 969, he promised to deploy medical advances to make "90 the new 50 by 2030."[4]

Starting in 2011, de Grey served as the chief science officer of the Silicon Valley SENS (Strategies for Engineered Negligible Senescence) Research Foundation. Its website claims that by "inspiring the next generation of biomedical scientists," it is "building a future free of age-related diseases."[5] De Grey was accused of meddling in a probe about his sexual harassing two women and lost that position in 2021. He then cofounded and served as head of the Longevity Escape Velocity Foundation.[6] For a period beginning in 2017, he was vice president of new technology discovery at AgeX Therapeutics, which is developing a "revolutionary longevity platform aiming to unlock cellular immortality and regenerative capacity to reverse age-related changes in the body."[7] Reflecting the belief that science replaced religion by bringing heaven to earth, the copywriter for *Ending Aging* remarked that its author, "the most bullish" of scientific researchers who study the biology of aging, "believes that the key biomedical technology required to eliminate aging-derived debilitation and death entirely—technology that would not only slow but periodically *reverse* age-related physiological decay, leaving us biologically young into an indefinite future—is now within reach."[8]

De Grey's work inevitably encountered skepticism. In 2005 a group of eighteen scientists, writing in the peer-reviewed *EMBO Reports*, a publication of the European Molecular Biological Organization, responded critically to his claims. "Journalists with papers to sell or airtime to fill too," they insisted, "often fall for the idea of a Cambridge scientist who knows how to help us live forever with telomerase, allotopic mitochondrial-coded proteins and marker-tagged toxins." And anyone who tries to explain "why de Grey's programme falls into the realm of fantasy rather than science is easily cast as a Luddite, an enemy of creativity and noble ambition, and someone whose prissy reluctance to confront de Grey's ideas might prevent us from living forever."[9] A more mixed appraisal came in an essay about the 2017 book by William Bains, a serial entrepreneur with a PhD in molecular biology, who was sympathetic to de Grey's commitments but skeptical of some of his excesses. *Ending Aging*, he writes, "is unashamedly a polemic and a plea for support for this grand vision, and its partisanship, first-person conversational style and occasionally immoderate comments may distract some readers from its message." That would be unfortunate, he continues, because though he found "the vision unrealistic in its extreme version," it was both "worth pursuing for its more modest aims" and "worth reading for its bold ideas and its ability to stimulate the receptive mind to think about how its grand vision might be reduced to practice, to the benefit of us all."[10] On Amazon, the appraisals are overwhelmingly positive. One reader remarks that "the basic strategy is quite sound, given the exponential progress in technology and especially bio-tech that we are seeing today."[11] In contrast came a handful of critical dissenters, including one by H.H., "a medical doctor practicing integrative medicine," who comments that the solutions were either "impractical," such as cell therapy, or commonplace, such as exercising or eating well.[12]

In striking contrast to de Grey, Elizabeth Blackburn and Elissa Epel, the authors of *The Telomere Effect: A Revolutionary Approach to Living Younger, Healthier, Longer* (2017), have sustained vitally important scientific work centrally related to understanding and promoting longevity. This is especially true of Blackburn, the senior of the two authors, who shared the Nobel Prize in Medicine or Physiology in 1999 with Carol W. Greider and Jack W. Szostak for their work on telomerase and telomeres. The latter, in the words of the National Genome Research Institute at the National Institutes of Health, "protect the ends of chromosomes from becoming frayed or tangled."[13] The Australian-born Blackburn received her PhD from Cambridge University based on work she did in a molecular biology lab. She continued her research, initially at Yale and then at the UC-Berkeley and University of California, San Francisco (UCSF). In 2015, she began a three-year stint as president of the Salk Institute for Biological Studies in La Jolla, California. Over time, she cofounded and then severed her relationship with Telomere Health, served on national committees, was featured in award-winning science documentaries, and focused her research on the relationship between telomeres and mindful meditation.

Epel, who received her PhD in psychology at Yale, is currently a professor in UCSF's Department of Psychiatry and director of the university's Aging, Metabolism, and Emotion Center. Much of her work focuses on the impacts of stress on telomeres. In 2017, the year *The Telomere Effect* appeared, Epel and Blackburn received the Alliance on Aging Research's prestigious Silver Innovator Award for what a writer for UCSF described as their "groundbreaking work on the psychological, social, and behavioral processes related to chronic psychological stress which accelerate biological aging."[14] As was true with *Ending Aging*, the responses to *The Telomere Effect* on Amazon's site were overwhelmingly favorable, with one reader, for example, writing that the book "should be of interest to anyone interested in healthy living and healthy aging. One of the authors got the Nobel Prize for her work in this area, nevertheless, the book is written in a manner that is readily understood by us mere mortals!" In contrast were the few critical responses. "Shame on them," wrote one reader, lamenting that "folks with these credentials fall prey to the 'quick buck' mentality of the pop-health crowd." Then this respondent continued by noting that "the book is full of 'maybe' 'could' 'might' and all the other safe words that allow them to say 'Hey, I never said it'd work . . .'"[15] Undaunted by criticism, near the end of 2022, Epel published *The Stress Prescription: Seven Days to More Joy and Ease.* Compared with *The Telomere Effect,* this book exists closer to the hyped, popular genre that focuses more on practical advice than scientific analysis. As the Amazon webpage for the book notes, "Epel distills decades of research, infused with wisdom, into a practical yet transformative seven-day plan of science-based techniques that can help you harness stress through more positive challenge and purpose."[16]

Next chronologically comes David A. Sinclair's *Lifespan: Why We Age—and Why We Don't Have To* (2019), written with the help of Matthew D. LaPlante, a professor of journalism at Utah State University and an author of books on science on his own and with other writers. Like Blackburn, Sinclair is an Australian American, in his case having earned his PhD in molecular genetics at the University of New South Wales and eventually becoming a professor of genetics at the Harvard Medical School, where he codirects the Paul F. Glenn Center for Biology of Aging Research. Like many of the authors under discussion, he has led nonprofit organizations, especially the Academy for Health & Lifespan Research, and has been a serial entrepreneur—in his case, often controversially so. Most recently, he has served as cofounder of the journal *Aging*, sponsored by the Academy and by Tally Health, whose website announces, "Welcome to a New Age," and invites you to "meet your personal longevity coach" and "become a member to start your journey to healthier aging."[17] In 2004, *Time* named Sinclair as among the "100 Most Influential People," calling him "the geneticist who is making age reversal real."[18]

Inevitably, Sinclair hyped the potential of his work. In 2004, using religious language to describe scientific findings, he remarked of one of his discoveries that it was "as close to a miraculous molecule as you can find" and that "one hundred years from now, people may be taking these molecules on a daily basis to prevent heart disease, stroke, and cancer."[19] Then, in 2020, he predicted that "one day it will be normal to go to a doctor and get a prescription for a medicine that will take you back a decade," before doubling down by stating, "there is no reason we couldn't live 200 years." In response, a writer in the *MIT Technology Review* noted, "It's this type of claim that raises so much skepticism. Critics see ballooning hype, runaway egos, and science that's on uncertain ground." Yet, he added, "the doubters this year were drowned out by the sound of stampeding investors," who were pouring billions of dollars into biotech companies, some of which were focusing on remedies for aging. Among the investors was "the cryptocurrency billionaire Brian Armstrong, the cofounder of Coinbase," who helped bankroll a corporation whose mission, he claimed, was "radical extension of human health span."[20] In a similar vein, Jeff Bezos and the Israeli billionaire Yuri Milner have invested $3 billion in Altos Labs, which *MIT Technology Review* described as "Silicon Valley's latest wild bet on living forever."[21]

On Amazon's website, most readers fully embrace what *Lifespan* offers. The book, one comments, did "a great job of transferring a ton of information to the reader (in this case, me!) and yet still managed to make it a very lighthearted and enjoyable book to read." Then, he continues celebratorily, "I have a feeling my life here on Earth not only got longer, it got a whole lot healthier too." Only a few, about 2 percent of almost ten thousand respondents, fully express skepticism. "The book is 95% scientific jargon and an exercise in Sinclair's self-aggrandizement." Another disappointed reader announces that the book had few "suggestions for enhancing longevity," most of which, like eating healthily and exercising, were hardly new.[22]

In 2020 came *Age Later: Health Span, Life Span, and the New Science of Longevity*, written by Nir Barzilai with the help of Toni Robino, in this case, as in some others, a cooperation involving a scientist and a writer. Robini advertises herself on LinkedIn as "The Book Architect, Concept Creation/Development, Book Writing Coach."[23] Barzilai earned an MD at Technion, the Israeli Institute of Technology. He migrated to the US in 1987 to take up residency at Yale and six years later joined the faculty at Yeshiva University's Albert Einstein College of Medicine. There he founded the Institute for Aging Research, the Nathan Shock Center for Excellence in the Basic Biology of Aging, and the Paul F. Glenn Center for the Biology of Human Aging Research. It was as the director of the medical school's Longevity Genes Project that he studied the hundreds of long-living Ashkenazi Jews with whom I began chapter 2. As he has founded only one biotech company, CohBar, Inc., his corporate entrepreneurship is much more modest than his academic career and than that of most of the other authors of scientifically based popular books. Apparently more modest in his claims about the scientific basis of longevity, in 2004 he remarked, "People think I'm searching for the Fountain of Youth," but he insisted that he was only "looking for ways to make old age better."[24]

With this book, the responses on Amazon are fewer in number but, as with the others, overwhelmingly positive. Yet the favorable ones are also more measured in their appraisals compared with responses to the other books. As one reader observes, the book conveys "the complexities of geroscience in a very straightforward and engaging language," grounded in how a "humble and enticing narration of the scientific facts often adorned with witty rhetorics makes the book exceptionally enjoyable to read." At least one of the relatively few negative reviews reflects dashed expectations fostered by objections to experiments using animals, the book's brasher competitors, and visions of science gone wild. "Virtually the entire premise of the book seems to be that the secret to be a happy and healthy centenarian is to be blessed with good genes—so that you don't have to worry about smoking, lack of exercise, or being obese." Rather, the respondent hoped that someday there would be "a pill or treatment that will tweak our DNA to mimic that of the genetically blessed centenarians," alas "driven by cruel and painful experiments on mice and monkeys (ethics and compassion be damned) financed by big pharma." The response concludes with its author "shudder[ing] at the thought of creating a super race of long lived humans with manipulated genes derived from experiments littered with dead and suffering sentient beings."[25]

Next in line chronologically is Andrew J. Steele's *Ageless: The New Science of Getting Older Without Getting Old* (2020). From what I can tell, Steele is the least controversial and self-aggrandizing of the authors of these scientifically based popular books. Not boastful about himself, he optimistically promises more than ample results: "understanding the scientific implications of ageing could lead to the greatest revolution in the history of medicine—one that has the potential to improve billions of lives, save trillions of dollars, and transform the human condition."[26] After receiving a PhD at Oxford in physics and convinced that aging is the most urgent scientific challenge, Steele turned his attention to computational biology. Working at London's biomedical research center the Francis Crick Institute, he focused on what National Health Service records could reveal about the relationship between genetics and heart attacks. Intentionally without a position in a university, he found his audiences through newspapers and television shows, as well as through the Discovery Channel's *Impossible Engineering* and *Strangest Things* on Sky television and even as what he calls on his website "a science stand-up (yes, that is a thing)" at a London theater that has also featured performances by the Rolling Stones and Bruce Springsteen. Unlike so many of his peers, he has apparently refrained from involvement in corporate biotech firms, instead providing leadership to two organizations that advocate more robust funding of science: the now-defunct Science Is Vital and Scienceogram, which continues to "make sense of our spending against the personal economic or human cost of the problems it's trying to tackle—and it looks like our miniscule spending on science doesn't make sense at all."[27]

Amazon's ratings, though somewhat less positive than with others, largely follow the familiar patterns of mostly high marks and rare negative ones. They also reveal the ongoing debate between the relationships of science and self-help advice. Interestingly, for some commentators at both ends of the spectrum, the issue is the same: whether the book fits the how-to genre. On the one hand, Jeff L. remarked about *Ageless*, "It is NOT a diet book or a book on what to do to prevent aging (which I appreciated)." Rather, he admired Steele's desire "to educate the reader on the aging process" by presenting "different theories and hypotheses on aging and how it affects different species." On the other hand, Ron Knepper turned Jeff L.'s positive observation into a negative one when he said that *Ageless*, though providing "a nice description of the various ways we age," regrettably offered neither solutions nor suggestions on how "to slow it down except for the old dogmas of no smoking, eating well, no supplements."[28] Ironically, Amazon offers a cornucopia of products that use the moniker "ageless"—on one version of its website, ads for Instantly Ageless Facelift in a Box stand on either side of the offering of Steele's book.[29]

With varying degrees of success, the authors of these five books skillfully and patiently explain the dramatically developing scientific and medical discoveries that make the study of longevity so promising. How convincing their claims are only time will tell. Aside from the power of social, economic, and political forces, what will determine the ability of billions of people around the world to live longer lives, and live them healthily, depends on issues like funding, the practices of regulatory agencies, the effectiveness of drugs like metformin, and above all what is involved in going from theory to experiments in labs to practical applications. Yet, in the end, my focus remains on what these books reveal less about the science and promise of new discoveries than about how their promoters envision their cultural meanings.

To varying degrees, these books explain the science that promises healthier and longer lives that seem to keep illness and death out of the picture, usually by focusing on results of investigations into genetics on the molecular level.[30] Sinclair emphasizes the importance of how advances in knowledge about sirtuins, proteins central to metabolic regulation, can turn aging into a treatable disease. Understanding them better, he asserts, will help produce "vaccines against senescent cells, CR mimetics, and retrotransposon suppressors" that will make it possible to "reset the aging clock and prevent cells from ever losing their identity and becoming senescent in the first place."[31] Barzilai, having insisted that "environment and life style can carry most of us only so far," emphasizes the importance of advances in genetic engineering. Among his strategies is using metformin "to prove that a drug can target the biology of aging itself" through his "Targeting Aging with Metformin (TAME) study."[32] Steele focuses on malfunctioning on the cellular level. What he calls "biogerontology" will make it possible to get to "negligible senescence" by "renewing things that are broken or lost, repairing things that are damaged or out of kilter and, finally, reprogramming our biology to slow or reverse aging."[33] De Grey's SENS promises to deploy new antiaging therapies to repair and reverse molecular damage. Like others, he offers interventions at the molecular level by tweaking genes in ways that will eventually transform the processes of human aging, in his case by focusing on mitochondria mutations in DNA. He deploys "novel hydrolytic enzymes to clear out the junk in our cells, preventing or reversing the most debilitating health problems of old age."[34] Blackburn and Epel write that going "deep into the genetic heart of the cell, into the chromosomes" where telomeres reside, will make it possible to use healthy telomeres as a "secret weapon" against "premature cellular aging."[35] With an emphasis on science unhinged, these scientific and medical advances challenge religious commitments, as they raise profound questions about life, mortality, science, and ethics, ones that these writers do not often confront.

These writers' assessments of what is possible or likely range widely. Some, Sinclair especially, offer what we might think of as medico-optimism by insisting that dramatically longer lives lived healthily in the not-too-distant future will transform society in untold and beneficent ways. "Prolonged vitality," Sinclair predicts, "is coming sooner than most people expect," so that "by the turn of the next century, a person who is 122 on the day of his or her death may be said to have lived a full, though not particularly long life. One hundred and twenty years might be not an outlier but an expectation, so much so that we won't even call it longevity; we will simply call it 'life,' and we will look back with sadness on the time in our history in which it was not so." "If cellular reprograming reaches its potential," he continues, "by century's end 150 may not be out of reach." Indeed, he insists in a way that brings heaven to earth despite all the dangers that surround us, it is possible that there will come a time when there is no "upper limit" to how long people will live. Once people recognize that it is possible to modify "the universal regulators of aging" by an antiaging molecule such as NMN, banned in 2023 by the Food and Drug Administration (FDA), "or a few hours of vigorous exercise or a few less meals," then "aging is going to be remarkably easy to tackle": "Easier than cancer. I know how that sounds. It sounds crazy."[36]

Steele comes close to echoing Sinclair's optimism, both acknowledging the obstacles ahead and celebrating, as the title of his book suggests, a time when "we would, as individuals and as a civilization, be ageless." A "de facto cure for aging" would make possible what he calls "longevity escape velocity," "a one-year-per-year increase in life expectancy." While he acknowledges that "most scientists wouldn't blame you for being skeptical of its plausibility," he predicts that a time will come when "a succession of technologies . . . gradually improve life expectancy to the point that people will notice that they've stopped aging." Initially, "the first ageless generation probably won't realize their luck at first—they'll grow up expecting to die at 100, or 150, or whenever 'old' is for their society." Then eventually "it will be blindingly obvious with hindsight, surveying centuries of life expectancy statistics, and spotting the point where people just stopped dying of old age."[37]

In what was in these books a relatively rare mention of retirement, Steele hails the overturning of what he characterizes as the triple stage idea of life's course: education, work, and then departure from the workforce. He envisions a future when we will "take periodic sabbaticals to return to education, travel or take up new hobbies at different times in our lives." Not only longer lives but longer lives lived healthily would, he claims, mark the end of retirement as we have understood it.[38] Along similar lines, Blackburn and Epel write of "a new purpose during retirement" by signing up for "The Experience Corps."[39]

De Grey also shows little caution. "Once your pro-aging trance is no more," he remarks, "you—yes, you—can make a difference to how soon aging is defeated." Then we would witness the closing of "an immense gap between how people envision *modest* postponement of aging and their attitude to the . . . genuine *elimination* of aging as a cause of infirmity and death." At that point, "the defeat of aging is *feasible*." At last, we would arrive at what he refers to as his "well-publicized case that a lot of people alive today may well live to be one thousand." Throwing caution to the wind and putting death off for eons, he thus chooses an age that surpasses that of Methuselah.[40]

Somewhat more cautious but nonetheless perhaps too optimistic is Barzilai. Like some others, he sees aging as a curable disease. "We are finally able to say that aging—as we know it—is over," poised as "we are on the leading edge of a revolution that will dramatically change the way we age. It may sound like science fiction, but I promise you it's *science*." He cites the Jewish blessing "May you live until 120," the age Moses supposedly achieved. "Once, such sentiments were just wishful thinking," he continues, "but perhaps now they will become the new normal." Yet, at moments, he seems more cautious, as evidenced by his use of the word "perhaps" in the preceding quote, by his acknowledgment of difficulties in securing patents and funding, by his recognition that "for now, though, we can stick to the humbler but wonderfully joyous Hebrew toast: *l'chaim*—to life," and by the title of one chapter, "Making Eighty the New Sixty."[41]

It is Sinclair especially who throws caution to the wind when confronted with concerns that having hundreds of millions, if not billions, of people living longer would wreak havoc. He counters those who argue that social, political, and economic results will be terrible, bringing on, as others have predicted, overpopulation, the collapse of job markets, adverse climate change, and social insecurity. Indeed, he insists that overcoming disease and prolonging lives is "probably the single most impactful thing we can do to avert a global crisis precipitated by climate change, crippling economic burdens, and future social upheavals." Sinclair hails a future "in which prolonged youthfulness is the torch that lights the way to greater universal prosperity, sustainability, and human decency." Steele and de Grey also predict that longevity will solve rather than exacerbate problems, adding to Sinclair's boisterous promises that longevity would not, as de Grey insists, perpetuate the possibility of "dictators living forever, or of a wealthy elite benefitting."[42]

For a number of reasons, I find problematic what I see as overly optimistic predictions articulated by Sinclair, de Grey, Steele, and Barzilai. The publication date of Sinclair's book was September 10, 2019, three months before the first evidence of COVID-19 appeared in China. Sinclair claimed that his predictions would come true, "barring a war or an epidemic." He also remarked that the remedies science and medicine would bring would be "available to most people regardless of socioeconomic status."[43] Indeed, the Great Recession and the COVID-19 pandemic, to say nothing of wars in Ukraine and Gaza and tempestuous politics, remind us that real-world events intervene, in some cases lowering life expectancies precisely when books were appearing with their sublime confidence that science will greatly prolong lives of billions of people at some time in the future, usually sooner rather than later. Belying the confidence of Sinclair and others in a soon-to-arrive socioeconomic utopia is the work of the Princeton economists Anne Case and Angus Deacon, who have shown unprecedented drops in life expectancy, as drugs, alcohol, suicides, and rampant capitalism ravage the lives of Americans, especially those in the white working class.[44] More generally, I have to wonder about how it could be that hosannas to long and healthy lives coincided with the rise of authoritarian leaders, the prevalence of failed states around the world, and outbreaks of violent conflicts in so many places—to say nothing of the increasing evidence of climate change. Moreover, the likelihood that by 2035 there will be more older Americans than those under eighteen underscores the potential of tremendous and often adverse problems with the federal budget as well as the job and housing markets. Yet there seemed little to stop these authors from their confident expressions of optimism.

These books vary somewhat not only in their expressions of optimism but also in their style and capaciousness. The most comprehensively ambitious books and the ones that, if Amazon reviews are any indication, compel the most attention—especially Sinclair's—artfully but chattily mix personal stories, surveys of historical advances in science and medicine, wisdom of philosophers, serious science lucidly and carefully explained, and colorful reports from worldwide networks of scientific investigators.

Yet they all also offer lots of advice on how to live longer and more healthily, often as readers wait for scientific discoveries to kick in. The books vary in how they balance gains due to scientific advances and lifestyle changes. As Amazon readers note, these authors recommend familiar strategies, especially not smoking at all or drinking excessively, proper dieting, reducing calorie intake, achieving a healthy body mass index, smart exercising, adopting mindfulness strategies, and sleeping well. In some instances, they go further, advising strategies such as exposing yourself to cold temperatures; taking not only the usual vitamins but also supplements like resveratrol, metformin, NAD boosters, and NMH; testing regularly for biomarkers and heart health; avoiding microwaved plastics and excessive CT scans and X-rays; vigorous brushing and flossing of your teeth; and having the good fortune of being female.[45]

To me, the most wide ranging and at times and in some ways weirdest recommendations for how readers could live longer and healthier comes from de Grey. After presenting the usual advice, he ends his book with an unusual pitch. Offering minimal focus on tactics such as diet and exercise, he focuses dramatically more than most writers on regulation and funding issues that slow down or prevent what he calls "the War on Aging" that will involve "the destruction of the pro-aging trance." He calls on readers to write their political representatives and lobby for funding and lifting restrictions on embryonic stem cell research. Yet something else would most significantly advance his expectation that "many people alive today" will "live to one thousand years of age" and lead "ultimately to an endless summer of literally perpetual youth." "An even more powerful thing you can do is to donate to the Methuselah Foundation" in support of its "The Methuselah Mouse Prize." Then, in the book's final paragraph, he tells readers, "eat well, exercise, and support the Methuselah Foundation, and I shall look forward to" a time when "we can enjoy dramatically extended lives in a new summer of vigor and health, the dark specter of age plague driven away by the sunshine of perpetual youth."[46]

The most impressive and interesting approaches to linking science and advice appear in Blackburn and Epel's *The Telomere Effect* and Peter Attia's *Outlive: The Science and Art of Longevity* (2023). Several things mark how the authors of the former book break the mold. Unlike most writers, who make their recommendations at the book's end, Blackburn and Epel do so throughout and in ways similar to how popular books by nonprofessionals highlight their own nostrums. They offer questionnaires to fill out, for example, one that enables you as a reader to assess "your stress response style." You too, they emphasize, can become a researcher, in a way that will give you "the power to influence whether your telomeres are going to shorten early, or whether they are going to stay supported and healthy." They also emphasize the importance of positivity, resilience, and purpose in a world where self-governance seems to work more effectively than communal or governmental action. Like other writers, Blackburn and Epel echo what Norman Vincent Peale advocated in *The Power of Positive Thinking* (1951) and was emphasized later on by happiness scholars. Barzilai, for example, speaks of harnessing "the power of purpose" and focusing "on the positive." In addition to the familiar run-of-the-mill lifestyle choices, Blackburn and Epel emphasize how scientific investigations that focus on telomeres underscore the importance of a broader range of factors such as healthy pregnancies, "whether you were exposed to childhood stress, and even the level of trust in your neighborhood," the adverse effect of "racial discrimination" and of income inequality, as well as the importance of "friends and lovers."[47]

Nowhere are their communitarian commitments clearer than on the final page of *The Telomere Effect*. "Just as your body is a community of individual and mutually dependent cells," they observe, "we are a world of interdependent people." This leads to their recommendation of "large changes, such as implementing policies for societal stress reduction," with "helping to change our communities and shared environment" strengthening "that vital sense of mission and purpose, which itself may improve our telomere maintenance." They double down in the final paragraph when they state that "the foundation for a new understanding of health in our society is not about 'me' but 'we.' Redefining healthy aging is not just about accepting gray hair and focusing on inner health," they insist as they emphasize a somewhat broader circle of we: "it's also about our connections with others and building safe, trusting communities." So they state in the final sentence, "Let's get started."[48]

Farther along the spectrum from longevity advice books by pathbreaking scientists to wildly popular ones by professional writers are several by MDs and PhDs who have done little original scientific research. Several command our attention because of their immense popularity: Ray Kurzweil and Terry Grossman, *Fantastic Voyage: Live Long Enough to Live Forever* (2004); *How Not to Die: Discover Foods Scientifically Proven to Prevent and Reverse Disease* (2015) by the MD Michael Greger, with the help of the professional writer Gene Stone; and two 2023 best sellers: Mark Hyman's *Young Forever: The Secrets to Living Your Longest, Healthiest Life*; and Attia's *Outlive*, written with the help Bill Gifford, a book that almost immediately zoomed to first place on the *New York Times* list of best sellers and remained there for months on end.[49] Like Attia, Hyman has developed a major clinical practice that focuses on longevity.

With regard to genre and content, Attia's *Outlive* and Hyman's *Young Forever* are the *Summa Longaevitas* books that build on what others have written before them. Attia grew up in Toronto, the son of Egyptian Coptic parents. After earning his MD at Stanford, he took up his residency as a surgeon at Johns Hopkins Hospital early in the twenty-first century and then worked as a surgical oncology fellow at the NIH's National Cancer Institute. According to a podcast biography, he "faced a personal health crisis, which became a significant turning point in his life." Realizing he was "suffering from metabolic syndrome," he began a "quest to better understand the underlying cause of chronic disease and find ways to optimize health and longevity." Supported by the Laura and John Arnold Foundation, in 2012, with the science journalist Gary Taubes, he cofounded the relatively short-lived Nutrition Science Initiative (NuSi), dedicated to the exploration of the health risks associated with obesity and diabetes. Then, in 2014, Attia developed a medical practice focused on how preventative medicine can enhance longevity. His most contemporary activities include a podcast followed by many people, *The Peter Attia Drive*, which has had had over seventy-five million episodes downloaded, and his role as cofounder and chief medical officer of Biograph, which advertises itself as "the world's most advanced longevity-focused diagnostic platform." More up front about the relationships between his scientific commitments and corporate ones, he makes clear on his website that he serves as the adviser to two corporations, Athletic Greens and Moonwalk Biosciences, and as an investor in almost a dozen corporations whose work he considers consonant with his larger vision of health and longevity.[50]

Attia offers extensive scientifically based recommendations about how to achieve not just life span but health span—even though at moments, he is realistic about what his readers will actually do. After all, his recommendations about diet, exercising, supplements, and testing are so extensive that following them would seem to take a person hours upon hours per day. His plan for Medicine 3.0 focuses on proactive prevention. He opposes those who "want to take a short-cut, right to the tactics," by eating this, following that exercise plan, and taking these supplements. "There are warehouses full of books that purport to have the answers, but the one you are reading is not one of them." Instead, he advocates pursuing an objective first, then strategy and tactics—though I suspect most readers will skip the first two and go immediately to the to how-to recommendations, especially what he views as the most important tactic: exercise. "I now consider exercise to be the most potent longevity 'drug' in our arsenal, in terms of lifespan and healthspan," he writes. Then, of course, there is one more thing that helped *Outlive* zoom to the number-one position on the best-seller list in *The New York Times*. He conveys at length and with considerable intensity the impact of what he calls his own "very long and painful journey to come to terms with things that happened to [him] in the past." Pitching to an audience eager not just for advice but also for personal connections, he offers this: "If you take nothing else from my story, take this: *If I can change, you can change.*" He relates that, "angry beyond words" and having hit having rock bottom, he arrived at The Bridge to Recovery in Bowling Green, Kentucky, which now advertises itself as "a sanctuary for healing from trauma and codependency."[51]

Despite his dramatic story, Attila expresses some skeptical caution about what Medicine 3.0 can achieve. "I kind of hate the word *longevity*," he writes, because "it has been hopelessly tainted by a centuries-long parade of quacks and charlatans who have claimed to possess the secret elixir to a longer life. I don't want to be associated with those people, and I'm not arrogant enough to think that I myself have some sort of easy answer to this problem." He rejects the idea that longevity, "barring some major breakthrough that, somehow, someway, reverses two billion years of evolutionary history and frees us from time's arrow," might involve "living forever. Or even to age 120, or 150." Without naming names, he refers to some "true believers" who say that if you follow their recommendations about diet, exercise, and meditation, "then you will be able to avoid death and live forever. What they often lack in scientific rigor they make up for with passions."[52]

Hyman is a prominent medical entrepreneur whose work focuses on living long and healthily. His best seller *Young Forever*, its title eliminating death from view, is by my count his nineteenth book, most of them about what we should eat but this one more wide-ranging, earning him a place along with Attia as an author who has brought robust findings and recommendations to abundant audiences. After earning his medical degree at the University of Ottawa, Hyman trained in family medicine and then began to practice as a family physician in rural Idaho before moving to the Berkshires, where he was medical director of Canyon Ranch, a health resort in Lenox, Massachusetts. There he founded the UltraWellness Center. He has also served as president of the Institute for Functional Medicine, was at one time the editor in chief and is now a contributing editor of *Alternative Therapies in Health and Medicine*, serves as a senior adviser to the Cleveland Clinic's Center for Functional Medicine, and is a podcaster for *The Doctor's Farmacy*. One production was a podcast episode titled "Death Is Inevitable but Aging Is Not with Dr. David Sinclair." Hyman remarks that he was joined by Sinclair "to explore the topic of longevity and antiaging and how he reduced his own internal age by more than twenty years." And here was an offer listeners could not turn down, unless they followed Greger's advocacy of a plant-based diet. "New subscribers to ButcherBox," Hyman promised, "will receive ground beef for life. When you sign up today, ButcherBox will send you twenty-one pounds of 100 percent pasture-raised grass-fed, grass-finished beef free in every box for the life of your subscription. Plus listeners will get an additional $20 off their first box."[53]

Much of what Hyman writes in *Young Forever* resembles Attia's analysis and recommendations—as well as the views of the most optimistic scientists such as Sinclair—if not necessarily in all specifics, then in general thrust. "Is it possible to live into our nineties, hundreds, and beyond disease-free, active, and mentally sharp?" he asks at the outset, before answering with "a resounding yes!" Even to "150 or 200," he adds, "which is not beyond current scientific possibility." Acknowledging that "aging is scary," he writes of a life of "love and service": "To dance under the stars, to ride my bike around the world, to hike remote mountains, to learn new languages, to laugh and play and cry with those I love." "I plan to live to be 120, maybe even 180," he insists, as he uses religious language to describe a secular pursuit, "in good health, savoring the miraculous gift of this life every day," blessed by "the emerging research on longevity and the right mindset," before adding that he believes "that's possible for all of us." Throwing caution to the wind while acknowledging threats to "our extinction," he promises, "we are on the verge of living as long as Methuselah." Indeed, he seems to have presented as established facts that Methuselah, Adam, and Noah lived well into their nine hundreds.[54]

Like others, Hyman mixes stories, about himself (including a highly personal one of his recovery from near-death conditions in his mid-fifties) and his patients, with accessible discussions of science, hyped promises, and extensive recommendations. Like others, he addresses readers with the personal "you." Asserting that aging is a treatable disease, he writes that "the extraordinary ability we have to unlock the key to disease reversal, rejuvenation, and aging backward is not a science fiction fantasy but science fact."[55] He joins others in insisting on focusing on advanced prevention rather than waiting until it is too late to take advantage of rapidly changing scientific discoveries, involving interventions on the cellular level, that promise, in relatively short order, to provide longevity to so many people. Yet, familiarly, he makes clear that what matters is not just living longer (life span) but doing so in good condition (health span).

Hyman follows Sinclair in insisting that spreading longevity in populations will solve rather than exacerbate socioeconomic problems. Mixing underlying science with specific recommendations, Hyman discusses what he has practiced with his patients for over thirty years and now offers you, the reader: his "Young Forever Program," based on "functional medicine," aka *the science of creating health.*" Focusing on root causes, his program relies on "the body's own healing and repair mechanisms, turning on the right genes, activating the right molecules, and providing the right inputs to rebuild and renew our bodies." Most of his specific recommendations are familiar enough, often with themes on a variation and greater specificity than other writers offer. Like Blackburn, Epel, and others, he talks of the importance of meaning, purpose, giving back, and connecting with others. Yet, at times, he is more expansive, including when he advises readers "to create a vision statement" and "transform your struggles and pain into purpose."[56]

Yet some of Hyman's more extensive and unique recommendations strike me as ones that would challenge my allocation of time and finances, to say nothing of my willingness to cross the line between conventional, widely accepted options and more experimental ones. He recommends that readers take the chance to obtain "a baseline panel of longevity laboratory testing" through his huckster-like Young Forever Functions Health Panel, ordinarily costing $15,000 but, for you, only $499. He suggests that they adopt a range of ways of monitoring their health through screening and testing as well as wearing a device like Fitbit. He recommends a full range of tests to determine your biological age and ascertain if you have cancer or heart diseases. He offers the chance to "add the Young Forever Supplements for Longevity" and drink "Dr. Hyman's Healthy Aging Shake." He pushes the envelope even further by, hold on a minute, recommending "advanced longevity-enhancing-strategies, . . . such as ozone, hyperbaric oxygen therapy, and Peptides" and, for the more venturesome, "exosomes, plasma exchange, natural killer cell infusions, and stem cell therapy. Use regenerative medicine to fix and heal pain and old injuries. Heal any traumas and your mind, heart, and soul by exploring emerging tools such as dynamic neural retraining, ketamine therapy, stellate ganglion block, and soon-to-be-available treatments of MDMA (also known as Ecstasy) and psilocybin." Farther off on the horizon are "Advanced Longevity Innovations" such as restoring stem cells by "intravenous infusions of injections into worn-out body parts."[57]

Hyman signed off on his text in October 2022 for a book published in February of the next year. As he sent off the manuscript, Xi Jinping secured his third term as head of the Chinese Communist Party; Vladimir Putin announced the annexation of Donetsk; climate-related events wreaked havoc in Nigeria, Venezuela, and the Philippines; and more evidence emerged of Donald Trump's violations of laws. Hyman acknowledges all there is to worry about—such as authoritarian threats to democracy, the depredations of climate change, the intensification of polarization and hatreds, and how "manipulative algorithms" undermine our freedom. Yet, he insists, we are learning how "to solve our most audacious challenges through innovation, creativity, and the genius of the human mind and spirit." To be sure, he speculates, "The focus on longevity and life extension for its own sake might seem like a narcissistic pursuit of the wealthy or a distraction from the fear of death."[58]

Both Attia and Hyman offer abundant opportunities for them to expand their reach and for you to benefit from what they advise. Their websites—www.drhyman.com and www.peterattiamd.com—direct inquirers to ways to learn more through podcasts, newsletters, and recipes. Greger presents an example of even more unrestrained medically based entrepreneurship. He reflects much of what Attia and Hyman write, but what makes follow-ups to his best-selling *How Not to Die* notable but hardly distinctive is that Greger's website, https://drgreger.org, offers access to books, speaking engagements, videos, pamphlets, and "merch," which includes mugs, aprons, T-shirts, posters, hoodies, and tote bags that celebrate "The Latest in Evidence-Based Nutrition" and "Plants Are the Best Medicine," all in multiple languages.

By the time I encountered *Fantastic Voyage* by Kurzweil and Grossman, I knew what to expect from Kurzweil, a widely hailed, world-famous futurist who works at Google, and Terry Grossman, a longevity MD now heading the Grossman Wellness Center, where you can "begin a journey that will help you achieve an optimal level of health and wellness virtually every day for the rest of your life."[59] After all, so many of the books I have read resemble what they offer early in the twenty-first century. The book's subtitle, with its promise of living "long enough to live forever"—is the tip to what lies inside. They substitute the worldly scientific lab for the otherworldly heaven by going from the Alpha of living forever to the Omega of meaning and purpose. Later books by other authors do so formulaically, alternating chapters on the science and pharmacology that make possible living forever, stories of their own personal journeys, and recommendations about how to exercise and what to digest prominent among the goals of life on Earth. Like so many other authors, they had drunk from fountains of youth. Early on, in the section titled "Immortality Is Within Our Grasp," they assert that "the knowledge exists, if aggressively applied, for you to slow aging and disease processes to such a degree that you can be in good health and good spirits when the more radical life-extending and life-enhancing technologies become available over the next couple of decades." Eventually, "the nanotechnology-AI" revolution will arrive, which "has the potential to allow us to live indefinitely." Then, as they near the book's end, they focus on "challenge, commitment, curiosity, and creativity" as ways of countering the multiple stresses of living, by practicing "lucid dreaming," being optimistic, seeking out beauty, relaxing, meditating, and rather than retiring, "chang[ing] the nature of your work from time to time."[60]

The range of responses on Amazon to *Fantastic Voyage* is familiar. Samuel Johnson writes that the book is "filled with scientific and medical information, no hocus pocus or mysticism." In contrast, and much rarer, are highly critical assessments. Wtx identifies Grossman as a "quack," and William writes that he had enjoyed Kurzweil's stuff until now. "BUT," he continues, "this Fantastic Voyage stuff is NOT science."[61]

Of the longevity books that were written by professional writers rather than someone with professional training directly related to longevity and that have attracted a robust readership, the most outstanding is *Life Force: How New Breakthroughs in Precision Medicine Can Transform the Quality of Your Life and Those You Love* (2022), written by Tony Robbins with the help of Peter H. Diamandis and Robert Hariri. Although Diamandis earned an MD at Harvard Medical School, he soon emerged as a visionary, entrepreneur, and best-selling author. Hariri, the author billed below the other two on the title page and someone who holds both an MD and a PhD, is an entrepreneur in the fields of longevity and biomedical interventions on the cellular level. Yet the person who shaped the book is Robbins—motivational speaker, best-selling author, philanthropist, serial entrepreneur, and, as the book's dust jacket says, someone who has "consulted and coached some of the world's greatest athletes, entertainers, Fortune 500 CEOs, and four U.S. presidents."[62] The titles of previous books by Robbins and Diamandis underscore the authors' commitments to optimistic positive thinking: *Unshakeable: Your Financial Freedom Playbook*; *Money: Master the Game: 7 Simple Steps to Financial Freedom*; *Unlimited Power: The New Science of Personal Achievement*; *Awaken the Giant Within*; *Abundance: The Future Is Better than You Think*; *Bold: How to Go Big, Create Wealth and Impact the World*; and *The Future Is Faster than You Think*.

Endorsed by Sinclair, Kurzweil (who wrote the book's introduction), and Hyman—to say nothing of celebrities such as Oprah, Dr. Oz, Jack Nicklaus, Serena Williams, and Sylvester Stallone—*Life Force* breathlessly, carefully, and abundantly follows the already familiar patterns, including the story of how what Robbins now conveys to readers about stem cell therapy rescued him from seemingly irreversible impediments to a long and healthy life. First comes "The Life Force Revolution," with its promise of lives lived long and healthily; then a middle section titled "Heroes of the Regenerative Medical Revolution," about people who have made it possible to reverse aging; and finally "What You Can Do Now." Although aimed at an audience larger than the elderly, longevity nonetheless remains a key focus. As other writers do, Robbins celebrates medical advances—many of which, he insists, "are happening right now!"—that will "unleash the pure, vibrant, turbocharged energy of your life force." If only you learn to "function as the CEO of your own health," all this will enable you to "understand why many of the world's most respected scientists believe that 80 can become the new 50, and soon 100 the new 60."[63]

Life Force breaks fresh ground at a number of points. There is a chapter on how to look more beautiful in "ways that once seemed unimaginable." Three well-credentialed professional women—Jennifer Garrison, Carolyn DeLucia, and Lizellen LaFollette—contribute a chapter on women's health over the life course. The authors recommend using placebos as a way of empowering your mindset. Above all, more than any other book, *Life Force* offers an up-to-date version of what Norman Vincent Peale's *The Power of Positive Thinking* had presented seventy years before. "Regardless of what happens to us, our minds can make us sick or healthy, miserable or happy, fearful or faithful and grateful," Robbins insists. Then, using both boldface and underlining, he goes on to state, "The most important decision that you can make is to decide that life is too short to suffer and that you're going to appreciate and enjoy this gift of life, no matter what happens." Finally, on the second-to-last page, Robbins writes, "Before you turn the final page, I hope you really take a moment to commit to live in a beautiful state, no matter what happens."[64]

Though perhaps not as robustly extensive as what Greger has on offer, Robbins's website (www.tonyrobbins.com) points you to opportunities to connect with "Tony's Coaches," as well as shop for books, programs, apps, and supplements. You also have the opportunity to attend events and join programs. Among them is becoming a "Tony Robbins Platinum

Partnership member," which would enable you to "receive exclusive invitations to up to three incredible adventures per year," and on some of these trips, Tony and his wife, Sage Robbins, will join Partners "as they learn, network, and play in such diverse situations as a private palazzo in Venice, the cascading beaches of Bora Bora, a private session on top of the Great Wall of China, 100 mph boat races in South Beach, a private invitation to Scotland's Skibo Castle and even camel riding through the Great Pyramids of Egypt." And you can sign up for sponsored events in order to "UNLEASH THE POWER WITHIN" to "experience explosive growth" by getting "all the tools and strategies you need to break through barriers, harness your power, and create a life you love."[65]

In contrast to books by authors ranging from Sinclair and Attia to Kurzweil and Robbins, two take a very different approach to longevity, exploring as they do communities around the world where a significant percentage of the local population lives unusually long lives and does so healthily. With Héctor García and Francesc Miralles's *Ikigai: The Japanese Secret to a Long and Happy Life* (2016) and Dan Buettner's *The Blue Zones: 9 Lessons for Living Longer from the People Who've Lived the Longest* (2012), I felt relief from the hype, hard edge, and intensely scientific approach that demands so much of its followers with regard to money, time, and disciplined attention.

Compared with books in the more demanding genre (Robbins, *Life Force*, is a whopping 691 pages), García and Miralles's *Ikigai*'s is a brief, 194-page, charming book, one not burdened by highly technical explanations of scientific breakthroughs. Instead, it deploys approaches that are simultaneously specific and elusive. With its title (translated from the Japanese as "the happiness of always being busy") denoting the intricate combination of mission, passion, profession, and vocation as reasons for living, García and Miralles explore Ogimi, a Japanese village on Okinawa, inhabited by the world's longest-living people, one of whose "secrets to happiness" is that from early on, its inhabitants feel "like part of a community," practicing as they do "*yuimaaru*, or teamwork, and so are used to helping one another."[66] The authors, both citizens of Spain but García also of Japan, are, respectively, a software engineer who has lived in Japan for over a decade and an author of best-selling self-help books.

Living on "the island of (almost) eternal youth," the villagers were less likely to suffer from the usual afflictions and "enjoyed enviable levels of vitality and health that would be unthinkable for people of advanced age elsewhere," they write, as they celebrate the virtues of small communities that contrast with the lives of most Americans. Of course, proper dieting, sleeping, sociability, meditating, and exercising (as well as an attentive health care system) are factors that make it possible for almost 25 percent of the inhabitants of the island to be centenarians, but more important are a series of attitudes and commitments that stand in contrast to what most of us in the US experience. Lacking a word for retirement in the sense of no longer being in the workforce, many people living in Japan "keep doing what they love for as long as their health allows." Being in the flow, avoiding stress, finding meaning in things large and small, and drawing on Zen Buddhism make it possible for people to "pursue their passion no matter what." Recognizing the "beauty of the fleeting, changeable, and imperfect nature of the world around us" and the "impermanence of things" enables them "to focus on the present and enjoy each moment that life brings us," lived in the here and now. Inspired by "emotional resilience," "they adopted techniques that go beyond resilience to cultivate *antifragility*." García and Miralles note the importance of "redundancies": having more than one job and multiple friendships that compel you. They also highlight the significance of expressing gratitude, connecting with nature, and living in the present. Then, at the end, they bring it all together. "There is a passion inside, a unique talent that gives meaning to your days and drives you to share the best of yourself until the very end." And if you have not yet discovered your *ikigai*, then "your mission is to discover it."[67]

Dan Buettner's discovery of Blue Zones, more extensive than what García and Miralles explore, underwrites the other project emanating from knowledge about peoples around the world experiencing unusually long and healthy lives. Like García and Miralles, Buettner celebrates the simple, healthy, and communal life in sites unlike those where almost all Americans live. The holder of Guinness records for long-distance cycling, he began in 1995 to develop expeditions as a way of solving mysteries. He founded Blue Zones LLC in 2003 and started leading expeditions in search of locations where people live long lives, an enterprise supported by *National Geographic* and the National Institute on Aging. Two years later, in 2005, he published a front-page story in *National Geographic* titled "Secrets of Long Life."[68]

Before long, he was off and running, as he built an empire, not unlike those of Greger and Robbins, that underscores how longevity entrepreneurship might help satisfy the apparently unquenchable thirst for some semblance of hope that readers might live long and healthy lives that could help them forget a range of social, political, and economic problems at home. The first in a series of longevity books published by *National Geographic*, *The Blue Zones: Lessons for Living Longer from the People Who've Lived the Longest*, appeared in 2008, updated four years later with *The Blue Zones: 9 Lessons for Living Longer from the People Who've Lived the Longest*. These books rapidly earned Buettner a coveted place on the *New York Times* list of best sellers; appearances on shows hosted by Oprah, Dr. Oz, and Anderson Cooper; and the opportunity to give a TED Talk titled "How to Live to Be 100+," which has attracted close to five million viewers. Other books and related enterprises followed, among them *Thrive: Finding Happiness the Blue Zones Way* (2010), *The Blue Zones Solution: Eating and Living like the World's Healthiest People* (2015), and two even more practical offerings: *The Blue Zones Kitchen: 100 Recipes to Live to 100* (2019) and *The Blue Zones Challenge: A 4-Week Plan for a Longer Better Life* (2021).[69]

Writing in *The New York Times*, Dana G. Smith captured the extent of the Blue Zones empire. "In the 20 years since blue zones were first introduced," she wrote in October 2024, "the Blue Zones brand (now trademarked) has spawned eight books, a Netflix series, product partnerships (Langers Blue Zones iced tea, Bush's Blue Zones canned bean soups) and a multibillion dollar program for other cities to become 'Blue Zones certified'—all in the name of helping people attain their longevity goals, ostensibly by mimicking the lifestyle habits of the individuals living in each region."[70]

Buettner captures the long lives of citizens of five Blue Zones—the Barbagia region of Italy's Sardinia, Japan's Okinawa, Costa Rica's Nicoya Peninsula, the Greek island of Ikaria, and in Southern California among Seventh-Day Adventists in Loma Linda. Although he draws on the work of experts in a wide range of fields, he writes in an accessible, even breezy style, laced with travel narratives. Endorsed by Drs. Oz, Andrew Weil, and Sanjay Gupta, Buettner distances himself from unnamed exaggerators. He strongly criticizes those who promise more than they can deliver. "The idea of discovering a magic source of long life still has so much appeal today," as when Ponce de León arrived in Florida in 1513, "that charlatans and fools perpetuate the same boneheaded quest, whether it comes disguised as a pill, diet, or medical procedure."[71] He goes on to quote a statement, discussed shortly, by "more than 50 of the world's top longevity experts," who insisted that "there are no lifestyle changes, surgical procedures, vitamins, antioxidants, hormones, or techniques of genetic engineering available today that have been demonstrated to influence the process of aging."[72]

Unlike writers such as Sinclair and Attia who insist on extensive, costly, and disciplined interventions, Buettner makes clear that moderation characterizes the advice itself, as well as the pace and extent to which readers should follow it—what he calls "an à la carte menu of sorts," from which "you can pick and choose the most appealing items." Unlike longevity scientists discussed earlier, Buettner makes no promises that following the advice he offers gives you a good chance of living well past one hundred. Instead, to counter what he calls "the brutal reality about aging," he notes that adopting "the right lifestyle . . . could add at least ten good years" of healthy living. "When it comes to the science of longer living, however," he cleverly remarks, "centenarians can no more tell us how they reached age 100 than a seven-foot man can tell us how he got to be so tall."[73] Or, as Thomas T. Perls, director of the New England Centenarian Study at Boston University and coauthor of *Living to 100: Lessons in Living to Your Maximum Potential at Any Age* (1999), writes when he points in Buettner's book to "mostly hucksterism and charlatanism," "a good start to adding more good years to your life would be to get rid of the anti-aging quackery."[74]

From the stories of folks who live long and healthy lives, Buettner insists, it is possible to "learn how to create our own personal Blue Zones, and start on the path to living longer, better lives." Most of what the lives of those in the five Blue Zones represent is familiar enough: diets that limit caloric intake and rely on plants, living purposefully, sustaining social connections with friends and family, giving back to others, and exercising not in a gym but as part of one's daily routine. Some lessons learned, based on specific local patterns, are more unusual, such as drinking goat milk or red wine, ingesting more soy products or herbals, planting a medicinal garden, eating dinner early, drinking hard water, and fasting. Then Buettner offers his own "nine deceptively simple but powerful things you can do today to create a lasting Blue Zone in your own life," all of them more modest than what people like Sinclair and Attia recommend and most of them simple and familiar, such as moderate physical activity, having a sense of purpose, leading a less stressful life, and connecting with family and like-minded friends. A few build on what he discovered in his travels, such as participating in a faith, religious, or spiritual community.[75] After he dispenses such wisdom comes one recommendation rarely heard from longevity experts. "Old-age homes don't exist in the world's Blue Zones," he observes, even though they do exist, sponsored by Adventist Health.[76] Nonetheless, he correctly insists that "a combination of family duty, community expectations, and genuine affection for elders keeps centenarians living with their families."[77]

Well, in light of books offered by scientists, motivational speakers, and those who explore places where people live long and healthy lives, how can you drink from the fountains of youth? The simplest and least expensive way is by reading one or more books—any one of which you can take out at your local library or buy at your local bookstore or online. Next up would be partaking of some of the offerings available from the Longevity Commercial Complex. Among the amplest are from Buettner's Blue Zones world. On Netflix, you can watch *Live to 100: Secrets of the Blue Zines* (2023). Among books, there are not only those on thriving and inspiring but also those on how to cook and eat like the people living in Blue Zones. You can buy herbal teas, a Blue Zones MOVE Activity Cube, Earth-friendly skin-care products from Immunocologie, or apparel such as a T-shirt or a tote bag.[78]

In addition to (and often based on) all these popular books are longevity clinics that draw on science and appeal to converts. Expanding and proliferating, they might well make you anxious, revealing as they might information that is worrisome even if accurate. Most of them, notes Jessica Hamzelou, "are expensive and currently only cater to the wealthy," costing between $5,000 and $50,000 annually. She explores all this and other issues in a 2024 issue of *MIT Technology Review* after attending a December 2023 conference that focused on establishing longevity medicine as a legitimate and formally recognized field like pediatrics or cardiology. A visit to a clinic can start with half a day of testing that includes blood work and bone density scans. With you on a treadmill, doctors measure the amount of oxygen you use when exercising. Then there are assessments of cognitive abilities and lifestyle choices. A whole-body MRI scan will reveal other data, including warning signs to track. Tests will examine your microbiome and genome. Clinicians will prescribe varieties of supplements. They will deploy problematic aging clocks to assess, among other things, how close you are to the end of your life. Nutritionists and physical therapists will coach you on what you eat and how to become more fit. They might deploy, Hamzelou writes, "a variety of stem cell-based treatments offered with vague promises of repairing and rejuvenating a person's body." Later appointments will examine data from devices you have worn since the initial appointment. Most of the people involved in the effort to legitimize the field and promote its clinics, Hamzelou reports, "believe that the majority of people can live to around 100 in good health, providing they eat, sleep and exercise well, identify their personal health needs and address the earliest signs of age-related diseases long before they start to develop symptoms."[79]

If you are a true believer and have time and money to spare, there is more. Peter Attia reportedly charges $150,000 annually for the highest level of his services.[80] The Tony Robbins Platinum Partnership membership costs $85,000 for the first year, a figure that goes down to $75,000 in the second year and then a mere $65,000 for the third and fourth years.[81] I cannot easily determine the cost of longevity programs at the Grossman Wellness Center in Glendale, Colorado, but surely it is not inexpensive to take advantage of all it offers, including multiple types of IV therapies, ozone therapy, bio-energy TM testing, hormone replacement therapy, nutritional supplements, longevity evaluation, and low-level laser therapy. But I do know that the center advertises a book by Grossman and Kurzweil, *Transcend: Nine Steps to Living Well Forever.*[82] This is all a somewhat roundabout way of saying that robust longevity programs are available only to those who can afford the costs, not only in money but also in time.

In other ways, fountains of youth remind us of their political and socioeconomic dimensions. With their emphases on positive thinking, personal practices, small communities, and the power of the science of longevity, longevity books for the most part recommend strategies that minimize the importance of acting collectively through the federal government, broad-based communal institutions, or major nongovernmental organizations. To be sure, some of the authors, notably Blackburn and Epel, embrace communitarian commitments without making explicit any reliance on government action. Moreover, there is one notable exception, seen in the frequent call on the FDA to label aging a disease, a decision that would open the floodgates to funding for research and make it easier to advance the science of longevity.

Moreover, when contemplating the possibility that tens or even hundreds of millions of Americans living well past one hundred would adversely affect the climate and government funding of Social Security, Medicare, and Medicaid, authors remain confident that entrepreneurship, as well as people's resilient choices, will counter the dangers of long and healthy lives. From what I can see, having more people work for longer periods of time is the one remedy often mentioned to solve fiscal problems. More typically, despite the books' optimism, they frequently acknowledge that medical advances will outpace society's ability to grapple with their consequences. When faced with the challenges of aging, these books emphasize that individuals and society should rely principally on highly structured collective action in labs but not elsewhere.[83] In addition, it is hard to square their optimism about solving the problems caused by so many people living so long with the current state of US politics, marked by partisan rancor, let alone how racism and inequalities afflict so many Americans.

Inevitably, divisions and critical assessments of the organized passion for longevity have emerged. The key division is between scientists engaged in biogerontological research and those involved in what is known as the Anti-Aging Medicine movement, best represented by the American Academy of Anti-Aging Medicine (A4M). To this cultural historian, it is sometimes difficult to distinguish between what Robert H. Binstock has called "the Gerontological Establishment" and those involved in A4M.[84] Both groups claim the scientific mantle, advocate a wide variety of longevity strategies, and, at least to me, sometimes embrace exaggerated claims. Perhaps the best way of differentiating the two groups and approaches is this: People like Blackburn are bench scientists who run labs supported by universities and biomedical investors. If their work began in labs, it was not long before they broadcast the results and applications of their scientific findings through popular books and amplified organizations. Whatever the connections with one another that they have established, these scientists by and large remain a group of individual researchers/entrepreneurs who work to develop and then apply scientific findings in order to promote longevity. A4M is more like an organized social movement that relies on scientific advances, but compared with what emerges directly from the work of scientific laboratories, it offers a wider range of longevity strategies. Currently not recognized by established medical groups such as the American Medical Association, A4M trains and then certifies practitioners, currently twenty-six thousand of them in 120 countries. Legally a nonprofit organization, A4M spreads its offerings through lobbying, public relations, conferences, publications, and the sale of products and procedures. Neither group has avoided controversy over its claims, but A4M faced more than its competitors.

In 1992, well before the publication of the books already discussed, two osteopathic physicians, Ronald Klatz and Robert Goldman, founded A4M which offers itself, according to its website, as "the established global leader for continuing medical education in longevity medicine, metabolic resilience, and whole-person care."[85] In 1999, Klatz published *Ten Weeks to a Younger You*, whose cover promised to increase your IQ and enhance your memory and sexual performance, by offering "age reversing benefits of the youth hormones."[86] At first glance, the goals of A4M and those who are more well established professionally in biomedicine and gerontology, including the National Institute on Aging, may seem parallel or even similar, yet for decades, the conflicts between the two groups have been intensely bitter.[87]

Nowhere are controversies clearer than in the 2002 article in *Scientific American* titled "No Truth to the Fountain of Youth," authored by three academic scientists who had conducted research on aging: S. Jay Olshansky, Leonard Hayflick, and Bruce A. Carnes. Without naming names, they write, "The hawking of anti-aging 'therapies' has taken a particularly troubling turn of late," with "disturbingly large numbers of entrepreneurs . . . luring gullible and frequently desperate customers of all ages to 'longevity' clinics, claiming a scientific basis for the anti-aging products they recommend and, often, sell." They add that the internet, then less than ten years old, "has enabled those who seek lucre from supposed anti-aging products to reach new customers with ease." They insist that "no currently marketed intervention—none—has been proven to slow, stop, or reverse human aging," and some on offer "can be downright dangerous."[88] Their statement achieved wide circulation—endorsed by fifty-one international physicians and scientists, reprinted in professional journals in the US and abroad, and the subject of the lead article in the *AARP Bulletin*.

The battles persisted. Well-established groups drew boundaries between the kosher and the treyf and embarked on educational efforts to highlight what they considered dangerous and incorrect approaches, as they attacked those whom they felt were chasing profits by preying on uninformed and vulnerable consumers. The people involved in A4M returned fire by calling into question the work of gerontologists and biomedical scientists. For example, they issued a statement that described Olshansky as "part of a 'multi-billion gerontological machine' that, without any basis in truth or fact, seeks to discredit tens of thousands of innovative, honest, world-class scientists, physicians, and health care practitioners."[89] Nor did A4M stop there, insisting, "Simply put, the death cult of gerontology desperately labors to sustain an arcane, outmoded stance that aging is natural and inevitable. . . . Ultimately, the truth on aging intervention will prevail, but this truth will be scarred from the well-funded propaganda campaign of the power elite who depend on an uninterrupted status quo in the concept of aging in order to maintain its unilateral control over the funding of today's research in aging."[90]

Valerie Reitman's January 2004 *Los Angeles Times* article "A Rift in Business, Science of Aging" makes clear what is at stake. More than a thousand doctors, dieticians, and physical therapists who attended a A4M conference in Las Vegas "had paid more than $1,000 to learn about the latest anti-aging therapies, from human growth hormone treatments to nutritional supplements to 'cosmeceutical' creams." Their clients are "clamoring for such treatments to make them look and feel better. And there is money to be made: By some estimates, the market for aging-related products is $42 billion annually." She observes that the organization's critics "contend that there is more at risk in the debate than A4M's viability and credibility. They fear that support for scientifically rigorous research into aging—examining topics such as why muscle mass diminishes and we become frail as we age—may be tainted by a group that welcomes companies that sell wrinkle creams, hair-growing potions, sexual enhancement pills and hormone treatments such as those on exhibit at last month's conference."[91]

Entering the fray of debates about longevity and science in a 2024 article in *Nature*, Olshansky and his colleagues marshal evidence to argue that the initial dramatic increase in life expectancy is now over. They recognize that "a second longevity revolution is approaching in the form of modern efforts to slow biological aging. . . . Until it becomes possible to modulate the biological rate of aging and fundamentally alter the primary factors that drive human health and longevity, radical life extension in already long-lived national populations remains implausible in this century."[92] In the meantime, enhanced health span—rather than longer life span—is possible, albeit that conditions, especially widespread obesity, have actually shortened the lives of so many people.[93] Indeed, Olshansky insists, with an upper limit to how long lives can be extended, those who had set on 120 as the number of years millions of people would live had pulled such a figure out of thin air—expecting many to live to 100 seemed possible, even likely, but 120, out of the question. Moreover, like skeptical me, he believes that the earlier distinction between "the Gerontological Establishment" and A4M that Binstock identified, which decades earlier seemed clear to him, had eroded. Like me, he worries that some scientists have crossed over into a danger zone and, like unscientific exploiters of people's fears and hopes, are selling longevity.[94]

Also in 2004, Olshansky, in response to Grossman and Kurzweil's *Fantastic Voyage*, criticized what he called "the cult of immortality." What they and others were doing, he wrote, was "weaving once again the seductive web of immortality, tantalising us with the tale that we all so desperately want to hear, and have heard for thousands of years—live life without frailty and debility and dependence and be forever youthful, both physically and mentally." Such seductive hopes, he insisted, "will no doubt last longer than its proponents."[95]

Early in the twentieth century, Olshansky established the Silver Fleece Award for Anti-Aging Quackery, with the first award going to A4M and to Clustered Water, a company based in Washington State that offers a "nontoxic water solution" to reverse aging.[96] I learned of this from reading Andrew J. Scott's *The Longevity Imperative: How to Build a Healthier and More Productive Society to Support Our Longer Life* (2024), the third of his books on the topic.[97] *The Longevity Imperative*, endorsed by Sinclair and Steele, is a learned, cautious, and capacious book. It is cautious in that Scott, relying on "short-term pessimism combined with long-term optimism," distances himself from "the charlatans and visionaries who flock to the subject" of "defeating the aging process." He embraces neither the expensive and so-far-untested nostrums others endorse as a way to extend life nor the promise that so many will live a decade or more beyond age one hundred. It is capacious in the sense that his analysis encompasses the scientific, political, economic, and highly personal aspects of living longer in good health.[98]

What Scott calls his "evergreen agenda" involves embracing a shift from seeing ourselves living in an aging society where focus is on "spiraling health costs, a pensions crisis, dementia and care homes" to being in a longevity one "that prepares us for longer lives and ensuring that the quality of life matches the newly found quantity." Emphasizing intergenerational commitments involves forcing not only how elders live but also how others do as well. His embrace of a "second longevity revolution" during which geroscience causes rates of mortality to fall even among the oldest citizens promises to impel so many of us forward "to a radical new era for humanity." Rather than going "straight to the new and exotic and potential wonder treatments," he emphasizes more humdrum and traditional approaches, such as exercising, eating and sleeping well, developing social connections, and reducing inequalities.[99]

Scott offers a comprehensive set of recommendations about how individuals and nations will thrive under new and transformative conditions. What will drive change will be "not just the elixir-chasing billionaires" but "decisions of billions of ordinary people" about how they live their lives, gain an education, and spend their money and leisure time. Yet he also advocates a robust and precedent-breaking public agenda in which over the long term, benefits will offset costs. He calls on experts to shift health care from intervention to prevention and public health to enhance health span in a world where life span has already increased. People will work longer, and the job market will have to accommodate older workers. Education should become a lifelong venture. Public policy will need to move away from age-based policies. To be sure, Scott seems overly confident that, even if desirable, developed nations can bring all this about successfully.[100]

Yet few are those who have asked the more fundamental question about longevity, one that both camps of longevity seekers rarely, if ever, even consider: Is the pursuit of longevity, so prominent an issue today, even desirable?[101] No one has raised this question more thoughtfully than Leon Kass, who earned a PhD in biochemistry and an MD, served as chair of the President's Council on Bioethics from 2001 to 2005, and is now retired from a professorship at the University of Chicago and is a Senior Fellow Emeritus at the American Enterprise Institute. In the May 2001 issue of *First Things*, he offers his thoughts in an article titled "L'Chaim and Its Limits," referencing in its title that raising a glass "to life" represents how "the celebration of life—of *this* life, not the next one—has from the beginning been central to Jewish ethical and religious sensibilities." Aware of the possibilities of the emerging scientific discoveries that promise longevity and drawing on the wisdom of literary, religious, and philosophical texts, Kass insists that "this beloved biomedical project, for all its blessings, now raises for Jews and for all humanity a plethora of serious and often unprecedented moral challenges." Acknowledging the usual warnings, especially about the social-economic consequences of longer lives, he instead focuses on how "our growing power to control human life may require us to consider possible limits to the principle of *L'Chaim*."[102] As Susan Jacoby writes in *Never Say Die: The Myth and Marketing of the New Old Age*, "what seems to concern Kass is not so much the length of life as the temerity of researchers who wish to manipulate the process of aging and give themselves credit, in God-like fashion, for the extension of longevity."[103]

In some ways convincingly to me, Kass identifies four "virtues of mortality," insisting "that the finitude of human life is a blessing for every human individual, whether he knows it or not." He identifies how mortality would intensify *"interest and engagement,"* promote *"seriousness and aspiration,"* sustain engagement with *"beauty and love,"* and finally, enhance "the peculiarly human beauty of character, *virtue and moral excellence.*" Thus, he calls on people to "resist the siren song of the conquest of aging and death" that "biomedical technology" has promised and instead "cleave to our ancient wisdom and lift our voices and properly toast *L'Chaim*," to the lives of family members of the future who, he hopes, "God willing . . . may also know the pursuit of truth and righteousness and holiness. And may they hand down and perpetuate this pursuit of what is humanly finest to succeeding generations for all time to come." As elegant and probing as what Kass wrote is, there is the offsetting evidence that little will stop the promise of longer lives lived more healthily, promises made by scientists, gerontologists, and charlatans.[104]

Cogent and more recent critiques of the pursuit of longevity are also available. In "No Time to Die: When Does the Quest for a Healthy Life Become Unhealthy?," published in *The New Yorker* in April 2024, the physician Dhruv Khullar casts an informed and skeptical eye on the work of Peter Attia. He notes how "the increasing obsession with longevity" has "inspired a backlash" that sees "many in the life-extension movement" as "quacks or hacks who peddle pills, potions, and false promises" instead of seeing "the loss of our capacities as something to accept, not avoid." He calls attention to perhaps "hundreds of specialized 'longevity clinics'—including some that charge six-figure annual fees— which claim to offer more of the world's most valuable commodity: years of healthy life." He focuses on Attia, "perhaps the most prominent longevity evangelist," whose "telemedicine practice" offers, "for an undisclosed price, . . . health advice, diagnostic tests, exercise protocols, and supplements to a wealthy and exclusive clientele." This was so, Khullar insists, even though Attia's emphasis on the term "longevity movement" "just smells like snake oil." Also in opposition to Attia stands the health policy expert and oncologist Ezekiel Emanuel, who characterizes many of the longevity nostrums as "hocus-pocus." In addition, Emanuel trenchantly argues that "doctors should focus less on 'getting rich people from ninety to one hundred' than on improving health in communities where people died young." When Attia was asked for his response to such advice, he responded, "I've never concerned myself with that."[105]

In the end, it is possible to understand the celebration of longevity as an example of the quest for successful wellness and aging that often reflects steroidal hucksterism. As such, it displaces religion and relies on the power of scientific and medical advances and the feel-good optimism so familiar in popular books on retirement. It promotes scientific extremism when populist animus against science is so visible outside university and corporate labs and the books that emerge from them. Those who promise that scientific and medical advances will help millions live well past one hundred rely un-self-reflexively on an ageist revulsion against those who cannot live long and healthy lives and, more explicitly, on celebrations of independence, self-governance, and continued productivity. At times, it seems to allow the living to put mortality out of mind. The critical gerontologist Stephen Katz terms impulses like the promise of longevity part of a vision of "postmodern aging" that stems from "culture industries that distribute pleasure and leisure across" an eager population and, as a result, "recast the life span in fantastical ways, in particular, in the masking of age and the fantasy of timelessness." This vision of successful aging, which insurance companies hope will prompt people to rely more on self-care than on expensive medical procedures, depends, again un-self-reflexively, on opportunities open to affluent people living in North America and western Europe, relying on what Katz calls "an illusion of consumer democracy."[106] Or, as the writer Joe Kloc remarked in *The New York Times*, the day before Trump's second inauguration, "The longevity industry is coming off perhaps its best run on record," at a time when American life expectancy at seventy-eight was the same age as what Trump had reached. Scientific studies, supplements, diets, and podcasts pointed to "the same mix of solid science, quixotic experimentation and questionable advice that has, for much of recorded history, defined the pursuit" of living forever.[107]

However optimistic, the celebration of longevity and successful aging cannot make problems of inequality, racism, pandemics, climate change, dangerous authoritarianism, and contentious political battles disappear. Solutions in biomedical labs, robust entrepreneurship, and far-off small communities provide alternatives to a sense of the fragility of life in the US. Unbound commerce—seen in support of potentially life-changing medical interventions developed in labs and then offered as costly procedures—opens up the possibility that in a troubled world, we should focus on how we can control our bodies. The power of individualistic positive thinking can take our attention off the prevalence of negative collective events. In celebrating the power of science on Earth and keeping death distant, the quests for longevity reveal how much, for so many Americans, heaven, religion, and belief in afterlife have lost their power.

4

Aging Organizations

Gray Panthers, Gerontological Society of America, AARP, National Institute on Aging, Research Centers, and Business Organizations

Inevitably, issues as significant as retirement and longevity have led to the launching of a series of organizations that underscore how aging is a significant social and political concern. Together they serve as advocates for older Americans by focusing on issues such as ageism, health care, and Social Security. Among the most important ones developed in the period after World War II were the Gray Panthers, the Gerontological Society of America, the American Association of Retired Persons (AARP), the National Institute on Aging, corporate and universities centers, and enterprises that helped businesses sell products and services to older people. Such a list hardly includes all the relevant organizations. Among others are the National Council on Aging, the Leadership Council of Aging Organizations, the Federal Council on Aging, Second Wind Dreams, the National Commission of Senior Citizens, the Family Caregiver Alliance, the Older Women's League, Caring Across Generations, and the Alzheimer's Foundation of America, as well as state and local agencies. The work of these organizations has both challenged and confirmed trends seen elsewhere in this book.

As James Chappel has shown in his 2024 book *Golden Years: How Americans Invented and Reinvented Old Age*, by the late 1960s, no major extensions to government programs for elders were in sight, something confirmed by the fractious and increasingly conservative politics of the following years. Despite the often heroic efforts of advocates for the disabled, people of color, and mostly female caregivers, by and large the powerful organizations for seniors that now gathered strength focused on white, middle-class and above, and able-bodied seniors. Trade unions and the Democratic Party, once among the most important supporters of more robust state programs, were themselves weakened. The result,

Chappel shows, was that "a loosely organized interest group" and private corporations stepped into the vacuum left by a once powerful "organized old-age movement" to improve the lives of elders. What resulted was "a crisis of care" that the more fortunate elders could solve through a combination of privilege and entrepreneurship but that left the less fortunate largely unprotected by a patchwork of programs that avoided resolving the challenges of diverse and disadvantaged populations, long-term care, and both institutions and people who were frail.[1]

This discussion begins with the Gray Panthers, a movement that, unlike the others, never fully developed into a major and stable organization. It deserves initial and special consideration because the story of its development under the leadership of Maggie Kuhn is so compelling, the issues it illuminates so important, its impact on public awareness so significant, and its connections with other organizations so revelatory.

In 1970, Maggie Kuhn (1903–95) took the lead role in the founding of the activist organization that soon came to be known as the Gray Panthers, which was among the most important groups that advocated for the elderly and more generally a host of progressive causes. Essential to its history are the connections between gerontology, social movements, and the role of women. Especially interesting is how over time, gender, olders, and ageism intersected uneasily.

To begin to understand what Kuhn and the Gray Panthers were up against, we can take a look at the life of Bernice Neugarten (1916–2001), who well before Kuhn emerged to launch the Gray Panthers had established herself as a pioneer in the study of the aging. She was the first person in the US to teach a course on "adult development and aging," which she did at the University of Chicago for thirty years beginning in the early 1950s, well before the aging of the baby boomers brought key elderly issues to the fore. Dispelling myths about later stages of life, she countered the belief that menopause was inevitably traumatic and, for men and women alike, offered nuanced and varied treatments of getting old and doing so successfully. Writing in *The New York Times* in 1975, she raised the possibility that changing demography, distinguishing the frail, "old old" from people living longer and increasing numbers of what she called the "young old"—people from fifty-five to seventy-five who lived with "continued vigor and active social involvement"—might "produce a society liberated from outmoded stereotypes of the so-called declining years." Rather than conforming to the stereotype of seniors as "sick, poor, enfeebled, isolated and desolated," they, along with some of those who were even older, might take leadership roles in an attempt to move "toward the society in which age is irrelevant." In doing so, they would help "create an attractive image of aging, reduce how people worried about aging, and thus "help to eradicate those age norms that are meaningless and those age attitudes that are divisive."[2]

For some reason, Neugarten did not acknowledge the existence of the Gray Panthers when she wrote that essay for *The New York Times*. The organization would hold its first national convention in Chicago in October 1975, not far from where she lived and taught. It is possible that she neglected to acknowledge its existence because of how she viewed the politics of aging. Indeed, tracking how over time Neugarten developed her views about women and aging reveals how little attention she paid to ageism and discrimination against elders. Writing in 1965 with two colleagues, she used the phrase "age discriminations" not to describe how the people in power marginalized seniors but as a term governing how observers discussed people at different stages of their lives. In a similar vein, she deployed words like "sanctions," "norms," and "expectations" that governed age distinctions as facts of life rather than acts of prejudice. Gender weighed lightly in her analysis, yet she seemed to pay no attention to the special situations elderly women face.[3] Then, in 1974, she remained neutral on whether ageism was increasingly or decreasing.[4]

In 1982, Neugarten intensified her call to fight against exacerbating tensions between elders and those who were younger than them, something the Gray Panthers were also committed to doing. Later, in 1988, as generational fights over federal programs for the elderly intensified, Henry Fairlie coined the phrase "Greedy Geezers" for a 1988 article in *The New Republic*, following the theme of its cover, which Robert N. Butler later called out as picturing "the advancing army of angry-faced older persons wielding garden trowels, fishing poles, and golf clubs," who "looked menacing, poised to assault America." Fairlie's essay, Butler noted, "described what the cover expressed visually: Older people are selfish and drain the country of resources that might otherwise be channeled elsewhere, especially to children."[5] The Gray Panthers were among those who offered a more positive view of aging, which one observer described as relying on "empowering values of independence, activity, well-being, and mobility."[6] Six years earlier, Neugarten had channeled those who worried about a "political backlash that will be harmful to older people" because their political power was growing. Rather than policies that focused on age, she preferred those that concentrated on non-age-related issues of what people needed and were able to do.[7] Four years later, now writing with her daughter, Dail Neugarten, she acknowledged age discrimination but principally as a legislative fact. Yet they did not use the word "ageism," and the word "feminism" appeared nowhere in their essay.[8]

The Gray Panthers had already emerged as an activist organization that fought for a whole range of progressive causes and against discrimination based on age, all the while emphasizing the importance of intergenerational alliances. Maggie Kuhn played a pivotal role in its founding in 1970 and remained its most prominent figure. Her "spirited advocacy on behalf of older Americans, and especially older women," writes Susan J. Douglas in *In Our Prime: How Older Women Are Reinventing the Road Ahead* (2020), "constitutes the origins of the quest for visibility for those over fifty."[9] From her mid-twenties until 1970, she had worked for a series of organizations—especially the Young Women's Christian Association (YWCA) and the Presbyterian Church—where she deployed a progressive version of Christianity on a range of issues. Her interest in the problems the aging faced grew in 1961 when, as an observer, she attended the White House Conference on Aging. Not long after, she came to recognize, she noted later, that "the Church's interest in the old was largely confined to administering to the sick and dying and running retirement homes for well-to-do Presbyterians." When she visited the former president of the Princeton Theological Seminary John MacKay, he told her that one of the church's retirement homes they visited was a "glorified playpen" that he hated. She encountered him in the late 1960s when she began to serve on the board of what she called "rather posh Church retirement homes," whose top-down and male-dominated governance she unsuccessfully fought to change.[10]

As if to underscore that the personal is political, Kuhn's role in launching the Gray Panthers emerged not only from lifelong social justice commitments but also from a specific situation she encountered as her sixty-fifth birthday approached. She had not yet come to see herself as old, a perception that might have changed when at age sixty-four, a little more than half a year before she turned sixty-five, the head of the Council on Church and Race asked her to retire. She was aware that others had been allowed to remain in their jobs on a year-to-year basis and worried she would be totally absorbed in caring for her ailing brother. And having not considered retirement, she could not envision herself "with no serious purpose in life and cut off from the wide circle of friends at work."[11] Her employer could force her to retire because until the US Congress in 1978 made mandatory retirement illegal at seventy and then altogether eight years later, it was legal for employers to terminate employment at sixty-five.[12]

Initially "dazed" and before long "outraged," she soon understood that her "problem was not [hers] alone": "I came to feel," she reported retrospectively, "a great kinship with my peers and to believe that something was fundamentally wrong with a system that had no use for people like us." As a retirement present, her colleagues gave her a sewing machine, "a beautiful gift," she recalled, "but a miscalculation of how I planned to spend my time."[13] Instead of a sewing machine, she preferred a copying machine she could use for political purposes. She organized with widening circles of friends and colleagues. They debated the tactics and scope of a movement dedicated to social action—whether it should focus on a range of generational issues such as the Vietnam War and the 1972 presidential election or those of interest principally to members of their generation, such as poverty, health care, housing, pensions, and discrimination. In the end, given their lifelong commitments against wars abroad and for social justice at home, as well as their interest in connections across generational lines especially over the Vietnam War, they decided to commit themselves to a capacious, inclusive set of goals.

Context is crucial here. In the months before Kuhn turned sixty-five on August 3, 1970, she and her comrades were intensely aware of events at home and abroad. The US invasion of Cambodia on April 29; a few days later the, Ohio National Guard's killing four Kent State students and wounding nine others who were protesting the Vietnam War; the May 15 killing by police of two students and injuring twelve at Jackson State College; on June 22, the Methodist Church for the first time allowing women to become full ministers; in the fall, the intensification of antiwar protests on college campuses; Nixon's rejections of the report by the Commission on the Causes of Campus Arrest that he had earlier established; and the ascendancy of the Black Panther Party and the ways governments responded, on both sides marked by violence.

The activists initially named their group the Consultation of Older Persons. This changed in the fall of 1971 when Kuhn met the Reverend Reuben Gums, a TV producer who began his career as a member of the Dakota Conference of the Evangelical United Brethren Church and now headed the New York Council of Churches' Department of Radio and Television. He listened to what in a 1982 interview he called Kuhn's "need for militancy on the part of older people." Aware that "a good name is important in public relations" and that the Black Panthers had recently taken over a church in Harlem and were, as Gums noted, "getting attention beyond their numbers" (but perhaps not of Tom Wolfe's June 8, 1970, scathing report of the Black Panthers' presence at a party organized by Leonard Bernstein, as reported in *New York*), he responded by saying, "Why don't you call yourselves the *Gray Panthers*." Kuhn, he reported, "practically fell off the seat, laughing. She liked it, and a few months later her colleagues were using it." His was a sympathetic suggestion but perhaps a provocative and risky one.[14] Indeed, one woman from South Carolina objected, remarking, "I don't want to become involved with bomb throwers."[15] Yet the new name reflected Kuhn's embrace of radical positions. In late 1970, she called political activity "more energizing than Geritol."[16] A few months later, reporting on discussions among members of the Consultation about the name change, she acknowledged that to most of them, the new name "conveys an immediate message to society and to old people [them]selves." After attention to "disagreement about its effect on the people [they were] trying to reach," the assembled group "decided if people were turned off by the name, [the group] should not try to change their minds. Obviously," she continued, "they are not ready for *action* that creates a stir and changes things."[17]

A socialist in college, Kuhn from then on opposed the United States' military involvements abroad. She developed programs that promoted a robust sexuality. Never married, she had affairs with a married man, as a white woman with an African American man, and late in life with a man four decades younger than she was. Long committed to labor unions, she joined forces with them and, in the early 1970s, with Ralph Nader, whose Retired Professional Action Group moved into the basement of her Philadelphia house. Once she played a critical role in launching the

Gray Panthers, she advocated and participated in what she spoke of as outrageous tactics, including guerilla theater and boisterous growls. Throughout her adult life, she was passionately committed to antiracism, something reflected in her work for the Gray Panthers. For example, in early 1971, as she rode in a hotel limousine to the Annual Conference of Aging, she met Hobart C. Jackson Sr., who was the administrator for the Stephen Smith Home for the Aged in Philadelphia, a retirement home for African Americans. Together they worried that the upcoming Second White House Conference on Aging would not adequately focus on the challenges elders faced. After all, they were sure that, as she recalled years later, "under Nixon the event would be a political charade," and with "the heavy participation of gerontologists and social service professionals who were not usually themselves old, the emphasis seemed paternalistic."[18] With Jackson, she helped plan a Black House Conference on Aging and worked on forming the National Caucus on the Black Aged. She found "senior citizen" an acceptable term only if it involved an acknowledgment of the robust political engagement expected, but she preferred, as she said in the early 1980s, the term "older people."[19]

Thus, Kuhn's radicalism shaped her own, and in turn the Gray Panthers', agenda. She and her colleagues felt that well-established organizations such as the AARP and the National Council of Senior Citizens "didn't encourage older people to take control of their lives or to concern themselves with larger social issues." Instead, "fighting for services and privileges for their members, many organizations for the old fell into the special-interest pit, as if the old were saying, 'We worked damned hard and we're going to get ours.'"[20]

Kuhn led the fight for pension and nursing home reform; for strengthening federal programs such as Medicare, Medicaid, and Social Security; for changes in banking policies that made accounts available for the poor elderly; for improvements in medical education and mass media representation; and for more adequate voting rights, housing, legal representation, and access to transportation. In addition, she campaigned against militarism and for nuclear disarmament. Undergirding all these efforts, she later wrote, "in the tradition of the women's liberation movement, the common mission of the Gray Panthers was consciousness-raising," in a struggle against ageism that had led to "the segregation, stereotyping, and stigmatizing of people on the basis of age."[21] US society, she remarked, was not only racist and sexist but also ageist. And she defined ageism as "the arbitrary discrimination against people on the basis of their chronological age. Ageism," she continued, "in this new age of self-determination, is a crucial problem of alienation and oppression."[22]

A 1972 statement captures so much that was central to Kuhn's visionary commitments. Crediting the impact of struggles against racism and the importance of the women's liberation movement, she pointed to "the group of older people who are fighting ageism" as "the newest liberation movement." As she insisted, "The subject of age affects everybody." When older folks were "no longer young" they were "immediately confronted with the fact that . . . society makes a fetish of being young." In response, Gray Panthers were "out to make old a beautiful thing, not something to be hidden, but something to be declared and affirmed," something enhanced by their having time, wisdom, experience, and numbers. She properly insisted "that life is a continuum and age is a period of fulfillment, of continued growth and creativity where the inputs, the experience of a lifetime can be related to the group of people who are coming into their creative productive years, and to our young people." Confidently, she predicted that the Gray Panthers were "going to change things" for themselves and others: "We're going to make our neighborhoods, our communities, our state, our nation better, not just for us but for all human beings." The combination of older and younger people "can help to change society and move it to a new sense of values— human-based values rather than thing-centered values."[23]

Kuhn and others opposed not only national politicians but also the gerontological establishment. Gray Panthers, she wrote in the 1970s, were "deeply alarmed that members of the burgeoning field of gerontology looked upon the separation of the old—from work, from families, from communities—as a normal part of life." The Panthers stood in opposition to disengagement theory, which emerged in the 1960s and assumed that "the detachment and isolation many of the old feel is an inevitable and necessary prelude to death." Gerontologists saw elders as problems to society, rather than as persons experiencing problems created by society. Public issues and controversies, thus reduced to private problems and complaints, were believed best dealt with by a system that, Kuhn argued, "increased the dependency and powerlessness of the old."

She lamented the way, as she saw it, that gerontologists, viewing the old "as mere guinea pigs, had a vested interest in maintaining the illusion that people become incapacitated by age. Government dollars flowed to researchers who documented this illusion and to service providers who sustained it." They do not see older folks as "resources, consultants, and experts in the field."[24] Disengagement theorists, she remarked, advised older people to withdraw "from what you did when you were younger" and did so "in deference to your aging body and failing physical strength." Though eventually discredited, this perspective was nonetheless "firmly embedded in public policy—especially in age-segregated housing and in the present service programs, which assume that people have no power and which keep them powerless and disengaged."[25]

Kuhn's long fight with gerontologists came to a head at the 1978 meeting of the American Gerontological Society. Standing on the stage with its president, George Maddox, she called on the organization to "take stands on public issues—a new socialized health-care system, affordable shared housing, elimination of mandatory retirement." Kuhn hoped that its members would show "some awareness on the part of [gerontologists] of the social questions they ask," and, she added, "evidence a genuine concern for the nature and shape of our future." Maddox responded as he made his opposition clear. There was, he said, a "natural source of tension between advocates and scientists. The Gerontological Society is primarily dedicated to research in aging; the Gray Panthers are primarily dedicated to restructuring the social order. . . . It is not obvious, at least not to me, that a primary dedication to advocacy or to science on the part of any particular individual or organization is morally superior or effective in achieving social change."[26] Seven years later, Maddox persisted in seeing aging as presenting a series of problems—"disease, impairment, disability, and illness"—to be managed by professional experts.[27]

Maggie Kuhn emerged serendipitously onto the national stage. In May 1972, as a volunteer and only informally as a Gray Panther, she was attending the General Assembly of the United Presbyterian Church. One morning, the publicity director of the church called and asked her to stand in at the last minute for someone who had to back out. He asked her, as she reported later, to "talk about those old folks." She talked for an hour and a half, she remembered, "about retirement, about 'senior citizens," about nursing homes, about sex at seventy-five, about gray-haired activists picketing for justice, about young people who felt powerless." But also, as Eleanor Blau, a reporter for *The New York Times*, wrote, she focused on issues of more general concern, such as poverty, war, and race, as well as "the curious and wonderful" empathetic connections between the "cubs" and people of her generation and older. Her performance launched her and the Gray Panthers into the national media limelight—with coverage and appearances on the wire services, major newspapers, NBC's *Today Show*, and Johnny Carson's *Tonight Show*.[28]

Assessing the historical significance of the Gray Panthers as an organization and social movement poses interpretative problems. By the mid-1970s, it had begun to take shape—holding its first national convention in Chicago in October 1975, with two hundred people attending from thirty-seven states. It expanded its office in Philadelphia and created one in the nation's capital as its staff grew and its publications (especially *Network*), activities, and outreach efforts expanded. Its membership, much of it white middle-class women, peaked in the early 1980s with six thousand to seven thousand. At most, it had 122 or so local chapters, called "Networks." Some of them existed mostly on paper or involved only one person. Crises on the national and local levels emerged and got resolved, or not. Local groups waxed and waned—or just disappeared. Some Networks thrived, such as those in metropolitan New York or Berkeley, California—though even those were on rocky roads. Groups emerged abroad, but the Gray Panthers was essentially a US phenomenon. At several points, including in the mid-1990s, the Gray Panthers seemed at death's door. It turned out that it was not, continuing today fighting the fights that concerned Maggie Kuhn as it survived but did not flourish.

Several factors made the Gray Panthers' vitality and future uncertain. Kuhn was an extraordinary figure whose energy, media visibility, and leadership were remarkable, even though the organization was overreliant on a seemingly irreplaceable individual. Then, by the mid-1980s, before she died at age eighty-nine in 1995, as someone who entered the world of the old old who struggled with several health problems, she was increasingly unable to keep up the pace that drove the founding and early success of the Gray Panthers. In addition, there was a persistent, albeit varying, tension between the national office and local Networks.

Sometimes relationships across generational lined frayed, as some at either end questioned the commitment to intergenerationalism and to a major focus on issues other than those that compelled attention of the olders. Over time, among young and old, fewer new recruits replaced those who were initially involved. Most of the organization's members were white and middle or upper middle class. Rarely does an insurgent national movement make the transitions needed as an organization to ensure the impact that embodied its original vision. Finally, the times they were a-changin', and over the years, issues and the political contexts in which their advocates fought for them made it difficult to successfully sustain momentum and achieve more and more successes.

However, to focus on these issues obscures the notoriety, reach, and importance of the Gray Panthers. Avoiding becoming a single-issue organization and one that focused only on the problems olders faced, it remained a cross-generational, grassroots movement committed to a capacious progressive agenda. Locally and nationally, in ways that are hard to quantify, it inspired people to act on issues such as health care, housing, transportation, pension reform, medical care, and media representations. It is possible to cite some specific accomplishments. Its Media Watch Task Force revealed the prejudicial stereotypes deployed against older people. The Gray Panthers helped create the Older Women's League and the National Citizens Coalition for Nursing Home Reform. As its skilled chronicler Roger Sanjek writes, Gray Panthers "played a catalytic role in ending mandatory retirement." Numbers can hardly convey its historical importance, and as Sanjek correctly insists, it "offered a vision of old age counter to the prevailing stereotype: active, zesty (Maggie's word), connected to others, politically engaged, savoring life, leaving 'no stone unturned' in the struggle for social justice."[29]

A few years before Kuhn died, in *The Fountain of Age* (1993), Betty Friedan offered a vivid picture of her as a "feisty" woman who advocated that if older women "were going to have sex, it would have to be with younger men, someone else's husband, other women, masturbation." She also told of Kuhn's sustained dedication to a broad range of progressive issues—all within the context of intergenerational commitments.[30] She praised the Gray Panthers for pointing the way toward "a model for age as a special interest group" that would constitute "the needed political paradigm shift: a new movement that will use the wisdom and resources of older women." Friedan attacked several powerful institutions that she believed undermined the way seniors could achieve autonomy and live lives decently. She also criticized the AARP for focusing "mainly on improving 'care' for the elderly, not on mobilizing the political power of people over sixty to demand new roles in society or to change the political priorities of the nation" and "confront the larger social and economic questions in terms of radical *change*," though she offered no blueprint for such a prospect. She expressed "suspicion that the science of gerontology itself was perpetuating the fear and dread of age." Then she contrasted the wisdom of elders with "this strange predilection of gerontological experts for dealing with age only in terms of pathology, and what appeared to be a serious discomfort with any view of positive aspects of aging."[31]

Friedan explored alternatives to institutional care that would enable her peers to live meaningful independent lives, and she criticized senior communities like the one her mother lived in, which she had described elsewhere as an "adult playpen." She excoriated nursing homes and retirement communities that attempted to "profit on the fear of being old and alone."[32] She wrote of places like Leisure World that incorrectly assumed that "mere participation in all those clubhouse activities would provide the satisfaction and continued sense of self considered essential to vital age." After all, "those preferring to interact only with the aged turned out on the average to be less active, lonelier, less confident, and *less satisfied with life*, and also *less healthy* than those who preferred interacting with all ages in the larger community."[33] She admitted her "own reaction of dread to those institutional settings," as she referred to "research which shows that people who choose to retreat to such enclaves, though they have more formal activities, and report more 'friends' than those who move among all ages in larger communities, experience *more* 'loneliness' and lower self-concept."[34] She cited the work of the psychologist Morton Lieberman, who reported that studies "suggested that *the more total the institution* (scheduling of activities, rules and standards of conduct, decision making about the use of private and congregate property), *the greater its depersonalizing effects*." Yet, she insisted, "profit-making corporations continue to promote and run highly structured congregate lifetime care communities" whose marketing relies on fear.[35] Echoing her problematic reference to the "Comfortable Concentration

Camp" in *The Feminine Mystique*, she insisted, "*Beware the final solution. There is none.*"[36]

Friedan discussed discrimination and aging but rarely, if ever, connected them to gender or to an insurgent political vision. So it is not surprising that looking back on *The Fountain of Age* in 2006, the gerontologist Ruth E. Ray offered a critical assessment. She underscored Friedan's optimism in a book "full of words like *zest, vitality, exhilaration, strength, adventure, vision, personal realization, transcendence,* and *freedom.*"[37] Ray objected to Friedan's othering residents of nursing homes but mostly to her "unwillingness to explore, with the same open-minded curiosity, the darker side of aging," what gerontologists call the "Fourth Age" or "deep old age," which includes isolation, poverty, and cognitive loss. She chastised Friedan for not discussing the elderly in all their diversity and instead focusing mainly on "white, educated, and middle-class adults with the health, finances, social resources, and time to explore new vistas." Friedan's "own ageism," she insisted, significantly limited her book's "potential to instigate social change. . . . Rather than increasing public optimism regarding the growth potential in later life, *The Fountain of Age* actually plays into people's *fear* of aging. . . . Friedan does not muster the same passion for age that she held for gender, and she did not fully realize that the 'age mystique' is an identity crisis of the same magnitude as the one underlying the feminine mystique."[38]

Ray was part of a generation, younger than Neugarten, Kuhn, and Friedan, whose members, shaped by the events and social movements of the last third of the twentieth century and beyond, connected the dots between the lives of seniors, feminism, ageism, and institutional life, which they often did from a feminist perspective even as they lamented how, as Toni M. Calasanti and Kathleen F. Slavin say, "an inadvertent but pernicious ageism burdens much of feminist scholarship and activism."[39] "A society as warped by ageism as ours is in the United States, or elsewhere," writes the critical aging studies advocate Margaret Morganroth Gullette in her compelling *Ending Ageism; or, How Not to Shoot Old People* (2017), ageism can be "transformed only by a movement that attracts increasing numbers of passionate members."[40] A year earlier, in *This Chair Rocks: A Manifesto Against Ageism*, Ashton Applewhite offered a vigorous and wide-ranging call for opposing ageism, which she defined as "the relegation of older people to second-class citizenship, . . . discrimination and stereotyping on the basis of a person's age." Acknowledging the importance of feminism, she admitted that ageism was not "a household word yet, not a sexy one, but neither was 'sexism' until the women's movement turned it into a howl for equal rights." It was, she insisted, "the last socially sanctioned prejudice," one that served "powerful commercial and political interests." Embarking "on a crusade to overturn American culture's dumb and destructive obsession with youth," she announced "that ageism is woven deeply into our capitalist system, and that upending it will involve social and political upheaval."[41]

This Chair Rocks nonetheless told readers, and not just olders (the term Applewhite preferred), how to fight ageism and lead fulfilled lives, including as workers, lovers, friends, citizens, and even as those facing death. Applewhite acknowledged how varied were the lives and experiences of people of all ages, including those younger and older than she was, sixty-four, in 2016. She made clear how important it was for people to join hands as activists across what were often generational divides as she criticized those who were inclined to "rail about olders sucking up 'entitlements'" they had earned. Instead, she called on people of all ages to see themselves as "an Old Person in Training," which would derail "shame and self-loathing" and promote cooperation and empathy. She cast a skeptical eye on how some others viewed aging, ranging from some olders themselves who expressed self-hatred to those who blithely celebrated its successful version, an embrace of denial whose adoption of the "high-end version that tends to overlook the very important role of socioeconomic and potential disability in shaping how 'successfully' we age." She hoped to set "an example of radical aging": "acknowledging my mortality; embracing aging as a natural process; wrestling with the countless paradoxes this involves; . . . and rustling up companions along the way." She emphasized that ageism was rooted "in deeply human fears about the inherent vulnerabilities of old age," even as she touted the advantages people her age and older brought to the table—greater wisdom, knowledge, contentment, and happiness among them.[42]

Born in 1974, four years after Kuhn launched the Gray Panthers, Ai-Jen Poo, a much honored activist, offers another example of a woman who focuses on older folks—in her case, in a way that combines gender, anti-ageism, elder care, and labor organizing among workers who are predominantly immigrants and/or women of color. She is director of the

National Domestic Workers Alliance (founded in 2007) and codirector of Caring Across Generations (founded in 2011), which bring together care givers and recipients of their work. With more than two hundred thousand members in more than seventy local organizations, the National Domestic Workers Alliance had worked to pass legislation, make sure workers receive at least the minimum wage, and provide adequate insurance protection, as its campaigns, its website announces, work "to win respect, recognition, and labor rights and protections for the nearly 2.5 million nannies, housecleaners, and homecare workers who do the essential work of caring for our loved ones and our homes." Day by day, "*domestic workers do the work that makes all other work possible. They are the nannies that care for our children, the house cleaners that bring order to our home, and the care workers that ensure our loved ones can live with dignity and independence.*" Primarily immigrants, themselves mothers, women of color, and workers paid low wages, "they are impacted by almost every policy affecting the future of our economy, democracy and country."[43]

With Ariane Conrad, Ai-Jen Poo laid out her vision of a more just society in *The Age of Dignity: Preparing for the Elder Boom in a Changing America* (2015). Their advocacy of robust provisions for supporting elders provides a compelling cross-generational vision that differs from more facile and reassuring approaches.[44] Their success stands in tragic contrast to the heroic but dramatically less fruitful efforts of African American gerontologists to advance the fight for Black elders.[45]

* * *

Maggie Kuhn's 1978 debate with George Maddox, the head of the Gerontological Society of America (GSA), came a third of a century after that organization's founding as the most influential one committed to the support of professionals engaged in the field of aging. In 1994, Bernice Neugarten had remarked that she was "greatly tempted to predict that the field of gerontology is going to disappear over the next couple of decades" because "chopping up the life cycle" into age-based segments "was not a very good idea to begin with," and "in its place, there will be a proliferation of need-driven, age neutral politics and programs."[46] Now, more than thirty years later, we can see that has not happened. In the meantime, debates have emerged over the GSA's mission.

The back story of the development of the GSA starts at least to when Élie Metchnikoff, a Russian who in 1908 won the Nobel Prize in Medicine or Physiology, in 1903 coined the term "gerontology." At the time, he believed that since the existence of toxic bacteria in the gut caused aging, the consumption of lactic acid, like what Bulgarian peasants digested in their yogurt, promoted longevity.[47] In the United States, gerontology as a scholarly field would only begin to emerge decades later, probably in response to the passage of legislation establishing Social Security in 1935. A 1937 meeting in Woods Hole, Massachusetts, involved a gathering of twenty-four scientists and physicians who created the Club for Research on Ageing. The publication of E. V. Cowdry's *Problems of Aging: Biological and Medical Aspects* (1938) is another important marker in the development of gerontology as a field.[48] At a 1945 meeting in Manhattan, the Gerontological Society of America was officially launched. In 1948, the Social Science Research Council began to support research on aging. In 1946, the first issue of *The Journal of Gerontology* appeared, and then, in 1949, Manhattan was the site of the GSA's first annual meeting. Other changes marked the development of the GSA: its 1952 division into four sections (Biological Sciences, Psychological and Social Sciences, Social Work and Administration, and Health Sciences); over the decades, the proliferation of publications and interest groups; in 1970, the move of its headquarters from St. Louis to Washington, DC; and its role in 1974 in the founding of the National Institute on Aging.

"GSA is the oldest and largest interdisciplinary organization devoted to research, education, and practice in the field of aging," its website announces. It has fifty-five hundred members from fifty nations, and its central mission "is to promote the study of aging and disseminate information," relying as it does on the "interdisciplinary collaboration among behavioral and social scientists, physicians, nurses, biologists, psychologists, social workers, educators, economists, policy experts, practice leaders, those who study the humanities and the arts, and many other scholars and researchers in aging."[49]

The GSA has had its share of problems, perhaps in part because, unlike the other aging organizations under discussion here, no single commanding figure has shaped its development. Among the issues the GSA has struggled with are the limits to multidisciplinary research, problems with governance and border protection, struggles over definitional issues, the balance between research and advocacy, and its reputation in the scientific world. Or, as one critic asserted more generally about gerontologists, they "seemed intellectually stymied by the data-driven, bio-medically dominant, and unreflexive conventions of their research community."[50]

Scholars in critical gerontology, a field that gained traction in the late twentieth century, have explored fundamental methodological and ideological issues they feel the people involved in the GSA have succumbed to. Writers such as Carroll L. Estes, Meredith Minkler, and Stephen Katz have made clear that at least well into the twentieth century, gerontologists and the organizations that support and promote their findings have seen elders as problematic people who have to be studied but also controlled. Relying on the work of Pierre Bourdieu and Michel Foucault and others, Katz remarked that even late in the century, "representations of the aged body [had] become resources for the professional expansion of gerontological knowledge."[51] Estes and Minkler have emphasized that gerontology must involve not only political and economic questions but also perspectives grounded in moral economy.[52] Proponents of critical gerontology have forcefully argued that historically, gerontology has warned about "greedy geezers," which in turn has injured cross-generational relationships; minimized the agency of older folks by emphasizing their neediness; seen the elderly as a homogeneous cohort and as a result not focused of how race, class, and gender have shaped aging; empowered professionals by disempowering elders; failed to recognize the vibrant agency of a range of institutions that care for and house elders; pathologized and biomedicalized their bodies; not understood that aging is a social construction; and relied on research, much of which emphasizes how needily problematic their lives are—discipline and punish, as Foucault night say, rather than celebrate, complicate, and liberate. Or as Minkler and Estes write, "Popular notions such as 'productive aging' and 'successful aging,' the false dichotomy of 'dependence' and 'independence' in old age, and the impoverishment of public discourse about reciprocity and the common good are among the areas ripe for rethinking."[53]

* * *

Along similar lines, Maggie Kuhn criticized the AARP, the behemoth of aging organizations, for wanting "to organize older people just to keep them together, as a lobby on old folks' issues," rather than, as she advocated, "using gray power with the young for issues on the cutting edge of social change."[54] Kuhn is to the Gray Panthers as Ethel Percy Andrus is to the AARP, both visionary founders and leaders of important aging organizations, even though what Kuhn helped create and shape was much more progressive and what Andrus helped create and shape was significantly more powerful.

Born in 1884, Andrus graduated from the University of Chicago in 1903. She studied and taught at what is now known as the Illinois Institute of Technology and volunteered nearby at Jane Addams's Hull House, an experience that helped inspire her progressive political commitments. Eventually she moved to Southern California, where she ended up as the principal at Abraham Lincoln High School, the first woman in the state's history to head an urban high school. There she applied what she had learned at Hull House about building community and providing social services to the underserved. Soon after she retired as principal in 1944, she volunteered and then became an employee of the California Retired Teachers Association, an experience that exposed her to how inadequate were the pensions and health insurance of supposedly middle-class retirees. That led her in 1947 to found the National Retired Teachers Association (NRTA), which over time welcomed members other than teachers and then became the AARP in 1958. To secure health insurance for retirees, she tried to find a company that would write insurance policies for older people. With more than forty companies turning her down, this effort was unsuccessful until, in 1955, she connected with Leonard Davis, whose enterprises, which eventually became Colonial Penn, relied on direct marketing to offer such policies. For years, the companies Davis headed were the only ones that provided insurance for AARP members, something that helped retirees and enriched Davis. Then, in 1958, with the help of Davis, Andrus began the process of transforming NRTA into the AARP.[55]

Over time, the AARP grew into an extraordinarily large, wealthy, and powerful organization that cleverly and carefully balanced competing commitments. It developed an ingenious business model. Low membership fees, which account for 20 percent or less of its revenue, are among the factors that make it possible to now enroll thirty-eight million members. Such a bulging roster enables it to make lucrative arrangements with enterprises that want to sell their products and services to members of a targeted, easy-to-reach audience. Most of its funding comes from licensing its name and logo, especially to insurance companies. Perhaps you have seen advertisements for UnitedHealthcare insurance programs offered to the AARP's members, to which more than four million subscribe.

The AARP is the nation's largest interest group, and *AARP: The Magazine* is the publication with the largest number of readers. The organization achieved such goals by clever marketing—reaching out to potential members when they reach a targeted age, which the AARP eventually lowered to fifty as it insisted on using the vague term "older people." This shift, along with calling itself "AARP" without using the word "retirement," James Chappel notes, meant that the AARP "saw itself less as a pressure group for those over sixty-five than as a lifestyle organization for those over fifty."[56] With so many members still working, the organization dropped "retirement" from its title and simply called itself "AARP," without emphasizing what the "RP" letters meant. Over the years, it has played a major role in promoting a positive vision of aging and of those who have aged, fighting as it has, as Andrus wrote in 1960, "the stereotype of old age as a disease, increasingly costly and troublesome," something "contradicted by the host of happy and productive oldsters participating and serving beyond the call of duty."[57] Rather than seeing itself primarily as an organization fighting for the expansion of government programs for olders or aligning itself with disenfranchised groups, it focuses instead, as Chappel notes perceptively, on ageism, a prejudice that undergirded "legal and cultural disenfranchisement by a society that disrespected the old," and yet it also projects "a sunny outlook of aging and a refusal to identify with 'old age.'" Moving to the center in a politically conservative environment, the AARP, he shows, as he correctly emphasizes its elevation of private solutions over public ones, "in its business model and its magazine, . . . was devoted above all to the creation of a fun, consumerist, and antidiscriminatory ideal of aging."[58]

More tangible are the benefits the AARP offers its members. Among them are seminars, social gatherings, volunteering opportunities, various kinds of insurance, financial tools such as mutual funds and annuities, help with taxes, and special deals and discounts on a range of goods and services. Its publications—now online and on paper—provide stories and advice, with *AARP: The Magazine* now offered in three versions for different age cohorts. The AARP moved its headquarters from California to the District of Columbia in 1967 and, thirty years later, opened a splendid building there to house its operations. Over time, the AARP grew more sensitive to the needs of women and ethnic groups. Its lobbying presence is legendary, even if its success has been uneven. Though it has persisted in supporting Social Security and Medicare, the AARP differentiated itself from so many other aging organizations as it, Chappel notes, "primarily sought private-sector solutions to the problems of senior living" by connecting "older people with for-profit companies to improve their lives."[59]

Inevitably, the AARP became enmeshed in controversies, initially over its use of questionable tactics to market products of questionable value. The outsized role Davis and Colonial Penn played ran into trouble, especially after 1978, following Andy Rooney's exposé on the CBS program *60 Minutes*, which revealed the excessive influence Davis had in selling the AARP members noncompetitive policies. Soon thereafter, the AARP terminated its relationship with Davis and then with Colonial Penn. In the 1980s and 1990s, the AARP became embroiled in political controversies. The rising costs of government programs for elders, the image of "greedy geezers," the rightward turn in national politics, and the rise of conservative organizations that focused on issues that the AARP had long dominated led to fierce battles in an increasingly divided political world. Congressional investigations ensued, resulting in the last decade of the twentieth century in the legal separation of the AARP's taxable, profit-seeking activities from its nonprofit ones that provided member services and social services.[60]

"To serve, not to be served" was one of the founding slogans Andrus used to celebrate what the NRTA and the AARP would aspire to accomplish. In the ensuing years, the AARP used its foundation and its emphasis on volunteerism to fulfill what Andrus hoped it would achieve.[61] In the halls of the AARP's headquarters, Davis is absent, but the memory of Andrus is ever present. Reading the AARP's publications and looking at its website, I have to wonder if the commitment "to serve, not to be served" gets lost amid the welter of a commercially dominated pursuits of successful aging.

* * *

Maggie Kuhn first met Robert N. Butler in 1975, the year he became the founding head of the National Institute on Aging and won the Pulitzer Prize for *Why Survive? Being Old in America.* A psychiatrist, he was moved by the endurance of the elderly grandparents who raised him and saddened by the contempt toward older people that some of his medical school teachers displayed. In 1963, he was one of the editors of *Human Aging: A Biological and Behavioral Study,* a book that sympathetically explored ways to improve the conditions that influenced the aging processes. Then, in 1969, he published "Age-ism: Another Form of Bigotry," to parallel sexism and racism, which as ideas and discriminatory forces were then increasingly prominent. A year later, Kuhn founded the Gray Panthers.[62] Ashton Applewhite dedicated *This Chair Rocks* to Butler as "mentor, activist, physician, humanist—who kicked the whole thing off," and Betty Friedan credited him with providing questions for her to work on in *The Fountain of Age.*[63] Kuhn and Butler remained friends and colleagues until she died in 1995.

In his 1969 essay, Butler told of how affluent whites had recently opposed a public housing project for the elderly poor in a Chevy Chase neighborhood near the nation's capital. Although only later would the term "intersectionality" emerge, Butler well understood how racism, classism, and ageism came together in this controversy, although in the end, as Chappel notes, this "was a missed opportunity to forge an intersectional account of aging, one that would aim to understand the relations between, in this case, age and race." Butler described ageism as "the subjective experience implied in the popular notion of the generation gap. Prejudice of the middle-aged against the old in this instance, and against the young in others," he continued, "is a serious national problem," reflecting as it did "a deep seated uneasiness on the part of the young and middle-aged—a personal revulsion to and distaste for growing old, disease, disability; and fear of powerlessness, 'uselessness,' and death." Butler went on to mention other expressions of ageism, among them mandatory retirement and discrimination in employment more generally, negative phrases such as "old fogeys," the view that Social Security and Medicare were a burden on the young and middle-aged, and the disproportionately small amount of research funds (less than 1 percent) devoted to the study of aging by the National Institutes of Health. Perhaps, he speculated at the end, people over sixty-five will begin to become politically active. Then, he hoped, "we will be hearing of Senior Power." After all, he remarked in the final sentence, "we don't all grow white or black, but we all grow old."[64]

"Fortunately, legislation establishing the National Institute on Aging (NIA) was passed in 1974," Butler noted in *Why Survive?*, "though moderately funded."[65] The history of the NIA goes back at least to 1940 with the creation of the Unit on Aging within the National Institutes of Health, directed by Nathan W. Shock. In 1951, Shock, who since the early 1940s had headed what came to be known as the Gerontology Research Center of the NIH, had proposed the establishment of a National Institute of Gerontology. By the mid-1950s, a Center for Aging Research was created within the NIH, and in the ensuing years, its location, alliances, and scope developed. In 1961, the initial White House Conference on Aging recommended the creation of an Aging Institute, something the 1971 conference again called for, this time as a separate National Institute on Aging at the National Institutes of Health. A year later, President Richard M. Nixon vetoed a bill authorizing its creation. Finally, in 1974, legislation marked the establishment of a National Institute on Aging, which Butler directed from 1976 until 1982.[66] The budget at the NIA began modestly enough, at $70 million initially, and recently stood at $4.4 billion, slightly less than 10 percent of the budget of the NIH.

According to the NIA's website, its "ongoing mission" is to "support and conduct genetic, biological, clinical, behavioral, social, and economic research on aging" and then to broadcast the findings "to the public, health care professionals, and the scientific community, among a variety of audiences." It does this by "funding extramural research at universities and research centers across the U.S. and around the world; maintaining an active communications and outreach program; and conducting a vibrant intramural research program at" its labs in Baltimore and Bethesda. It also serves "as the lead federal agency for research on Alzheimer's and related dementias."[67] Focusing on diverse populations of older folks, it has produced widely disseminated and often pathbreaking research on how we age, on diseases that afflict elders, and on socioeconomic factors that shape their lives. Over the years, it has significantly advanced how we understand aging, which in turn has helped enhance the health span and life span of millions of Americans.

Some of the work the NIA has supported reflects the issues that critical gerontologists have identified. With so much of its funding going to problems defined as medical, Alzheimer's especially, Carroll L. Estes and others have criticized gerontology generally and the NIA specifically for "the biomedicalization of aging." By focusing on "individual organic pathology and interventions," she wrote with Elizabeth A. Binney in 1989, medicine had "become a powerful and pervasive force in the definition and treatment of aging. The resulting 'biomedicalization of aging' socially constructs old age as a process of decremental physical decline and places aging under the domain and control of biomedicine." By "equating old age with illness," they wrote, society has thought "about aging as pathological or abnormal," a viewpoint that shaped elders, often leading them to "such behaviors as social withdrawal, reduction of activity, increased dependency."[68]

Moreover, the power of biomedicalization, developed and amplified by the NIA, had led, Estes and Binney wrote, to how members of the public had a "tendency to view aging negatively as a process of inevitable decline, disease, and irreversible decay (as opposed to the reversible, remediable, and socially constructed aspects of aging)." One result was that both the elderly and their families "'buy into' the belief that the problems of aging are primarily biological and physiological, while ignoring the socially produced nature of many of these and other problems that occur in old age." Among the results were "the interpretation of public issues as private troubles, and the resulting social construction and production of helplessness and dependency," which were "then bolstered by public policy that does little to redress these issues." The power of the biomedicalization of aging meant that "older persons find themselves blamed for the health care crisis (and indirectly, for larger economic crises of the state), as well as the poverty of children" because of the costs of Social Security and medical care. Such blame, they insisted, was "due in no small part to the unwillingness of the proponents of the biomedical model of aging to relinquish their power or control, while the model remains inappropriate to (and hence ineffective in) addressing the inherently social phenomenon of the problems attendant to an aging society."[69]

Yet Binney and Estes saw some reason for hope. They pointed to "sources of resistance" to the biomedical model among growing numbers of older people "that directly or indirectly challenge it and produce some alternative models." In addition, "improved awareness about nutrition, exercise, and other life-style modifications" were challenging "notions of the inevitability of disease, disability, and decay in old age. More important," they concluded, "a number of organizations, ranging from the moderate to the radical, are promoting different images of aging as they advocate for the elderly. Not only are groups like the Gray Panthers, the American Association of Retired Persons, and the Older Women's League serving as role models for vibrant, active, and intelligent elders, they are working on issues such as income, housing, intergenerational interdependence, retirement policies, spousal impoverishment, and health insurance that belie the biomedical construction of aging."[70]

* * *

"Another momentous moment in San Francisco," Maggie Kuhn remarked, referencing her encounter with George Maddox at the Gerontological Society of America in 1978, came when Carroll Estes invited her to talk to her class at the University of California, San Francisco (UCSF). Kuhn noted that Estes had established UCSF's Institute for Health and Aging, which was then in the planning stage and "which has highlighted the urgent need for health care in late life." Kuhn called out Estes's book *The Aging Enterprise: A Critical Examination of Social Policies and Services for the Aged* (1979) as "the first of a lively, significant critique of America's response to 'the demographic revolution.'" Estes had criticized gerontologists and social scientists for supporting "the existing order by overemphasizing research that locates 'the problem' within the older individual and his or her aging process, diverting attention away from the social and political production of the problem." Kuhn noted that they had become "loving friends" but might also have pointed out that among gerontologists, Estes was a pathbreaking feminist.[71]

Centers like the one at UCSF that focus on aging, longevity, and retirement are another example of aging organizations. There are scores and scores of them, many of which arrived on the scene well before the one Estes founded and led. Relatively few of them are related to corporations, such as TransAmerica's Center for Retirement Studies, a nonprofit foundation funded by money from the Transamerica Life Insurance Corporation, which offers customers life insurance and retirement services. Others are nonprofit nongovernmental organizations (NGOs)—such a list would include the Milken Center for the Future of Aging, the MacArthur Research Network on an Aging Society, the National Bureau of Economic Research Retirement and Disability Research Center, the AARP's Public Policy Institute, the Brookings Institution, and the Robert and Arlene Kogod Center for Aging at the Mayo Clinic.

University centers are the most numerous. They vary greatly in sponsorship (though I suspect that the National Institute on Aging often provides major funding), leadership, scope, size, and focus. No list can be complete, but here is a sampling: California State University, San Bernadino's Center on Aging; Duke University's Aging Center; the Multidisciplinary Center on Gerontology at Howard University; the University of Michigan's Institute of Gerontology; UCLA's Longevity Center; Northwestern's Buehler Center on Aging; Rutgers University's Institute on Health, Health Care Policy, and Aging Research; the University of Kansas's Landon Center on Aging; Case Western Reserve University's Center of Aging and Health; New York University's Next Phase Adult Caregiving and Retirement; the Yale Center for Research on Aging; the Hinda and Arthur Marcus Institute for Aging Research, a Harvard Medical School affiliate; UMass Boston's Center for Social and Demographic Research on Aging; and UConn's Aging Center. *Dayenu*, the Hebrew word for "enough already."

Two centers—at Boston College, the Center for Retirement Research; and at Stanford University, the Center on Longevity—can begin to reveal the range represented by a greater number of them. The economist Alicia H. Munnell has until recently directed the former. Founded in 1998, it receives funding from three federal agencies, nine state and local governments, sixteen foundations, seven research and educational institutions, and seven corporations. Aside from thirteen affiliated researchers, it employs fifteen scholars. In podcasts, congressional testimony, books, and articles, it explores issues such as the funding of retirement by Social Security as well as local, state, and private pensions, work patterns following the usual retirement age, and programs for health care including Medicare, Medicaid, and long-term insurance.[72]

One publication, Munnell's July 15, 2024, "Do We Have a Retirement Crisis?," directed to members of the general public, gives a sense of the scope and tone of the center's work. Published on the financial website *Market Watch I* and drawing on the center's National Retirement Risk Index, which in turn relies on the Federal Reserve's Survey of Consumer Finances, Munnell translated complex issues into easy-to-understand terms. Over the past two decades, she noted, the figure for how many Americans could sustain their standard of living in retirement, influenced by fluctuating housing and stock market prices, rates of inflation, and powerful forces such as COVID-19, had fluctuated between 39 and 51 percent. And in 2024, it rested uncomfortably at the lower number. She noted that only 50 percent of Americans in working households with folks from age fifty-four to sixty-four had any investments in 401(k)s or IRAs and that Social Security alone was highly unlikely to provide adequate income. Yet surveys revealed that 80 percent of older Americans responded that they had enough money to be doing okay, something explicable by the likelihood that "older people are reluctant to say that they are doing poorly and just adjust to their financial situation, whatever it is." Too many people existed day to day to set aside sufficient money for retirement. "The bottom line here," she concluded, "is that all the objective evidence indicates that between 40 and 50 percent are not saving enough and, when the question is put to retirees in a non-threatening fashion, about half admit they wished they had saved more." Munnell's sober conclusion might convince people on the right who believe that moral weakness and not social and political factors was responsible for such a dire situation.[73]

Although Munnell here offered no solution to what statistics revealed, six weeks before she had done so, the *New York Times* columnist Jeff Sommer described the eighty-one-year-old economist as someone "who is among the nation's premier experts on Social Security" and had been "doing serious research on Social Security since the 1960s," including as the founding head of Boston College's center. She advocated an increase of 3.4 percent to the existing 12.4 percent Social Security payroll tax, a levy shared equally by employees and employers. To this, in order to address income inequality, Sommer proposed raising the ceiling on income taxed to fund Social Security, currently at $168,600, and reducing the payroll tax increase.[74]

By and large, Stanford's Center on Longevity stands in contrast to the center at Boston College. It was launched in 2007, and its founding and current director is Laura L. Carstensen, a psychologist and not an economist. Its website does not offer much information about its sources of income. However, like its counterpart—and even more broadly so—it relies on and supports a more than ample group of scholars: 180 Stanford faculty members who are center affiliates. Boston College's center relies mostly on the work of economists, statisticians, demographers, and policy experts to focus on retirement; Stanford's, although it does focus on retirement, is more wide-ranging in its focus, something made possible because it draws on faculty members from schools of engineering, medicine, law, business, education, sustainability, and the humanities and social scientists. Almost forty people serve on its Advisory Council—not only Jane Fonda but also people from the academic and corporate worlds. If those who are involved in the center at Boston College are appropriately sober about the challenges people face in retirement, their counterparts in Silicon Valley envision promises of longevity.

"Longer lives are, at once, among the most remarkable achievements in all of human history and the greatest challenges of the 21st century," the Stanford center's website insists. Deploying a problematic but unnamed strawman, it remarks that most discussions assume that "older people are frail and infirm," and in contrast, the people involved in Stanford's center believe "that problems of older people demand solutions so that the substantial increase in life can ultimately benefit individuals and society." Therefore, its "mission is to accelerate and implement scientific discoveries, technological advances, behavioral practices, and social norms so that century long lives are healthy and rewarding." It predicted that "100-year lives will be common for those born today," even though "institutions, economic policies, social and cultural norms have not kept pace," something the center would work to remedy. The hope was that there would be "a future in which all people, regardless of socio-economic status, can make the most of the advantages afforded by increased lifespan—resulting in lives infused at every stage with a sense of belonging, purpose, and worth." That is, "if we act now," though what this would involve in political economic terms seems unexplored. Even so, it is clear what individuals have to do, including following "7 Lifestyle Pillars" that rely not on more experimental and interventionist nostrums that people like David Sinclair and Peter Attia recommend but on exercising, eating, and sleeping well, in addition to committing oneself to amplifying social connections, expressing gratitude, enhancing cognitive powers, and managing stress.[75]

Although Carstensen's 2011 book *A Long Bright Future: Happiness, Health, and Financial Security in an Age of Increased Longevity* was cautious about the future, its title and much of its contents, if not throwing all caution to the winds about economic conditions and human capacities, were optimistic. She wrote appreciatively of her involvement with a group of Gray Panthers who had created the Over 60s Health Center across the Bay in Berkeley and of Erik Erikson's writing about "making peace with life in the later years." Though neither as specific nor as extensive as standard how-to books do, she nonetheless offered advice on "ensuring a long bright life" by working longer, saving more, investing wisely, developing satisfying social relationships, committing oneself to lifelong learning, and making healthy choices.[76] She told her readers, "The story is ours to write. Life stages," she continued, "are social constructions, not absolute realities. We have the opportunity to rethink life's stages in profoundly novel ways." When she used the word "we," she apparently meant "boomers," whom she called on to "rekindle the creativity and out of the box thinking we've been claiming to have since the 1960s and 1970s": "We proclaimed that our generation would start a revolution," but focusing on family and careers distracted them. "We've got the smarts and we've got the numbers," she believed. "Think of it as the boomers' last revolt."[77]

Retirement and longevity centers abound, but the Leonard Davis School of Gerontology at the University of Southern California (USC) is the largest and oldest school devoted to these subjects. In addition to Andrus, several people were central in its origins and development. In 1963, Davis had founded the insurance company Colonial Penn, the pioneer in selling life insurance to older Americans—a private solution that sidelined advocacy of government programs. Ross Cortese developed the Rossmore retirement communities. And USC's chancellor Norman Topping in 1965 brought James E. Birren to USC as the founding director of the Ethel Percy Andrus Gerontology Center.

A key moment occurred in 1964 when USC and the Rossmore Corporation embarked on a joint research project that focused on retirement, creating the Rossmoor-Cortese Institute. Andrus died in 1967, and a few years later, USC created the Ethel Percy Andrus Gerontology Center. The center was to serve as a memorial for Andrus, with Ross Cortese leading the fundraising efforts. The AARP, to honor its founder and support research on aging, contributed about $2 million, which significantly financed the design and construction of a fifty-five-thousand-square-foot building designed by Edward Durell Stone. Then, in 1975, a center became a school and housed the Ethel Percy Andrus Gerontology Center as the focus of research projects at the Leonard Davis School of Gerontology.[78]

USC's Leonard Davis School website boasts that it is "the world's first, largest and most renowned educational institution on aging," one that offers "first-class interdisciplinary studies, the most diverse and cutting-edge course offerings anywhere, close working relationships with top professionals, both from our faculty and in the working world and outstanding internships and career placement." Students can enroll in four undergrad programs, eleven at the masters level, and three doctoral degree programs including a doctorate in longevity arts and sciences, in which students will "will explore the possibility of finding meaning and relevance in the elongated lifespans human beings are enjoying in the 21st century."[79] Twenty-six regular faculty members teach students at a range of levels, while researchers carry out their work in any one of eleven centers or institutes, including those on elder justice, life-span science, fall prevention, Alzheimer's disease, longevity, and global aging. Even more so than Stanford's Center on Longevity, USC's School of Gerontology reaches across a wide range of disciplinary fields.

* * *

Writing in the *Huffington Post* in 2012, Ken Dychtwald celebrated the life of Maggie Kuhn. He did so as a psychologist, author, and both founder and CEO of Age Wave, an educational and consulting organization that, among other things, helps businesses benefit from the rapidly increasing number of older people. Kuhn was, he wrote, "a woman far ahead of her time. She was both a visionary and a role model for young and old, attesting to our potential for strength, worth and beauty in the later years. I'm also honored," he insisted, "to say that she was my friend and mentor." Relying on interviews he had carried out with Kuhn in 1978, he recounted how she identified the myths that people had about elder Americans. Among them were, she told him, "stereotypes [of] old age as a disastrous disease which nobody wants to admit to having, but which affects us all" and that that people in their old age were mindless, sexless, useless, and powerless. She also lambasted seniors-only communities as "glorified playpens." Instead, she emphasized, "We who are older have enormous freedom to speak out, and equally great responsibility to take the risks that are needed to heal and humanize our sick society. We can try new things and take on entirely new roles."[80]

When Dychtwald was twenty-three, he was teaching at the Esalen Institute in Big Sur, California. Soon after, he was the cofounder of the Sage Project. Funded by the National Institutes of Health, it helped elders learn to enhance their lives by more actively working on their physical and mental health. In 1986, with his wife, Maddy, he created Age Wave, which, as its website claims, guides "Fortune 500 companies and government agencies in product/service development for boomers and mature adults."[81] In a series of books, he enthusiastically celebrated the healthy longevity of growing numbers of Americans and coached public and private organizations how to market successfully to them. As he wrote in 1989, "the Age Wave is beginning to pull American business in new directions," influenced by Americans fifty years and older, who "will turn out to be the most powerful and affluent consumer group in history," spending money especially on leisure, housing, financial services, and health care.[82]

If Dychtwald's grounding in the human potential movement has shaped Age Wave as a private corporation that helps a variety of organizations market to elders, then MIT's AgeLab, founded in 1999 and led since then by Joseph F. Coughlin, is a university-based lab that aims to do the same, albeit shaped less by exuberant psychology than by more cautious academic commitments, influenced by both Abraham Maslow's hierarchy of needs and pathbreaking technology. Coughlin not only teaches in MIT's Department of Urban Studies and Planning but also serves on the Board of Directors of the AARP, offers advice to federal agencies and major corporations worldwide, and writes for business publications including *The Wall Street Journal* and *Forbes*. Staffed by twenty-three faculty and researchers, the AgeLab promotes itself as "a multidisciplinary research program that works with business, government, and NGOs to improve the quality of life of older people and those who care for them. The AgeLab applies consumer-centered systems thinking to understand the challenges and opportunities of longevity and emerging generational lifestyles to catalyze innovation across business markets."[83]

In Coughlin's 2017 book *The Longevity Economy: Unlocking the World's Fastest-Growing, Most Misunderstood Market*, he began by talking about what he called the "longevity paradox"—the contrast between so many people living longer and more healthily, on the one hand, and on the other, negative and highly problematic views of elders. "It's so enormous," he emphasized as he pointed out how business leaders had to realize the importance of what was happening, that "it's as though a new *continent* were rising out of the sea, filled with more than a billion air-breathing consumers just begging for products that fill their demands." And deploying Maslow's hierarchy of needs, he made clear that the demands would not be only for physiological needs such as food and clothing but also for "higher-level needs like the desire for human connection, personal or professional ambition, contemplation, and yes, fun," as well as items that enhance "independence, happiness, and the pursuit of meaning."[84]

The products developed would "need to leverage cutting-edge technology and make it available in a way that is highly usable without seeming blunted and dumbed-down," ones that "simply excite and delight [people] in old age." Therefore, the job of the AgeLab was to enable corporations "to harness the heightened expectations of baby boomers craving a better old age and," by not focusing so much on those in younger cohorts, "to avoid being left in the dustbin of creative destruction." In doing so, it had to pay special attention to tech-savvy middle-age and older women, pioneers who blurred "the line between producer and consumer to identify products capable of solving the true demands of older adults" as it helped businesses develop products that relied on generation connections, "radical empathy," "lead-user innovation" normally found among consumers, and "*transcendent design*—making things not just accessible for all types of users but so wonderful to use that people go out of their way to obtain them, even if they don't strictly need them." He often focused on needs for health and care that treated "those solutions not as end goals but rather as a stepping-stone on the way toward the accomplishment of older people's aspirations and goals." Among the many examples he cited are autonomous vehicles; "the Internet of Things, particularly as manifested in smart homes; and the on-demand and sharing economy"; and health and safety products that will become "automated and commoditized." Coughlin ended the book by calling on baby boomers and corporations to leave legacies by helping elders "chase their dreams, have fun, contribute, achieve meaning."[85]

My scholarly exploration through the world of aging organizations reveals just how varied, extensive, and often powerful they are. Corporate, nonprofit, scholarly, advocacy, and governmental, they range across much of the political spectrum—all products of the postwar world shaped by increasing numbers of people living longer. At the same time, Gray Panthers blossomed and faded, leaving the more practically and commercially minded AARP a relatively open field for advocacy, which it did more strategically than insurgently. As Chappel notes, the AARP was "a service-providing nonprofit that operated more through the mail than in the streets or on the soap box."[86] Of course, none of these institutions was consistently, significantly, or clearly ageist, though they varied in the extent and nature of their compassion—focusing as many of them did on able-bodied, white, and socioeconomically privileged elders. Above all, together they remind us of the limitations, power, and omnipresence of groups that make up the longevity industrial and commercial complex.

5

Housing Seniors

Over the course of US history, major changes have occurred in where seniors have lived. Several forces have driven shifting patterns, among them increasing longevity and wealth of millions of citizens and the varying roles played by family and religious, communal, and government institutions. Throughout, the clear majority of elderly Americans have lived in their homes, which over time grew more varied. Increasingly after 1945, many elders lived away from family members, making it necessary or desirable for them to seek residences where they would not feel lonely. Federal legislation underwrote new forms of residential real estate and thus opened up a wider range of opportunities, especially for those in the middle class and above. At the same time, dramatic increases in life expectancy and affluence for tens of millions of Americans helped create markets for new institutional arrangements. Especially beginning in the mid-1970s, an infrastructure for elders developed, including senior centers, Meals on Wheels, Elderhostel (now Road Scholar), and Osher Lifelong Learning Institutes.

Senior housing is the principal focal point of this chapter because postwar Americans saw the arrival and development of major alternatives. People fortunate with regard to wealth and well-being could choose among active 55+ communities, Naturally Occurring Retirement Communities (NORCs), Continuing Care Retirement Communities (CCRCS), and varied arrangements for aging in place. And for others, among the possibilities were young daughters caring for their aging mothers, often problematic nursing homes, subsidized affordable housing, nonmedical custodial care in a residential setting, and, at worst, the grim realities of incarceration or homelessness. In the literature of senior housing, more political, economic, and cultural capital sustains the focus on where and how the privileged live than on those who end up on the street, in substandard housing, in inadequately staffed nursing homes, or in crowded residences that house several generations.

Public policy, frailty, discrimination, and inequalities mean that some elders end up lonely, insecure, dependent, and neglected, while others can take advantage of opportunities for social engagement, comfort, and personal growth.[1]

Early in the history of the United States and well into the nineteenth century, religious and communal values mandated that many families take care of members of older generations. In addition, the fact that most Americans lived not in crowded cities but on farms or in small towns, that modern medicine could not prolong the lives of people inflicted by cancer, heart diseases, and other diseases, and that life expectancy was not as great as today meant that few among the elderly faced starvation or homelessness as they aged. To be sure, some, especially the poor, many African Americans, and unmarried women who had no close or supportive relatives struggled mightily to survive.[2]

Beginning in the 1840s, when factories and cities emerged and then increased in numbers and size, nonfamily custodial institutions grew in variety and capacity. For local governments struggling to house the elderly indigent, the most common solution was the almshouse or poorhouse, institutions supported initially by town taxpayers and eventually also by counties and states. They housed paupers unable to support themselves, including the elderly. Over time, worries about high institutional costs drove the poorer among the elderly into government-supported large institutions, in some instances mingling with those seen as insane who lived in asylums that an 1845 federal law had helped fund. Reformers and officials moved to separate children and people seen as mentally ill from the deserving poor, a category that included the elderly, whether dependent or independent, ill or healthy.[3]

Especially after the Civil War, other alternatives emerged. Some of the elderly and infirm ended up living in hospitals, including homes connected to the main building. The federal government provided facilities for aging disabled veterans. On a lesser scale and in small numbers, elderly people who needed supervised care lived in places such as medical boardinghouses or even rooms in a private house. More common were residences for seniors developed by private organizations. Wealthy benefactors provided for some of them in their wills. Religious, ethnic, and fraternal organizations founded others. Examples abounded, such as those run by Jewish, Italian, or Irish benevolent societies, local churches, or fraternal organizations like the Independent Order of Odd Fellows. Such groups relied on contributions from their members, in some cases dues paid in anticipation of future needs. In some instances, they helped make it possible for the elderly to remain in their homes. And they built their own "homes for the aged"—places that were often paternalistic but hardly punitive, in some cases spare and in others offering comfortable accommodations, with a range of options from independent living with communal resources to hospital wards, and funded by varying combinations of charitable contributions, family resources, or even by the elderly turning over pensions or life savings.

Near the end of the nineteenth century, other options emerged. There was a small number of dedicated retirement communities. A rare example was the William Enston Home in Charleston, South Carolina, which dated to 1889. According to the National Park Service Register of Historic Places, it was "comprised of 24 residential cottages; Memorial Hall, a community building; and an infirmary"—all on "spacious, landscaped grounds" on which were located "neat and convenient two-story brick cottages" that housed "residents" who were "old and sick, from 45 to 75 years old, of 'good honest character,' and not suffering from 'lunacy.'"[4] More common, especially in big cities, were settlement houses that accommodated some elders. In addition, with the rise of nursing as a profession and the emergence of visiting nursing associations, the elderly could receive professional care at home or elsewhere.

In the late nineteenth century and the first three decades of the twentieth, the patchwork set of arrangements for the elderly persisted, some changes accelerated, and a few innovations occurred. The number and size of old-age homes increased, most of them built by nonprofit organizations. One example was the Masonic Home in Utica, New York. Opening in 1893 to house Masons and their family members (including their widows and wives), it is now available to all as the Masonic Care Community, where it houses more than five hundred elders. Its mission, the current website says with pride, "is to support, nurture and educate those whose lives we touch by providing exceptional care and services with compassion and pride guided by the Masonic Principles of brotherly love, relief, truth and integrity."[5]

In these years, increasing numbers of people resided in cities, with many of them living in crowded tenements. In 1910, the economist

Henry R. Seager underscored the consequences for the elderly. "The cost of maintaining an aged relative in the country is so small as to seem an insignificant burden," he noted, as he contrasted this with the situation "in the crowded tenement houses of modern cities." Not only would "an aged person" over sixty-five find it difficult to have gainful employment, but "the cost of maintaining an aged relative in the city is an appreciable item in a wage earner's budget, and even when the burden is cheerfully borne, it means so much less for other necessary family expenditures."[6] If family members could not shoulder the burden of providing for elders, including those whom employment-related injuries forced out of the workforce prematurely, then other options came into play. Provisions varied. Retired schoolteachers or clergy members might live in small group homes. Around 1900, state and local governments began to build sanatoria for the increasing number of people inflicted by tuberculosis, many of them indigent or elderly or both. State and local governments, private insurance, and families themselves provided home care for elders by visiting, private-duty, or public health nurses. In an effort to keep elders out of almshouses, state, county, and local governments provided means-tested cash allotments to the indigent elderly on a patchy and limited basis. Yet by the 1930s, the number of people over sixty-five was modest—estimated at 5.4 percent of a population of 132 million, dramatically less than the 17 percent in 2022.[7] In the earlier period, perhaps as high as 3 percent of people over sixty-five lived in institutions—whether charitable residences or proprietary ones, poorhouses, or places for the mentally ill.

Still, before the Great Depression, most Americans over sixty-five either were financially independent or relied on help from friends and family. According to one study, in 1929, 44 percent of that cohort were financially self-sufficient—with well over half of them continuing to work and the rest relying on pensions or savings. Of the remaining 56 percent, the lion's share (87.5 percent) relied on friends or relatives. The rest lived in communities but depended on private or public charity, resided in government institutions, especially poorhouses, and in proprietary or nonprofit homes. If my calculations are correct, this means that in 1929, a vast majority of Americans over sixty-five, a figure perhaps as high 93 percent, either were financially self-sufficient or relied on friends and family. And perhaps 5 percent lived in institutions. Indeed, Carole Haber and Brian Gratton have shown that, rather than being increasingly isolated, before the coming of the twentieth century, "a higher percentage of elderly resided in complex or extended households than had their preindustrial peers," enabling them to benefit from cross-generational connections.[8]

The Great Depression of the 1930s and World War II drove changes that over time would play major roles in shaping the future of senior housing. Already in the 1920s, criticism of almshouses as inhumane intensified, and proposals for old-age pensions gained wider acceptance. Truth be told, the numbers of people in almshouses were small, less than 1 percent of seniors. In the 1930s, such a figure paled in comparison to the millions of the elderly who saw their savings depleted, which, along with the weakening of charitable and state-based programs for elderly assistance, made precarious where seniors dwelled. The 1935 Old Age Insurance (OAI) provision of the 1935 Social Security Act would later profoundly shape housing possibilities, including making it possible for couples to live alone or only with their children.[9] But in the short term, its means-tested Old Age Assistance (OAA) program, by barring the use of federal funds for folks in poorhouses but allowing their use for those living in proprietary old-age homes, helped underwrite the growth of what was initially a small-scale cottage industry providing for care of the elderly and others in something resembling what we know as nursing homes. In the 1940s, federal programs increasingly impacted where and how people resided. The expansion and more adequate funding of OAA, OAI, unemployment insurance, and veterans' benefits enabled increasing numbers of people to reside in nursing homes, which were, the scholar Bruce Vladeck has written, "almost entirely a creation of public policy." From then on, government policy relied increasingly on the belief that inadequate income and not character flaws dictated funding, which relied more and more on cash grants that enabled seniors to decide where they would live.[10]

In 1939, OAI was expanded to include coverage for dependent children, widows, and widowers, and by 1947, 22 percent of Americans over sixty-five were receiving support from OAA. In many cases, this meant that the elderly, women especially, were able to live independently rather than with family members. In addition, by helping to fund the building of nonprofit and public hospitals, the 1946 Hospital Survey and

Construction Act (aka the Hill-Burton Act) made possible the conversion of older facilities into nursing homes and, over the longer term, served as a model for the funding of retirement communities. Like the transformation of other existing buildings, such as hotels, this helped drive up the number of people, including the elderly, who could live in nursing homes, a capacious and often confusing term that ranged from facilities connected to public and private hospitals to what we would now call assisted living facilities and even to private homes housing only a few seniors.

What had happened during the Depression and the immediate postwar period set precedents for the ensuing decades. Federal funding, often in connection with state and local support, provided increasing numbers of the elderly with more generous financial assistance. This made it possible for more of the indigent and infirm among them to live in public and for-profit facilities. At the same time, with family size affecting the lives of seniors, federal legislation helped finance buildings that housed the elderly in settings that increasingly provided a combination of housing and medical care, considered not as welfare but as health care. Over time, programs, including those launched by the Great Society, such as the 1965 Older Americans Act, expanded as more and more federal agencies got involved in supporting shelter for the elderly—eventually in nonprofit (sometimes launched by religious and fraternal organizations) and for-profit facilities that ranged from nursing homes (now increasingly larger and mostly proprietary) to congregate settings where people could live independently. All these arrangements raised but often left unresolved issues of standards and government supervision.

In the postwar period, new options emerged for housing seniors, although keep in mind that about 97.5 percent of seniors live in their own homes or in the residences of someone they know—most frequently a relative.[11] Among those who own or rent their domiciles are millions of Americans aging in place, living in NORCs, 55+ communities, and CCRCs. These options are among the most innovative and attention-grabbing possibilities, whose numbers of residents are often growing most rapidly. Housing vouchers and subsidized rents are among the varied programs sponsored by governments or philanthropy that make it possible for some seniors with few financial resources to live in public housing. Yet, given the power of inequalities of wealth and income in the United States, these provisions hardly help all in need, disproportionately people of color with low incomes.[12]

Aging in place is one option, one that it is likely that millions of Americans who want to remain in their own residences as long as possible hope to achieve or actually do. In some instances, they do so without much planning or forethought, while in others, to some degree or other, they plan appropriately, often with the help of social workers employed in Area Agencies on Aging. They might take steps to make their homes as safe as possible by, for example, installing grab bars in showers. They can identify and then contact individuals and organizations that provide home-based care when needed; talk to their friends, family members, and physicians about contingencies; and prepare documents that will govern arrangements for finances and health care.[13]

I often think of my parents, who in the 1980s moved into a CCRC, Evergreen Woods in North Branford, Connecticut. They did so because my somewhat-frail mother felt it was too much of a burden to take care of my father. They were living in an apartment within blocks of the Yale New Haven Hospital and had nearby many people who cared deeply for them, including many MDs. What they lacked and we now have access to are home delivery of groceries, streaming of movies, telemedicine, and, above all, easily available coordination of home heath care. On television now, I often see ads for agencies like Home Instead and A Place for Mom. Founded, respectively, in 1994 and 2000, they are private corporations that connect providers of health care with seniors and their families—including for those who want to remain in their homes. The medical practice that Helen and I use in Cambridge provides us with access to several social workers who help patients, if they choose to remain in place, gain access to coordinators of care.[14]

NORCs are one step up from aging in place.[15] Credit for inventing the term "NORC" goes to an architect, Michael Hunt, and a social worker, Gail Gunter-Hunt, who in 1986 defined them as "housing developments that are not planned or designed for older people, but which over time come to house" many of them. Differing "from the stereotypical retirement community," they observed, in the United States, they were the "most common form" of "community-based housing," offering a "supportive neighborhood" to their residents.[16] Living in Madison, Wisconsin, and associated with the University of Wisconsin, they realized that seniors, especially widowed women, were not flocking to retirement communities. Instead, they were moving into older apartments in the Hilldale neighborhood that provided easy access to conveniently located stores and a public library.[17]

In the ensuing decades, the numbers of seniors who lived in NORCs were probably greater than those in 55+ communities or CCRCs. In the early 1990s, the AARP estimated that well over one in every four seniors lived in a NORC.[18] What complicates any accurate figure is that standard measurements vary, with some using ages lower than sixty-five, sometimes as low as fifty-five. In addition, though the commonly accepted figure for the percentage of seniors living in a NORC is 40 percent, there is hardly agreement among analysts. In 2006, the federal government stepped into the definitional thicket when it defined a NORC as "a community with a concentrated population of older individuals, which may include a residential building, a housing complex, an area (including a rural area) of single-family residences, or a neighbourhood composed of age-integrated housing," in which a minimum of 40 percent of older Americans or "a critical mass of older individuals exists," that, relying on varied factors, make it possible "to achieve efficiencies in the provision of health and social services."[19] There are surely such communities elsewhere, but information is readily available only for those in the United States and Canada.

Of the social categories that drive who lives in NORCs, age is the most obvious one. In addition, there are likely to be more women than men, a factor driven by gendered differences in rates of mortality. NORC residents are more likely to be white and relatively well-to-do, not only because of the generally more precarious financial situations of others but also because, as a 2022 survey revealed, "especially those with lower incomes, those living in rural areas, and Black or Hispanic older adults" are leerier "about the services in their area that support aging."[20]

Most commonly (but not exclusively) located in cities, NORCs exist in areas in which significant numbers of the local population are seniors who have gravitated there because of individual decisions rather than top-down planning. Though usually unplanned, their existence is at least initially retrospectively explicable—driven by issues such as density of population and availability of transportation as well as shopping, communal, and health facilities. Some urban NORCs are vertical, an individual apartment building or a series of them somehow connected, by geography or design.[21] Others are horizontal, a series of geographically defined urban areas. Walkability, social networks, and opportunities for communal involvement are among the factors that enable senior residents to overcome isolation, benefit from mutual support from neighbors, remain active and independent, sustain healthy aging, and postpone institutionalization as long as possible.[22]

The Village Movement is one NORC model, in which a relatively small number of local residents (often in the low hundreds) of an urban neighborhood pay a fee, one that depends on local conditions and services offered, to gain access to services that a nonprofit, community-based organization provides. Members of the more than three hundred such Villages in the United States are mainly affluent and white, with more women than men. A small staff coordinates access to planned outings and referrals to services such as transportation to appointments, help with technology, home care, and household arrangements that help members live independently. Those who live in such Villages are more elite but far less numerous than those in NORCs.[23]

The Village Movement began with the founding in 2002 of Boston's Beacon Hill Village. With a paid staff of five, supplemented by volunteers, it now serves 360 members, who pay annual fees starting at $675. Its website describes this Village as "a member-led community of active, creative and independent adults aged 50 and older who connect with and care for one another," with a shared commitment "to grow older better in the homes and neighborhoods we love." It celebrates "social capital and member energy," committed to "the idea that together we're stronger," by emphasizing "peer-to-peer networking to promote an active lifestyle, improve health, and reduce isolation." Among its robust offerings are wellness activities, ranging from classes in meditation and exercise to medical referrals; social events that rely on affinity groups; access to resources such as tech support and home care that foster independence; "educational programs that include talks by local notables"; access to cultural resources that "provide ways to enhance and enrich lives"; and local and regional excursions that foster "life experiences and outlooks."[24] If the people pictured on its website are representative, then its staff is all female and white, and its members are all white and overwhelmingly female.

What emerged in the 1980s were NORC-SSPs (supportive service programs) that developed infrastructure arrangements—sometimes more or less spontaneously and more commonly with varying degrees of planning. Funding comes from many sources, prominently from governments, religious or ethnic organizations, neighborhood associations, philanthropies, fundraising efforts, and membership fees. Volunteers among neighbors work with professionals to build and coordinate activities that promote well-being and independence by enhancing social engagement through outings, clubs, educational activities, and congregate meals and by providing access to resources, especially health-related ones.

Manhattan's Penn South Houses was the location of the first NORC-SSP. The International Ladies' Garment Workers' Union had built Penn South in 1962. Composed of ten buildings that housed over six thousand residents, it evolved over time into an institution that catered to seniors. With them aging and hoping to age in place, at this location in 1986, a public-private partnership established the nation's first professionally managed NORC-SSP. Public-private partnerships were central in these developments. Beginning in 1986 in an existing series of ten cooperative housing buildings, it was financed initially by the United Jewish Appeal (UJA) and the United Hospital Fund. Three years later, the UJA worked to put finances on a sustainable basis by combining funds from multiple sources, including state and local governments, the housing company, residents themselves, and philanthropies.[25] New York State soon emerged as the location of the largest number of NORC-SSPs, something fostered by a 1995 law promoting them in apartment complexes that housed low- to moderate-income families. In Canada and the United States in the early twenty-first century, national and regional governments supported the development of dozens of NORC-SSPs.[26] Then the federal government enhanced the efforts of the Jewish agencies in developing NORC-SSPs in fourteen cities across the nation.[27] Funds and personnel came from local, state, and federal governments, which, according to one study, provided 57 percent of the finances. An additional 17 percent came from philanthropies, 13 percent from health care providers, 10 percent as a housing match, and smaller amounts from elsewhere, including membership fees.[28]

If Bruce Vladeck wrote the key book on nursing homes in 1980, in 2003, his wife, Fredda Vladeck, authored *A Good Place to Grow Old:*

New York's Model for NORC Social Service Programs, the key report on NORC-SSPs.[29] Relying on the work of the United Hospital Fund's Aging in Place Initiative in a cooperative arrangement with United Way of New York City, she charted the development of a new model that since 1986 has enabled tens, if not hundreds, of thousands of seniors to age in place. It was, she writes, "a model of care" that was "revolutionizing services for older people" by recognizing "the considerable strengths of the elderly" and their "overwhelming preference to remain at home, in the neighborhoods they have lived in for years, and the importance of community for successful aging." A number of characteristics distinguish them from the usual arrangements, notably "quite a departure from the then-current practice of separating programs for the well-elderly from services for the frail based on payer source and functional status." People were members by virtue of their age, residence, and strengths and not because they needed special care. They entered the system as active participants before a crisis forced them to do so. They benefited from the on-site presence of coordinated and ongoing services, sustained by a broad range of integrated amenities provided by government and nonprofit agencies.[30]

New York's NORC-SSPs housed significantly more diverse population than Villages, 55+ communities, and CCRCs. As Fredda Vladeck writes, the NORC-SSPs reflected "the diversity of New York's older population." Of the twenty-eight programs, sixteen housed "predominantly white seniors," including descendants of Irish, Italian, and eastern European Jewish immigrants and Russians who had arrived more recently. Then there were eleven "in mixed communities in which the majority of seniors are of African-American, Caribbean black, Hispanic, or Asian heritage, and some are recent immigrants," as well as one that housed mostly African American citizens.[31]

Vladeck reported on the extensive and coordinated services SSPs provided, both on-site and in connection to more distant locales. They enhanced the possibility that residents could sustain active involvement in place by creating "opportunities for seniors to remain active and involved in their community." Filling in the gaps of major federal program was help from social workers and health care providers. In addition, SSPs supported access to a wide range of recreational and educational activities. Inventively and extensively, they empowered residents. "Revitalizing a community," Vladeck insists, "can only be done from the inside and requires the active participation of the residents themselves. Residents are not just clients. They have multiple roles in NORC-SSPs and an ownership interest in their success. They play a key role in shaping programs through their participation in its governance structure. They are also program ambassadors, service providers, and consumers of services."[32]

The results of all these arrangements at Penn South and elsewhere, Vladeck reports, were impressive. "Residents at all levels of functioning," she writes, "are more engaged in the lives of their communities: those who remain capable of more extensive activities have a broader range of choices available close to home, many of which permit them to make tangible contributions to their own communities and their own neighbors; residents who experience acute or intermittent crises have familiar and trusted sources of professional assistance close at hand; those with increasing disability have trusted neighbors and supporters assisting them in navigating the complexities of the formal, 'old' service system, and in many instances are also able to draw on additional services that might not otherwise be available."[33]

There are also age-restricted communities, usually where at least one household member has to be fifty-five years or older and no young children are allowed on a long-term basis. Some RV parks or communities with immobile manufactured homes are one type. Although figures for how many seniors live in them are hard to come by, my guess is that they are home to around three hundred thousand.[34] Some spaces are rented, others purchased. Some of those who go to an age-restricted RV park do so for a short period of time, perhaps a monthlong vacation near the beach. Yet there are some, mostly in Florida, California, and Arizona, where residents live most, if not all, of the year. Some house small numbers of retirees, but others, such as Bradenton Trailer Park in Florida (opened in 1936 by the Kiwanis) and Trailer Estates in several Florida locations, house thousands in communities that offer ample educational and recreational opportunities. Early on, many of them excluded African Americans, Latinos, and people of Asian descent. The Bradenton currently and emphatically states, "We will not tolerate racism," although the pictures on its website display few, if any, nonwhites.[35]

More prevalent are age-restricted communities of what since 1975 are called manufactured homes. Produced in a factory and moved to a permanent site on a truck, double-wides with two thousand square feet or more and containing two bedrooms and two baths can easily cost $170,000, a figure less, sometimes dramatically so, than the price of a home constructed on-site. An exploration of the Friendly Village of La Habra, California, reveals what this type of 55+ community is like. Located in a city of sixty thousand in northwest Orange County, California, this outpost contains 271 residences. In the city, a two-bedroom, two-bath condo with just under 900 square feet costs $450,000, which makes clear why someone might purchase a 1,288-square-foot home in Friendly Village for a little more than half the price. I assume what explains the difference is that in Friendly Village you do not own the land and on-site construction costs are greater than factory ones. The website of Friendly Village touts its virtues, some of them unique to this property but most of them common to many 55+ communities. It emphasizes the importance of a lifestyle that is active, carefree, and inspired, one where making friends is effortless. This is a "charming neighborhood" that is "surrounded by scenic forested areas," albeit more likely by broad and busy suburban roads. More convincing is the description of "ornamental streams, sunny blue skies and an exclusive on-site amenity package." Among its elements are a community center, an eighteen-hole putting course, a BBQ area, a library, and a heated swimming pool. Beyond its perimeter, "just around the corner," are "[sub?]urban conveniences and attractions," with "dining and cultural venues just minutes away." Farther afield is Los Angeles, where you can "experience one of the most vibrant and diverse cities in America." Promotional material hypes diversity a few miles away without specificity; it could have mentioned centers of Asian American or Latino life within twenty miles. However, more prominently featured are "all the joys of small-town living, . . . a quiet setting [that] provides residents that cozy, small town feel," where they "live the ultimate California lifestyle."[36] Like other arrangements for seniors, gated 55+ communities remind us of how fear of crime drives community designs that appeal to many Americans. Ditto the evocation of life in small towns, seen elsewhere from how politicians like Jimmy Carter and Tim Walz have evoked the reassuring pleasures of seemingly simpler lives. Like so many other sites where seniors live, Florida's The Villages mixes traditional and nontraditional evocations of place, in this case small-town values in a highly developed, commercial setting.[37]

More prominent among 55+ communities than those featuring manufactured homes are the more than two thousand with residences located on hundreds and sometimes thousands of acres. A reasonable estimate is that at least one million seniors have relocated to them. They are mostly in the Sun Belt—Florida, California, and Arizona especially—although New Jersey has a sizeable number of these communities. Age discrimination in such communities became legally protected when lobbyists secured a 1995 amendment to the 1968 Fair Housing Act. The resulting 80-20 rule dictated that a minimum of 80 percent of residential units had to have at least one resident who was at least fifty-five years old. In addition, no offspring under eighteen could reside permanently, and in some instances, there were restrictions on how long a younger child could sleep over.[38]

Youngstown, founded in 1954 outside Phoenix, was perhaps the nation's first age-restricted community—all those who purchased homes had to be at least sixty-five, and young children were not allowed to reside there permanently. Unlike developments that followed, it had relatively few amenities or recreational facilities. It was Del Webb's Sun City, located on adjacent land, which opened in 1960, and Ross Cortese's Leisure World Seal Beach in Orange County, California, the following year that established the patterns that other developers of 55+ communities followed. They were, Jonathan Rauch writes, with some exaggeration, "a suburban dreamscape for a class of people who, only a generation before, were typically isolated, institutionalized, or crammed into their kids' overcrowded apartments."[39]

To be sure, there were differences among 55+ communities. Cheap land located far from settled populations made it possible to place homes on ample parcels next to or near golf courses, while different patterns marked developments located closer to already-settled communities. Some projects relied more or less exclusively on one-story single-family homes, while others included attached townhouses and multistory building. Walls and gates surrounded some, while others had more permeable boundaries. If some attracted mostly out-of-state migrants, especially those escaping cold winters, others attracted in-state residents who were downsizing. Amenities varied in their numbers, fanciness, and variety. Over time, developers built larger and more expensive residences. Some communities began with homes with less than one thousand square feet and eventually added many more than twice that size. With the average age of residents increasing, some 55+ projects began with and others added medical facilities and assisted living accommodations, sometimes within the community and in other instances in adjacent locations.

These differences aside, 55+ communities grew in prominence. Expansion built on patterns set by Del Webb's Sun Cities and Ross Cortese's Rossmoor/Leisure World brands. They pioneered schemes for land-use planning, congregate housing, and social engineering of communal life. Robust entrepreneurship and clever marketing helped increase corporate projects, some of them imperial in size. Yet exogenous factors were also in play—prominent among them were the growing number of seniors who benefited from longer lives lived healthily, postwar prosperity, corporate pensions, government programs such as Social Security, and support of home ownership through the tax codes and FHA mortgages.

Larger communities—when completed, Sun City's forty-eight thousand residents lived in 25,149 homes—offered more elaborate and numerous amenities, whose activities community staffers coordinated. Among them were multiple golf courses, community swimming pools, meeting spaces, performance venues, churches and eventually synagogues, small shopping centers, banks, newspapers, and provisions for adult education. Other things attracted seniors to 55+ communities, including how they turn away from responsibilities to family and society outside the walls of the retirement community. Except for California, state taxes are low. Almost everywhere, residents keep local taxes low by offering limited support for schools. Home owners who live in residences especially designed for seniors benefit from carefree maintenance outside. Bus systems but especially growing number of electric golf carts make it easy for people to move about within the community.

Along with other options that developed in the United States after 1945, 55+ communities helped transform the image and experiences of seniors. This is something the historian Judith Ann Trolander explores in her deeply researched and wide-ranging *From Sun Cities to the Villages: A History of Active, Adult, Age-Restricted Communities* (2011), a book that focuses not only on this approach but on others—trailer parks as well as beachfront condos that house ample numbers of seniors but others as well. Over time, she notes, Webb and Cortese shifted the promotional language used to describe residents from those enjoy-ing "active retirement" to people who were "active adults." Marketers promoted a capacious vision of how seniors could live—independently in ways that embraced key elements of an active late-in-life lifestyle, where on-the-ground residents reshaped what corporations offered. Other nations had age-targeted communities, but age-restricted ones were uniquely American. Trolander notes that these communities "popularized the legal device of common-interest communities to cre-ate amenity-rich developments with the ownership and use of the ame-nities limited to the residents." Above all, she concludes, "the greatest significance of these communities was to change the stereotype of the elderly from impoverished adults in physical decline to the image of 'active adults' who can afford a resort type of lifestyle. In the popu-lar imagination," and with the help of clever marketing that played on people living longer lives more healthily, "Grandma and Grandpa ex-changed their rocking chairs for golf carts."[40]

As Trolander makes clear, 55+ communities were hardly beyond re-proach. Critics underscore how age-based policies undercut the benefits of intergenerational experiences. They point out that 55+ communities celebrate problematic small-town virtues. Moreover, the Casserole-Brigade, which involves widows appealing to the appetites of widowers, hardly solves the issues arising from the gender imbalance prevalent among seniors. Betty Friedan, whose mother, Miriam, lived in a Cali-fornia 55+ community, characterized these developments as "adult play-pens," whose inhabitants rarely developed passionate commitments. In 1964, the *New Yorker* writer Calvin Trillin, who authored one of the earliest critiques and one that foretold later ones, characterized most of those who lived in Sun City as "almost belligerently happy," self-satisfied that where they had ended up was "the closest . . . there is to Utopia."[41] Critics also lament that developers and residents often em-brace conservative politics—antitax and antiunion positions prominent among them.

Like what some people called "ghettoes," these developments too often remained isolated and self-contained, disengaged from the wider communities that surrounded them. This was prominently clear with Sun City in Arizona, where locals kept their distance from adjacent Mexican American communities. Developers promoted and residents often preferred clubby homogeneity and familiarity, accentuated by many factors, including the systematic fostering of home-state identity. Some communities embraced more diversity than others, and in the twenty-first century, many of them have tolerated and even welcomed a wider range of residents—in some cases, especially Jews in Florida and Asian Americans in California. Yet, in many instances, white, Christian, middle- to upper-middle-class residents have dominated, what Trolander calls those with "above average but not lavish incomes," characterized by "relative social class homogeneity," even though over time, there has been a tendency of more affluent folks to move in. To be sure, some developments contain decent numbers of retirees from the upper reaches of the blue-collar workforce. Yet whiteness has prevailed. In 1964, Trillin reported that Sun City's vice president, Thomas Breen, remarked, "Let's face it, a Negro would be miserable in Sun City," and if an African American dared to buy a home in a California Sun City, the Del Webb corporation would offer relocation elsewhere locally.[42] Such exclusionary practices long remained in place. One 1990 survey counted Black, Hispanic, and Asian residents at less than 1 percent in Arizona's Sun City and Sun City West. Ten years later, there was not one African American resident among the 5,519 who lived in Sun City, California, and presumably not one Native American there or elsewhere.[43]

Webb and Cortese pioneered the development of 55+ communities, but The Villages exploded the model. Founded in 1982 by Harold Schwartz and amplified further by his descendants, starting with his son, H. Gary Morse, who sustained control through zoning, ownership of businesses, and media that spread news of its conservative commitments. Located forty-five miles northwest of Orlando, it has grown to cover fifty-seven square miles, sprawling over three counties and housing 145,000 people in seventy-one thousand residences. Called variously "A Disney World for Adults," "Sun City on Steroids," and officially "Florida's Friendliest Hometown," the complex contains a series of economically homogeneous villages or neighborhoods. Then there are several "downtowns" that, with their false fronts and clever signs, hype Disney-like fantasies. They contain shops, restaurants, and entertainment spaces.[44] The Villages also has its own hospital, over 230 pickleball courts, more than fifty golf courses, three libraries, and multiple and varied restaurants. "There are more than 3,000+ social clubs and resident lifestyle groups in The Villages," its promotional copy boasts, "including car clubs, state clubs, creative clubs, plus over 130 different types of single-specific clubs."[45]

Several characteristics mark The Villages. Many of its residents are retired veterans. The Midwest and Northeast are the main sources of relocators. Given its status as an age-restricted community, there are very few people there under age fifty-five. The median age hovers in the high sixties, with over 86 percent of residents sixty-five or older. Of course, there are more women than men (53.9 percent) and more Republicans than Democrats. The Villages attracts people who can afford to live there—from the mid-middle class upward to the upper middle class. The median household income is $73,415, but 3.7 percent supposedly live in poverty. Almost everyone has a high school degree, and 42.3 percent graduated from college. Ethnically the population is homogeneous: 97.4 percent of residents are white, with some Latinos (1.4 percent) and multiracial residents (1.2 percent). Remarkably but not surprisingly, there are few Asian Americans (0.09 percent) or African Americans (0.04 percent) and no Native Americans.[46] Promotional materials picture happy, smiling white folks, many of them heterosexual couples and more likely to be in their fifties or sixties than seventies or eighties. In a brochure titled "Dream a Little *Dream*," of the hundreds of adults featured, I could not find one Asian American (oh, perhaps an Asian Indian doctor) and only two African Americans—one of them perhaps a male tai chi instructor and the other probably a female professional singer.[47]

There are multiple renderings of what life in The Villages is like, and prominently contrasting ones come from its own website and critical responses, including in the 2020 documentary *Some Kind of Heaven*. The Villages, we read online at its own site, is a "collection of quaint retirement neighborhoods," each one "unique in its charm and personality and connected in ways where all the lifestyle here for you to enjoy is just a golf cart ride away." "Relaxing," "endless opportunities," "safety," "active lifestyle," "creativity," and "lives purposively led" are the words describing "a place where anything you can dream of doing, learning or becoming is possible. . . . Whether a place to unwind and rest from a fun filled day, gather for cookouts or find inspiration for your newest hobby." Connecting with new friends is easy, because "with so many unique interests, you'll find plenty of people with the same passions as you!"[48]

There are so many places where you can enhance your life. In "America's Healthiest Hometown," there are abundant health and wellness facilities that facilitate "nurturing the mind, body and spirit and taking steps to ensure a long, happy life." What makes "religious fulfillment in our hometown" possible are "churches and synagogues" that "await those residents who seek a friendly place to worship, . . . all accessible by golf cart." Then "at the heart of our community lie three old-fashioned town squares where you'll find plenty of modern day fun!" and "Where Good Friends Gather for a Great Time!" to enjoy "FREE nightly entertainment, modern movie theaters, and a colorful assortment of shopping and dining opportunities." And, of course, domestic bliss is possible in the home you will buy. They range from one-bedroom, one-bath residences in the low $200,000 range to a more palatial domicile costing as much $2.5 million. In addition to the cost of the home, there is a monthly fee, ranging from $881 upward, that in addition to covering utilities, taxes, and a "Development District Assessment," provides access to forty-two "executive Golf Clubs" and more than three thousand "activities and clubs."

Critical takes on The Villages that contrast what is on offer from corporate public relations emerge in the work of a few scholars. Hugh Bartling depicts residents as permanent tourists, writing that "unlike the theme park where visitors are implicitly asked to 'exit reality' to take part in a collective fantasy, the themed planned community is a heterotopia with a much more pronounced 'permanent' quality."[49] Pointing to signs on buildings that celebrate a historical site that never existed, Amanda M. Brian casts a well-trained skeptical eye on how "The Villages' faux history gives a patina of stability and continuity to a highly volatile region and stage of life."[50] Noting its "demographic singularity," the architect Deane Simpson raises ethical issues "over the 'benefits' of large mono-demographic enclaves such as local political evasion of tax burdens for public amenities including schools." In addition, he found that The Villages' "small-town metropolitanism" involved "a compact designed to send residents back to a constructed, idealised mental space of a less urban and more rural past—the space of their own youth where stimulation might be possible without alienation, and familiarity without boredom."[51] Others have explored the high rates of alcoholism and severe injuries from golf cart crashes.[52]

More numerous than scholarly articles critical of The Villages have been journalistic ones. Casting skeptical eyes on the authenticity of the built landscapes and relationships among residents, they are more likely to picture The Villages as "A Disney World for Adults" than as "Florida's Friendliest Hometown." They find problematic the lack of diversity along lines of age, social class, race, and ethnicity. They criticize the high cost of living there and the quality of health care available inside village walls. And they oppose how powerfully and extensively the private corporation that owns The Villages controls the flow of information, dictates design possibilities, and attempts to shape what people experience.[53] The frequent comparisons to the lands of Disney evoke how Jean Baudrillard emphasized the importance of the simulacra. In problematic but reassuring ways, The Villages and some other communities involve what he called "the generation by models of a real without origin or reality," although in this case, there is an evocation of a "hyperreal" reality nearby—Walt Disney World.[54]

Two journalists explored local politics in the context of the DeSantis/Trump years in probing and revelatory critiques. The first was "The Villages Vendetta: How a Grassroots Revolt in the Iconic Retirement Community Ended with a 72-Year-Old Political Prisoner," written by Ryan Grim and published online on February 5, 2023, in *The Intercept*. Grim told a story worthy of his last name. It began in 2019 when the people in charge of the Villages levied a 25 percent increase in local property taxes in order to finance not enhanced amenities for existing locations but purchase of new land "instead destined to subsidize further sprawl south of The Villages, ultimately benefitting the entity known locally either as 'the developer' or 'the family,'" increased taxes that would adversely impact so many of the residents who lived on fixed incomes. Three residents responded by running for positions on the county commission, two of them successfully, including Oren Miller. Those who controlled The Villages responded by marshaling political and economic power that drew on their long-standing connections with Governor Ron DeSantis. "The family," Grim noted, "owns the robust local newspaper, *The Villages Daily Sun*; owns the radio station, which pipes Fox News and right-leaning updates through speakers in common areas and at pools; owns the glossy magazine; and also owns local politics" and, one might add, politics beyond the local level. What ensued was a series of legal maneuvers that ended up with the imprisonment of Miller under conditions that significantly and maliciously threatened his health.[55]

In "The 'Disney' for Boomers Puts Hedonism on Full Display," published in *The New York Times* in early March 2022, Michelle Cottle, a writer and member of the Editorial Board of the paper, connected local, state, and national politics. When earlier visiting The Villages, Trump had, another *New York Times* reporter noted, "retweeted a video of one of his supporters yelling 'White power!'"[56] Almost two years later, Cottle went to The Villages, which had, she noted, become famous as a "MAGA stronghold." She weighed in on the issue of voter fraud, unable to convince local Republicans to take seriously the arrest of three of their peers for double voting, and observed that "the rise of Trumpism dialed up the tribalism," with politically driven vandalism in its wake. Much of what she wrote addressed political tensions that threatened the community's reputation for friendliness. She also offered a criticism that linked the generational dimensions of the intersection of politics and culture. She noted how shrewdly Trump had exploited "some people's nostalgia for a bygone era where the cultural hierarchy was clear and the world made sense." Many of the people in The Villages worked "overtime to maintain a replica of that fantasyland—a shiny, happy, small-town bubble where seniors can tune out the rest of the world and party like it's 1969," although I think an earlier date would be more appropriate given the explosive events in the late 1960s. She acknowledged that living there could make some progress in giving residents "a sense of belonging and purpose—of still being able to make a difference"— and tackle "head-on the scourges of isolation, despair and loneliness that are eating away at so many Americans as the nation's social fabric frays." Yet she zeroed in on how "this sense of belonging may flow as much from who is *not* a part of the Villages as who is." With its overwhelmingly white population, The Villages has "a time-warped quality," in which "the culture, like the overwhelmingly conservative politics, can feel like a scrupulously maintained bulwark against the onslaught of time and change." Living in a demographically homogeneous world, she insisted, "Villagers can maintain a distance from the demographic and cultural changes reshaping the nation and from many of its more intractable problems," such as inequalities of wealth and income, climate change, and racism. She might have also noted that folklore and rumor had together given The Villages the reputation as the "STD Capital of America." "The surreal effect of living in a bubble where everyone is encouraged to act as if on perpetual holiday," Cottle pointed out, was a focus of the 2020 documentary *Some Kind of Heaven*, for which the *New York Times* served as coproducer.[57]

That documentary, directed by Lance Oppenheim, explores and exposes the elusive and problematic dreams that many people in The Villages pursue. It begins with scenes that capture so many ways that residents engage in the pursuit of happiness. After an opening with lugubrious music, *Some Kind of Heaven* features drivers of golf carts riding in formation, seniors vigorously paddling a boat, women engaged in synchronized swimming, a resident who speaks of how he does not see slums, and someone who insists that the community comes close to being a self-contained heaven. "This is Nirvana," one resident observes, before another states, "The Villages is a place where you become younger." Five or so minutes in, alternative takes emerge as the film begins to focus on four central characters. Anne struggles with her husband Reggie's experimentation with drugs to protect himself against the inevitability of death. His habits endanger their marriage, as well as Anne's sense of well-being as she ponders what it means to remain committed in "sickness and in health, to love and to cherish, till death do us part." Recently widowed Barbara, her savings gone and "unfortunately" working full-time, hopes for a new life with a new mate. And eighty-one-year-old bachelor Dennis, illegally seeking his "last hurrah" while living in a van, tries to escape the authorities and find a wealthy woman who will be his sugar mommy. Their stories are interspersed with scenes of others chasing their dreams in a world filled with fake architectural fronts that serve as metaphors for a wider range of troubled pursuits of a better life though therapy, partying, playing, consumption, and religion. As the film nears its end, we learn that Reggie has avoided jail with the help of therapy as well as drug and alcohol counseling. Yet he is more confident than Anne of the future, especially what it means to face death. Dennis, choosing freedom over comfort, returns to life in his van when he leaves the home of Nancy, an old flame and not-very-wealthy woman. Barbara's hopes are dashed as a man she was flirting with, a golfcart salesman and Jimmy Buffett Parrothead, opts instead for what he must consider a more attractive woman. Barbara tells the story of how in her youth she complained to her mother, "God didn't answer my prayer." In response, her mother remarked, "God answers all our prayers. It's just rarely the answer we were looking for." Before the credits roll, we see Barbara dancing alone, surrounded by couples dancing together—all this against the background of unoccupied homes in The Villages, suggesting that new residents chase after false gods.[58]

More than almost all 55+ communities, many CCRCs attract the very affluent. Some of them grew out of much-earlier communities. For example, Villa Gardens in Pasadena, California originated in 1933 when a small group of retired teachers, supported by Ethel Percy Andrus, moved together into a house. Over time, their numbers and accommodations grew, but it was not until well into the postwar period that it became a full-blown CCRC, open to all who could afford to enter.[59] Nationally, the growth of CCRCs began in the 1970s. In the United States, there are now over nineteen hundred CCRCs in which well over nine hundred thousand seniors live. Many of them are nonprofits, many run by religious organizations. They range in size from those with fewer than a hundred units to some with well over a thousand; in between are those of the most common size, complexes with several hundred units. The long and powerful arm of the federal government is ever present—especially in financing real estate and through Medicare and Medicare providing for and controlling health care. States (to be sure, not uniformly) regulate what goes on in retirement communities, while private accrediting agencies monitor and certify them.

CCRCs vary considerably—in where they are located, how much they cost, how they are funded, and the levels of care and social amenities they provide. The most comprehensive offer three levels—independent living, assisted living, and memory care/skilled nursing care—with movement between them, or more problematically, discharge from the community, among the most vexing issues. Accommodations in independent living vary considerably, ranging from studios with fewer than four hundred square feet to large apartments or free-standing homes that can be two thousand square feet or more. Financing varies, depending on the market served, services provided, the nature of housing, and the luxuriousness of the facilities.[60] In some instances, seniors pay set monthly fees, which go as high as $20,000 (or more) for a couple. Then there are CCRCs where a couple pays a substantial nonrefundable deposit and then a monthly fee that can go as high as $10,000 or more. Or a couple can pay a monthly fee and also put down $2.5 million or more, with their estate getting 90 percent back and the facility having funds it can invest or rely on for cash flow or reserves. The extent and nature of health care provided also varies, with the most robust offerings including nurses and even MDs on-site. In some cases, a comprehensive fee covers virtually all medical and health care; others operate on a fee-for-service basis.

Facilities also vary considerably. The most comprehensive offer social and cultural opportunities that include movies, wellness opportunities such as exercise classes and meditation, seminars, lectures, and informative in-house publications. Physical amenities can also abound: multiple formal and informal dining rooms that at their best serve gourmet meals, with diners having plenty of choices; indoor and/or outdoor swimming pools; amply staffed and provisioned exercise palaces; banks; convenience stores; gardens to tend; and woodland paths to explore. Research reveals that occupants live longer, healthier, and happier, partly because CCRCs selectively admit upper-income, healthy, and educated people with greater longevity prospects and because CCRCs work to overcome the isolation that many elders experience, foster sociability and active lives, and make health care more readily available.[61]

Noteworthy are CCRCs based in or closely connected to college and university communities (aka UBRCs). Located on campuses such as Stanford, Penn State, the University of Florida, UC-Davis, and Furman, they now number fifty or more.[62] Seniors can experience the pleasures of intergenerational connections, participate in university life by taking classes, sing in a campus chorus, or work in a lab. Helen and I have visited and been impressed by Lasell Village, located on the campus of Lasell College in Newton, Massachusetts. Committed to a belief "that learning is not an activity—it is a way of being," it requires residents to participate in 450 hours annually of "enrichment activities" that include attending performances and lectures, volunteering, reading on one's own, and taking classes. In the summer of 2023, there were many, offered by both residents and Lasell College faculty, ranging from "LGBTQ+ Identities and Experiences" and "Bad Supreme Court Decisions and What We Can Learn from Them" to "Art of the Renaissance" and "Write for Your Life!"[63]

Eager to understand how operators of CCRCs and other retirement communities understand what they do, I discovered a book that many mangers rely on, Benjamin W. Pearce's *Senior Living Communities: Operations Management and Marketing for Assisted Living, Congregate, and Continuing Care Retirement Communities* (1998). Much of what he wrote focuses on topics common to any industry, such as developing and marketing a project, hiring and managing staff, and sustaining financial health. However, it was the distinctive aspects that captured my attention. "It can be a very difficult time for people who may have been living independently to take this first step forward declaring their own 'dependency,'" he insists, before he goes on to note that "the transition into a community lifestyle can be traumatic," with seniors dealing "with this trauma in a variety of ways." Pearce underscores the importance of this dynamic, hyping as he and others do how retirement communities celebrate successful aging by doing their best to hide evidence of dependence as well as aging and instead celebrate the wonders of the independent individual engaged in productive activities. "For many seniors," he insists, "seeking information about an 'independent' retirement community is in fact the first step toward declaring their own *dependence*." Here he was reflecting a common tendency that the gerontological sociologist Joyce Weil highlights: the paradoxical and simultaneous presence of opposite responses to a sense of place, in this instance, dependence and independence.[64] Without acknowledging his indebtedness to how Elizabeth Kübler-Ross in 1969 described five stages of grief, Pearce writes that "normally they begin the process in denial, then exhibit anger and hostility, then followed by bargaining and ultimately acceptance," although he neglects to mention depression between bargaining and acceptance. "It is much like a bereavement process," and "for many, this loss can touch their very identity, an identity that may have been developing for the past 75 years."[65]

Pearce emphasizes how staff members need to be aware of how emotionally fraught the decision of seniors is to move out of their homes and into a retirement community. Because they tend to deny what they faced, he tells those in charge of marketing to be patient, because "the decision to move into a senior-living community can be a long process." Hiring caring and compassionate staff could "help seniors accept their own aging and cope with everyday difficulties" and, at best, foster a reversal of "the depression and exert a genuinely recuperative effect." Robust programming also bolsters people emotionally. Because residents sense how restricted their lives are becoming, "a community's enrichment and activity program . . . must be designed to redirect their focus away from their limitations and toward productive educational and social" activities, "with a positive emphasis that will enhance the quality of life."[66] As Weil notes and as is applicable to life in CCRCs and other institutions, Pearce's observations reveal how olders simultaneously experience different senses of time in one place.[67]

To be sure, Pearce acknowledges, there are some rare occasions when employees and even other residents will encounter people having an urgently difficult time adjusting to a new situation—"'chronic complainers' or 'difficult residents.'" These are not "bad" people, and it is only their behavior that is so problematic. Perhaps some are "experiencing difficulty adjusting to the community, a difficulty that may be complicated by feelings of rejection or guilt" that derive from not being able to leave anything for their children because of the lavish lives they are leading in retirement. In other cases, troubled residents might "seek 'special' treatment or try to differentiate their situations from those of other residents. Any success in convincing management to 'bend' their rules for personal needs can be considered a triumph to be flaunted before other residents." They might be among those who "have a psychological need to get attention by disruptive and negative means. . . . It is almost as if they live in a constant storm, moving around in a vortex of anxiety from one place to the next. . . . If this behavior continues, residents and staff alike will begin to exhibit creative avoidance" or in other ways isolate "disruptive behavior problems." More generally, "the *feel, felt, found* technique acknowledges residents' feelings, substantiates the importance of their concerns, and offers solutions based on experience."[68]

There are several topics Pearce does not cover that reveal the realities that marketing hides. One is aggression and arguments between residents, something a June 2024 *New York Times* story noted under the headline "Conflict Is Common in Elder-Care Settings."[69] Another is the existence of sexually transmitted infections among residents. As a reporter noted in 2020, "It would seem retirement homes might not be such dull places after all."[70] Also of note are the implications of how investors finance retirement communities, including CCRCs. Not surprisingly, investment opportunities abound, and for profit-seeking enterprises, this includes crowdfunding, private equity, and large public corporations. Among the largest is Brookdale Senior Living. Listed on the New York Stock Exchange, it has a market capitalization around $1.1 billion, with the private equity firm Fortress Investment Group owning 51 percent. Its properties house in excess of sixty thousand seniors in more than one thousand locations, CCRCs prominently among them and located in almost every state. Its website carefully walks a prospective resident through making a decision to go forward. Talk to your kids and consider the lifestyle you want, it advises. Accentuating independence rather than dependence, it speculates, "Maybe you've always known you want to spend your retirement years improving your golf swing or working on the next great American novel." Our communities, it continues, offer "engaging activities," and "whether you want to jumpstart your day with a workout or have a loved one who could benefit from brain-stimulating games or a round of dominos, there's something for everyone to enjoy." Activities like dining with newfound friends or engaging in activities provide the "social connections" that studies show help so many seniors overcome "feelings of depression due to social isolation."[71]

Although Pearce does not discuss how to raise money for CCRCs, he offers advice on how CCRCs should describe themselves to potential residents. Remember, he cautions, you are "selling a lifestyle, not real estate." And given that CCRC shoppers "see themselves as at least 10 years younger than their true chronological age," it is essential to picture them not as doddering and feeble, people who rely on canes and walkers, but as "active, interested, and involved," because "they are in fact looking for empowerment so that they can live fuller lives and stay in control longer." They will reject "media attempts at communicating a catered lifestyle" because "the very idea of being catered to implies a loss of control." Consequently, promotional material needs "to show things that attract seniors' attention with pictures of people that tell a story, 'real' people who are active and involved, people whom they might like to meet." Yet, though they might understandably like to meet people like themselves, it is nonetheless important to offer some evidence of diversity among residents. "Understand the relevant regulatory requirements such as Equal Housing Opportunity (EHO) specifications," Pearce cautions, "and incorporate the appropriate minority mix into the models or resident subjects. There is not," he adds, "a discernable negative effect on the responses from ads that properly comply."[72]

What Pearce notes might remind us of what Erving Goffman explores in *Asylums: Essays on the Social Situation of Mental Patients and Other Inmates* (1961) or of Frederick Wiseman in films such as *High School* (1968). Notably, Goffman wrote of sleights of hand in representing what would happen and how to train staff to manage the behavior and emotions of seniors. Okay, nursing homes may not come close to resembling mental hospitals and prisons, which he described as "total institutions," or what James Chappel calls "the dark underbelly of sunnier developments that emerged for older Americans in the 1960s and 1970s." But other communities for seniors deploy a range in the degree to which rules and personnel regulate the lives of inhabitants. They go from arrangements where people age in place to an urban Village on Boston's Beacon Hill to NORCs and NORC-SSPs to self-enclosed 55+ communities and then CCRCs. To varying degrees, institutional life for seniors involves staff members trained to manage people in custody by deploying rules and regulations and what institutionalization foster in residents who are hardly inmates.[73]

There is an extensive body of scholarship that fosters what enhances the quality of lives (QOL) in retirement communities, CCRCs especially. Among the most recent, and one that provides access to other studies, is a case study of a CCRC in the northeastern US, written by two University of Vermont psychologists, Jacqueline S. Weinstock and Lynne A. Bond. They conducted a rigorous study, relying on surveys of residents and administrators in a community that housed residents who were affluent, in relatively good health, and almost all white. They conclude that there was widespread agreement that a "sense of community; resident-driven active engagement; and individual autonomy, independence, and respect" were critical factors that enhanced the QOL. To begin with, people responded by using words and phrases such as "feeling connected," "belonging," "sharing experience," and "knowing you're there for each other" to describe what a sense of community involved. Words such as "active, vibrant, engaged, curious, and involved" suggested the goals CCRCs aspire to achieve. And a "strong sense of dignity, privacy, and worth of each individual, calling for 'mutual respect' at the heart of the community," highlight the core values that needed to be stressed. Weinstock and Bond then identify six strategies that those whom they interviewed emphasized as critical to achieving these goals. They are the importance of "clearly stated organizational values," significant reliance on participation and advice of residents, the importance of "ongoing, mutually respectful interaction and consultation among and between residents and administration," regular meetings open to all member of the community, physical arrangement and activities that promote "interpersonal interaction," and attention to factors that promote a range of interactions. Weinstock and Bond acknowledge that although most seniors prefer aging in place, studying how to enhance the quality of life in retirement communities is important because there exist relatively few communities that make that possible, "and pervasive ageist beliefs and policies make this practice even more challenging."[74]

I thought about the advice Pearce offered and the work of Weinstock and Bond when I looked at the brochures provided by eight CCRCs—in Pasadena, the Boston area, and Charlottesville—that Helen and I have looked into. The key words, ones repeated again and again, are "independent," "engagement," "purpose," "community," "friendship," "active," "home," "wellness," "choice," "freedom," "comfort," "caring," and in some instances, even "luxuriousness." The infirmities and dependencies of old age seem buried, hinted at principally in references to the availability of conveniently located and multiple levels of care. The lineup of walkers that often appear at the entrances to dining rooms makes no appearances in the brochures. Rather, personal testimonials, accompanied by smiling faces of active and engaged people more likely in their sixties and seventies than eighties or nineties praise their newfound world for its vibrant and caring qualities.[75]

Some pitches capture the promise of lives well and fully lived. "We like to change the perception of not only what it means to grow old," insists the people involved in Lasell Village, "but what it meant to be young." The nearby Newbury Court strikes a similar note when it evokes "an active, independent lifestyle that's culturally rich, socially connected and full of enriching ways to grow, explore and have more genuine fun" in "An Extraordinary Place Where Living Comes to Life." Waterstone, also in the region, seems to violate Pearce's recommendation to avoid mentioning being catered to, a phrase it buries in copy promising "you every opportunity to continue living the life you love. Spend your days enjoying locally sourced chef-prepared meals, cultural and educational programming, fitness classes and more. Then, spend your nights in an open, stylized apartment. It's life, catered to you, right here, in your home."[76]

Locations distant from eastern Massachusetts strike similar notes. Villa Gardens in Pasadena, we learn, offers "the right combination of sophistication and small-town warmth" in "the community you'd create for yourself," one complete with "the personal comfort of home," the "friendship of neighbors," and "the inspiration of vibrant culture close at hand. And the ability to enjoy it all with ease." Helen and I also looked at places in Virginia, not far from where our daughter lives. One possibility was Westminster Canterbury of the Blue Ridge, its residences combining the new with "Jeffersonian character and appeal." With the Christian cross in between its two names, it reminds you of its connections to the Episcopal and Presbyterian Churches, offering "a sense of place that redefines your sense of home," "opens the door to retirement living as it should be—active, exhilarating, enriching, self-directed," and provides "a culture designed to nourish the mind, body and spirit." Nearby is Charlottesville's The Colonnades, "sponsored by foundations of the University of Virginia" and one of more than 270 facilities owned by Sunrise Senior Living. "We believe each day presents something new to explore," its brochure announces confidently, and "that is why we empower residents to engage with the community and build meaningful connections through a variety of activities designed to appeal to your curiosity, intellect, and spirit."

Despite how Pearce recommends that promotional material for CCRCs remind readers that all are welcome, materials I have looked at vary considerably in their sensitivity to inclusiveness. If most of them pay only the visual equivalent of lip service to diversity, there are some notable exceptions. Of the dozen or so residents pictured in The Colonnades' brochure, an African American man (presumably a resident) appears four times—playing golf, listening to music on his smartphone, walking with a woman who may be his African American wife, and raising his coffee cup at the dinner table. Newbury Court features Margie Yamamoto, pictured with her husband, Mark Hopkins, as someone who "spent her first two years, along with her family, incarcerated in an American detention center because they were of Japanese descent." Only Westminster Canterbury addresses the issue of inclusivity directly. "You're part of a diverse community of fascinating individuals," its brochure remarks as it backs up this commitment by including pictures of an African American couple and an Asian American woman. Of course, none of these CCRCs seems to recognize other dimensions of diversity, especially those involving socioeconomic class or gender identity.

In January 2024, with friends, Helen and I attended an information session at a Pasadena CCRC. Daring to pose the diversity question to our African American host, I found that approximately 5 percent of residents are African or Asian American. I neglected to include Latinos in my query, but I am reasonably sure that the percentage would not be much higher. This in a city where, of the residents in 2020, 7.78 percent were African American, 17.41 Asian American, 32.98 Latino, and 4.32 multiracial.

So I wondered whether there are retirement communities in the United States, especially CCRCs, that market themselves to people who might not feel welcome elsewhere. I turned to Google for help. Immediately, up came the website of "Aegis Gardens: Our Asian-Inspired Communities." Of the corporation's thirty-five communities, two—one in the Bay Area and the other east of Seattle—are "Asian inspired, culturally-authentic" CCRCs. They both feature "carefully curated décor, integrated feng shui principles, authentic Asian cuisine, and engaging traditional activities," with a "multilingual team members" making sure "that residents receive the care and respect they deserve." Rest assured, however, that they also welcome "all seniors who enjoy a home with international flair and global appeal."[77]

Looking for arrangements that serve Latino seniors, I happened on a program in Los Angeles that provides community health workers known as *promatoras* to those who remain in their homes, as well as run classes and make calls to help seniors manage the challenges they face.[78] I found some information on more institutional arrangements. Although I could not easily identify Latino-oriented CCRCs, I did find a website that talked more generally but principally about assisted living arrangements and the special challenges community members faced. For "Hispanic and Latinx adults living in the United States," it read, the challenges aging adults face, such as "finding the right health care, maintaining one's mobility, or choosing a senior living community, . . . may be exacerbated." Too many Latino seniors lack sufficient access to paid sick leave and adequate insurance and disproportionately end "in nursing homes that have inadequate care due to racial and ethnic differences." Alternatively, "some communities offer services and amenities that can make Hispanic and Latinx seniors feel at home."[79]

For gay, lesbians, and perhaps transgender seniors, the options seem much more abundant. The website I relied on noted that "regardless of sexual orientation, gender identity, and race, we all deserve to be our authentic selves!" and that "LGBTQ retirees are entitled to live comfortably without unjust discrimination." Acknowledging that there are many more, the site featured ten, each with different amenities and levels of care. Except for several in Florida, none was in the South. One welcomed only lesbians, while others were more inclusive, with one appealing to straight allies as well. Most of them were quite small, with one containing only twenty-one units. Some were designed for those with low incomes, but Fountain Grove Lodge in Santa Rosa, California, touted itself as offering "five-star living at its finest, . . . an excellent choice for LGBTQ retirees looking for a well-appointed and luxurious retirement community." Birds of a Feather, Stonewall, Rainbow Vista, Triangle Square, and perhaps A Place for Us use clever names to suggest who is welcomed.[80] Interestingly, when I Googled "African American retirement communities," most of the responses focused on cities. For example, in a May 2023 article in *Essence*, Jasmine Browley cautions readers against considering Florida because of "its recent gubernatorial politics," which "have polarized potential retirees of color." Instead, she focuses on "urban options available for Black people looking to reap the fruit of their labor." This and similar sites might focus on cities with substantial Black populations but are also likely to highlight affordability, quality of health care, and activities designed for seniors.[81]

That I know of, there is one memoir whose author explores life inside a for-profit retirement community, the retired high school teacher Sue Matthews Petrovski's 2018 *Shelved: A Memoir of Aging in America*. When mental and physical conditions afflicted her eighty-two-year-old husband, they moved into a corporation-owned independent living facility with almost two hundred residents that she called Planet X, "because it is so far out of the reality of what life was like when we were younger." "Old age," she laments, "is a sad and dreary time to endure and not enjoy," when "much of Western society sees old people needing to be shelved, a tagline that chronicles our culture's way of registering us as useless, expensive, and a difficult obligation." She immediately felt that she was "in a far-off world," with the shelf she inhabited "deep and distant": "a thousand mental miles from the active, doing world I had inhabited" before her husband's illness threw them into oblivion. "Instead of being a vigorous part of the adult world, we had suddenly entered a new, captive, unknown space."[82]

On Planet X, she observed cliques and listened to "chitter and chatter and a lot of superficial discussion and 'remember when' talk." Residents joked "about wobbly necklines and floppy arms, but death," she observed, "is seldom discussed," especially by corporate management. Indeed, the major and most interesting theme in her memoir is how those who owned and governed Planet X brooked no sensitivity to or input from aging residents. Lower-level staff, she notes, "are friendly and seem to accept us as human, and the upper management is pleasant and capable," but "the final corporate voice often speaks to those who carry out their desires in a manner that does *to* the elder resident instead of working *with* them," causing her to "question whether they see us as being capable of making decisions about our daily lives." Rules were often changed without taking into account the wisdom of residents, with management acting arbitrarily "rather than giving much attention to the needs and suggestions of those who live here." The result was that, absent challenges, an occupant was made "to feel like an old geezer" instead of as someone "passionately motivated to fill this period . . . with a wealth of living that has value and worth." Institutional arrangements in housing for seniors thus contribute to "the feeling of ineffectual aloneness, helplessness." The fact that the people in charge focus on what stockholders demand means that "the color of old people is green," because "professional care of the elderly is an industry, and make no mistake," she insists, "it acts as an industry."[83]

Pearce's *Senior Living Communities*, the study by Weinstock and Bond of one CCRC, the pamphlets describing others, and Petrovski's memoir offer very different and often contrasting pictures of CCRCs. At one end is the promotional exuberance of community brochures. At the other is the contrast between Petrovski's exposure of the tensions between residents and often-absentee management representatives and Pearce's combination of management expertise and acknowledgment of dependence and five stages of grief. In between are the aspirational and reassuring results of what Weinstock and Bond revealed from a sample of one, albeit probably a representative one. My suspicion is that the truth lies closer to what Pearce and Weinstock and Bond emphasize than what Petrovski and the fancy brochures reveal.

Nursing homes, NORCs and NORC-SSPs, an urban Village on Boston's Beacon Hill, the massive suburban The Villages in Central Florida, 55+ communities including those that house seniors in manufactured homes, and CCRCs—despite all these choices in the United States, today most elderly Americans live in their own residences, whether rented or owned, alone or with a partner or with family members of a different generation. Notable is the burden placed on family members, usually women, who live with and care for older family members in their eighties and older. As of 2021, the vast majority of seniors live in their own residences by themselves or with a spouse, including 9 percent living in the residence of another person, most commonly an adult child. These figures include those who own or rent a private residence or live in various kinds of retirement communities. More and more, they also live in NORCs, 55+ communities, and CCRCs. Only 2.5 percent live in group homes, nursing homes, residential treatment centers, skilled nursing facilities, or military or correctional facilities.[84]

Public policy, capital allocation, gender, ethnicity, race, location, and class shape the choices seniors face. Women significantly exceed the number of elderly men who live by themselves. Greater numbers of people of color, especially Latinos and Asian, live in multigenerational situations. Rental rates are especially high for senior African Americans and Latinos. And more generally, growing inequalities of wealth and income shape the choices available to members of these communities. The fact that so many have their incomes dramatically lower than those of their white peers (approximately 20 percent less), as a 2023 report of Harvard's Joint Center for Housing Studies stated, "fuel[s] disparities in financial security in older age." Living under even more precarious conditions is the relatively small but increasing number of unhoused seniors—some of them unsheltered and some sixty thousand sheltered.[85] Then there are about 186,000 Americans over fifty-five who live in prisons. These are small number—after all, 126 million Americans are fifty-five or older.

As Chappel makes clear, attention to arrangements for the relatively privileged, such as NORCs, 55+ communities, and CCRCs, though they house relatively small percentages of elders, "are worth remembering, if only to demonstrate that alternatives to our current system, or nonsystem, did exist."[86] Yet focus on retirement communities for the relatively affluent can all too easily hide how the other half or more lives—not only those who are incarcerated and unhoused but also those who are in crowded multigenerational homes, substandard residences, and nursing homes. And it can especially hide the importance of eldercare by heroic women, family members, and hired help.[87] The attention that policy makers, investors, journalists, and public relations experts lavish on places like The Villages in Florida or Dell Webb developments in Sun Belt locations minimizes how less privileged older people age and instead celebrates healthy, socially active, and engaged elders. Social isolation, cognitive loss, physical frailty, and loneliness afflict millions of elders who cannot benefit from the opportunities for sustained social engagement and individual growth afforded the more fortunate among us, me included.

From Long Books to Brief TikToks

So Many Old and New Media, So Many Aging People

Information on retirement and longevity floods the US marketplace, reaching expansive audiences eager for guidance and reassurance. It arrives before us in many media, from post-Gutenberg printed books hundreds of pages long to TikTok, launched internationally in September 2017 with videos that often last only seconds. The nature of specific genres shapes much of what tracking these depictions in multimedia reveals.[1] Many of these sources provide windows into issues that how-to books and celebrations of longevity minimize or avoid. They focus more amply and interestingly on dying and death. Some of them emphasize the dynamics of intergenerational support and exchanges. Others range more broadly within American culture and cross-culturally than do so many other sources. Storytelling and excursions into new media reveal what audiences even larger than readers of best-selling books learn about.

We can begin with whole books, focusing initially on *From Strength to Strength: Finding Success, Happiness, and Deep Purpose in the Second Half of Life* (2022). For ten years beginning in 2009, the author, Arthur C. Brooks, had served as president of the conservative American Enterprise Institute. In the book, he focuses on what he calls the "striver's curse," the difficulty people who are successful in the first half of their lives have in shifting to a new set of strengths in the second half. He insists that almost all highly skilled professionals face declines in their levels of achievement at some point between their late thirties and early fifties, at which point they need "ever-greater success to avoid dissatisfaction," precisely when their "abilities to stay even are declining." To deal successfully with this issue, high achievers need to shift from what he calls "fluid intelligence"—the ability to wrestle successfully with complex information by deploying reason—to "crystallized intelligence" by building on skills and knowledge acquired over a lifetime. One exception he notes is professional historians. In a career requiring "high stacks of knowledge and the wisdom to synthesize it," he writes in ways I am not sure applies to me, being a historian involves "almost pure crystallized intelligence." It is best to "take care of your health," he advises, "so you can write your best books into your eighties." For a striver to make the shifts necessary to live well in life's second half, he advises giving up the "addiction to work and success," ending the "attachment to worldly rewards," and abandoning the "fear of decline." He advises folks "to make the second curve better than the first" by developing relationships and starting a "spiritual journey," which seems irrelevant in my case.[2] Finally, like so much advice to retirees, he focuses on what an individual could do for themselves and not on our responsibility to build a more just society for others.

Nor does what Brooks writes apply to Nell Painter, whose *Old in Art School: A Memoir of Starting Over* (2018) is a compelling book about what it means to successfully execute a major shift in interest and careers. Born in Houston in 1942, she moved to Oakland, California, at ten weeks old with her parents as part of the Great Migration of African Americans to urban areas outside the South. She went on to a distinguished career as a historian—author of seven important books on race, gender, and region in the US and president of both the Southern Historical Association and the Organization of American Historians. With her PhD from Harvard in hand, she taught at the University of Pennsylvania and the University of North Carolina at Chapel Hill before joining the Princeton University faculty in 1988 and then retiring from there in 2005 as Edwards Professor of American History. Determined to pursue a career in the field that her surname references, she earned her bachelor of fine arts from the Mason Gross School of the Arts at Rutgers in 2009 and then a master of fine arts two years later from the Rhode Island School of Design (RISD).[3]

When starting over, Painter was drawing on tryouts as an artist earlier in her life, especially when she was in Ghana in 1964–65 and continuing when she was a historian at Princeton. Henry, one of her teachers at RISD, told her, "You'll never be an artist," the title of the book's first chapter. He said she "lacked an essential component, some ineffable quality necessary to truly be An Artist," and another professor insisted she was "not being 'hungry' enough to be An Artist," judgments they hurled at her right when she learned that her book *The History of White People* received praise on the front page of *The New York Times Book Review*. She continued to encounter skepticism about her endeavor because of her age. The people around her viewed her "as an exotic in art school, an exotic on account of age, the exotic old person." She stuck "out more on account of age than race," she notes; her "defining characteristic" was "not all the things [she] had done to become a historian—a goddam distinguished historian"—but "as an *old woman*," rather than what had been true earlier, "as a black person and as a woman." Yet, as her experiences in art schools reminded her, "much of the prejudice against black and women artists such as I was on my way to becoming was merely because they—we—were and are black artists in a racist culture and female artists in a sexist world."[4]

And An Artist she did become, someone who was steeped in the history of art, which she playfully explored, and who drew and painted with verve and imagination.[5] Nonetheless what she experienced and exemplified provided powerful lessons—not only what she accomplished when she started over (her art is admittedly harder for me to judge than her historical writing) but also the lessons she drew for the rest of us. Not surprisingly, despite her good health, being older impinged on her consciousness. And it did so both because of "other people's automatic assumption" that her work, "because made by an old woman, isn't interesting, even before being seen," and because "more than ever" she was "obsessed by age and the desire to un-age." "There's a wonderful freedom," she writes, "in not having to prove anything," albeit that she proved so much. She also poignantly explored the complicated relationships between being an accomplished and famous historian and becoming an artist. She realized she fit uneasily into the category of "an 'emerging artist,'" who "had moved into the twenty-first century," but she "still couldn't make *right nowness*'s grade." After all, she inhabited "a body old enough for an emerging artist's mother or grandmother": "I still had to push down that feeling of being superannuated, of suspecting people wanted me to go away, to disappear along with my disproportioned combination of new and old."[6]

Reinventing oneself is the first major issue that compelled my attention as I read books. Growing old at death's door is the second, with writings by May Sarton and Nora Ephron serving as bookends. They were both multitalented: Sarton as an author of poetry, novels, nonfiction, children's books, and journals; Ephron as a director, screenwriter, novelist, and essayist.

May Sarton was certainly busy getting, as Ephron remarked about herself, "the most out of life," as evidenced in *At Eighty-Two: A Journal*, covering the period from July 25, 1993, until August 1, 1994, which she dictated and edited. She died July 16, 1995, and the book appeared in 1996. "KAIROS. A unique time in a person's life; an opportunity for change" is the book's epigraph, albeit that death may not have been the kind of change she had in mind.[7] Her life at eighty-two was filled with pleasures and challenges. She lived alone in a house in York, Maine, albeit with helpers and guests buoying her spirits but also disrupting her routine or sapping her energy. She loved looking out from Oak Knoll, the residence where she lived for the last twenty-two years of her life and whose pleasures she had extolled in her 1977 memoir *The House by the Sea*. She relished the company of her cat, Pierrot. She enjoyed (but could also be exhausted by) a constant stream of letters from friends she knew well and from admirers with whom she connected only when she opened the envelopes containing their letters. She greatly enjoyed news of how well her books were selling or being reviewed. The arrival of a team of people from National Public Radio's *All Things Considered* to prepare for an airing gave her great pleasure. She loved the beautiful winter-landscape day, looking out at the ocean, and the arrival of spring. Yet on many days, she worried that contemporary critics were no longer paying attention to what she wrote. She struggled to reduce that pile of things to do on her desk as a result of her professional success, to get handymen to fix the furnace or clear the basement of flooded water, to straighten out her finances, to walk up and down stairs, and to find a doctor who could accurately diagnosis what ailed her.

And indeed Sarton's many and persistent health issues prompted her to contemplate the meanings of aging and death. The beginning of the very first entry set the stage for what followed. "I am more and more aware of how important the framework is, what holds life together in a workable whole as one enters real old age, as I am doing," she noted. "A body without bones would be a limp impossible mess, so a day without a steady routine would be disruptive and chaotic." Yet the ravages of old age often imperiled "a steady routine," something she highlighted when she recalled a poem by Wordsworth that contrasts how "We Poets in our youth begin in gladness," and "in the end despondency and madness" take over. Again and again, she confronted how depressed she was—sometimes because of what she called "the chaos of my life and all that is asked of me beyond my strength."[8]

Like many people in their eighties, memory loss could plague Sarton as she entered what she called "real old age." She had begun "forgetting where things are, forgetting names even of friends": "Forgetting so much makes me feel disoriented sometimes and slows me up." She struggled with the tension between dependence and independence that aging and ailments brought. Reading Betty Friedan's *The Fountain of Age* prompted her to think about that tension in relation to the world beyond York, Maine. "We still turn to the old because they have something to give us," Sarton noted, "and what is so terrible about the current state of affairs in America is that the old are relegated to a place where they are simply a burden." She went on to say that the young complain that they "have to pay for the old," even though "the old paid for the young years ago. If we were willing to admit that old people have a lot to offer, then they would not be such a burden."[9] In mid-November 1993, journal entries about medical problems emerge significantly.

Feeling pain that she worried may have signaled the return of cancer that had earlier caused a mastectomy prompted an extended series of diagnostic challenges for doctors and contemplation of death for Sarton. "When you are eighty-one and as ill as I feel," she wrote, "and have felt for the last four years, death is a friend." She shifted to how eager she was to write about her beloved cat: "without him, who knows?" In late February 1994, recalling a stroke she had recently had, she acknowledged that she had "entered a new phase" and was "approaching [her] death." "If I can accept this," she continued, "not as a struggle to keep going at my former pace but as a time of meditation when I need to ask nothing of myself," focusing on "nothing except to live as well as possible as aware as possible, then I could feel I am preparing for a last great adventure as happily as I can."[10]

Depression and frustrations continued, in part because doctors could not diagnose what ailed her and prescriptions for Prozac did not work. Despair was interspersed with hopes that she would soon feel well, so she could "start to live again." In the book's final entry, dated August 1,

1994, just short of a year before her life ended, she felt reassured by her doctor that she did not have cancer, even though she experienced pain from inflamed muscles and bones. "I am aware that very few solitary women of eighty-two who live alone are as lucky as I am," she observed, "surrounded by lovingkindness. How did it ever happen to this old racoon!" she concluded in the next-to-the-last paragraph. Then came these final optimistic, forward-looking words: "And now, the combination of slightly cooler weather and my being slightly better should be rousing. With that hope I close this eighty-second year." Death no longer seemed on the horizon.[11]

In the opening essay of Ephron's 2010 *I Remember Nothing*, she recounted her long-standing forgetfulness. But now at sixty-nine, she wrote, "I forget in a new way." If earlier she believed she "could eventually retrieve whatever was lost," that was something she could no longer do, for "whatever's gone is hopelessly gone." This made her "feel sad, and wistful," she continued, "but mostly it makes me feel old." She noted that she had "many symptoms of old age, aside from the physical," an issue we will get to later.[12]

Ephron ended her collection with an essay titled "The O Word," standing for "old." "I'm not really old, of course," she insisted. "Really old is eighty," even though the young surely saw her as old. She then referenced some symptoms of aging: losing height and gaining weight; "your hot flashes come to an end; things droop"; and taking "so many pills in the morning that you don't have room for breakfast." Then "there is a new conversation, about CAT scans and MRIs. Everywhere you look there's cancer." With friends dying, "you are suddenly in a lottery, the ultimate game of chance, and someday your luck will run out." She would lose the ability to speak, listen, eat whatever she wanted, or easily take a walk. Returning to the subject of her opening essay, she remarked, "My memory, which I can still make jokes about, will be so dim that I will have to pretend that I know what's going on." Moreover, that she may "have only a few good years remaining" had hit her "with real force." As a result, she reminisced about her life's pleasures, such as enjoying "a frozen custard at Shake Shack and a walk in the park. (Followed by a Lactaid)" or going to Los Angeles and watching hummingbirds, which she loved to do because, as she said in the book's final sentence, "they're so busy getting the most out of life."[13]

Janet Maslin characterized Ephron's book as "fluffy and companionable, a nifty airport read from a writer capable of much, much more."[14] Yet scattered in Ephron's essays were hints of what she was really facing at the time, not relatively minor symptoms of aging but death—hinted at when she wrote, "aside from the physical"; referred to the omnipresence of cancer that involved body scans and being in a lottery; and mentioned that the realization that she might "have only a few good years remaining" hit her "with real force." Ephron's book was published on the first day of 2010, and she died almost two and a half years later, on June 26, 2012. As far back as 2006, she learned that she had myelodysplasia, and her demise came from complications that resulted from that type of cancer.

In March 2013, Jacob Bernstein, the son of Nora Ephron and Carl Bernstein (whose Watergate reporting had focused on things more serious than the end of hot flashes), wrote of "Nora Ephron's final act." Understandably, as I know from my days at Smith College, when my dear friend Ron MacDonald knew his end was quickly coming, many people do not want the end of their lives to be the all-consuming topic of conversations with all but a few friends and family members. "The thing is," Bernstein wrote in an essay that detailed his mother's final days, "you can't really turn a fatal illness into a joke. It is almost the only disclosure that turns you into the victim rather than the hero of your story. For her, tragedy was a pit of clichés. So she stayed quiet."[15] The "fluffy and companionable" descriptions of aging that Nora Ephron wrote in her essays stand in remarkable contrast to her son's description of the agony that his mother and her friends and family experienced in her final weeks.

When I read what Jacob Bernstein wrote of his mother's last days, I thought back to 2014, when I read the recently published *Being Mortal: Medicine and What Matters in the End* by the *New Yorker* writer and surgeon Atul Gawande. My takeaway then, now confirmed and enhanced with a second reading, was that when a medical team suggests aggressive treatments for a patient nearing the end of life, the question to ask is, "And what will my life be in that added six or so months?" Now I understood the profundity that lay behind my simple takeaway. Hyped-up modern medical interventions, Gawande writes, are antithetical to the realization that death, rather than being a "failure," is "normal, . . . the natural order of things," since "we are all aging from the day when we are born." All too often, he continues, modern medicine "fails the people it is supposed to help," because in the "waning days of our lives," too many of us give our lives "over to treatments that addle our brains and sap our bodies for a sliver's chance of benefit." Building on stories of the final days of people's lives, including those of his own physician father, and underscoring the consequences of the transition of the aging spending their final days not in multigenerational households but in antiseptic institutions, he instead calls on caregivers and family members to "make life worth living when we're weak and frail and can't fend for ourselves anymore." As we age, we should see ourselves "as part of something greater: a family, a community, a society," "seek comfort in simple pleasures," and "become concerned for our legacy." Near the book's end, having stood by his father's side as he breathed his last breaths, he embraces how important it is to understand "damage we in medicine" do when pushing against "the constraints of biology." Rather than focusing on ensuring "health and survival," doctors and people like the family members who stood at Nora Ephron's bedside should have focused on enabling well-being by focusing on hopes and fears as they balanced the power and limitations of medical interventions. Honest but difficult conversations would make it possible to embrace personal engagement, dignity, and compassion in death as in life.[16]

In *Being Mortal*'s final pages, Gawande tells the story of traveling with his family to India, where, carrying his father's ashes, they embarked on a boat on the Ganges. He helped perform the rituals that would enable his father "to achieve *moksha*," a Hindu tradition that makes possible "liberation from the endless earthly cycle of death and rebirth to ascend to nirvana."[17] Jacob Bernstein tells a different and more American story of his mother's final moments. She understood that "the odds of the chemo working were below 50 percent, and even if it did, it would probably not buy her more than a year and a half or so." Although she confessed that she wanted to live to be a hundred, "she wasn't sure the chemo was worth doing for such a limited upside." Her son told her that he "hoped she would reconsider, that a year and a half is a lot of time during which something else may emerge as a viable treatment": "Still, I said I would respect whatever she wished to do, that it was her body, her life, her choice. I think this is what she needed to hear, that we wanted her to live more than anything but that she was still in control. Because within minutes, she seemed resigned to the idea that she was going to be nuked, as she put it." The end came on June 26, 2012, about five weeks after she entered the hospital. *Being Mortal* was published on October 7, 2014.[18] I wonder if all involved had read Gawande's book, whether the end of Ephron's life would have more closely resembled that of Gawande's father, perhaps with Jewish traditions substituting for Hindu ones. It is too much to expect that the secular and humor-embracing Ephron would on her deathbed have engaged in the *viddui* or confession of sin. Instead, she requested that her son bring her a pineapple milkshake. But the time between death and burial would have been shorter, and sitting shiva might well have followed.

Aside from books by Brooks, Painter, Sarton, Ephron, and Gawande there are scores and scores of others on aging and its end point. With *Growing Old: Notes on Aging with Something like Grace* (2020), at age eighty-seven, Elizabeth Marshall Thomas, an anthropologist who wrote the best-selling book *The Hidden Life of Dogs* (1993), gently but probingly explored a number of issues. Like so many others, she feared not death but what preceded it, because for her, the end of life was "our only escape" from how "we try to hide" from the ravages of aging "while our minds and bodies crumble." She decried how so many younger than she saw elders as social and economic burdens. In that context, she was especially caustic about how Donald Trump lowered taxes on the very rich at the same time that he cut subsidies for Meals on Wheels. "He didn't worry," she remarked, "that old people might go hungry—he knew if they were starved, they'd be too weak to get to the polls." She celebrated the advantageous recourses seniors have—how well they can adjust, the wisdom they have gained, and their powers of compassion. You are smarter, she observed—even if you "you forget people's names and lose thing, . . . you understand the world around you more deeply and clearly. You excel at interpreting your surroundings because of all you've learned." As an inveterate reader of obituaries in *The New York Times*, including the unpaid ones, I appreciated what she wrote of her own, parallel experiences. "The deaths I fear are those of others," and yet "the ability to trudge onward, no matter what, is a skill the elderly develop. . . . What else should we do? Lie on the floor, screaming and kicking? No. We note the date of the funeral because we plan to attend. Then we empty the dishwasher and put the dishes away."[19]

I track obituaries in *The New York Times*, but what pleases me more is the witty wisdom of drawings Roz Chast offers in *The New Yorker*. I took special pleasure from her graphic 2014 memoir *Can't We Talk About Something More Pleasant?* She offers a poignant, moving recounting of how as the only child of two aging parents, she took care of them until they passed in their nineties; her burden intensified because, she said, it was "against my parents' principles to talk about death." The title references the key issue: "So . . . do you guys ever want to talk about THINGS? *You* know THINGS." "Somehow," she noted, "they were able to see through the euphemisms." She organized their move from the Brooklyn apartment where they seemed to have lived forever. She spent hours and hours going through their possessions, "sick of the ransacking, the picking over and deciding, the dust, and the not particularly interesting trips down memory lane." She moved them to a retirement community near where she and her husband lived in Ridgefield, Connecticut, which she called The Place, where "everything took time and cost money. It was enraging and depressing," she remarked, with her mother adding, "We're not 'residents.' We're *inmates.*" She did her best to manage intergenerational tensions and responded as best she could to their fears (and hers) of running out of money and to their increasingly precarious physical and mental conditions. She arranged for caregivers, especially Goodie, a woman from Jamaica, to attend to them. "She and my mother had *bonded*," she noted. "My mother had surrendered control to a lovely stranger." A dutiful daughter, she cared for them until they passed, first her father and then her mother.[20]

Many are the magazines on retiring and living long and healthy lives, but none has more prominence than the AARP's *Modern Maturity*, in 2003 renamed *AARP: The Magazine*. In 1958, Ethel Percy Andrus, who had founded what became the AARP, launched the magazine with its October–November issue. "It would," according to the AARP's website, "provide a new image of aging, exploring common challenges and sharing stories of men and women who continued to strive, grow and enjoy life as they matured." And, as Andrus wrote at the time, the publication would emphasize how "aging is not just a problem; it represents a real and thrilling challenge. It is one thing to recognize that older people represent the nation's greatest single human resource available and it is quite another to do something about it." The magazine promised "to create a showcase for the achievement of our people; to build many bridges between the worlds of our needs and the powers that can answer those needs; to open the door to all the various human adventures we can picture for you; and to serve as a forum for the discussion of subjects of interest to retired persons." Among the articles were ones that told readers how to improve their bridge games, find a job even though they were sixty-five or older, and with "How a Queen Stays Slim," how to remain fit. Eleanor Roosevelt contributed an article on aging, and material promoting the AARP's group insurance plan took up almost 10 percent of the magazine's pages.[21] Here and elsewhere, the AARP offers buckets of optimism.

In 1997, two researchers published their study of advertisements in the AARP's magazine for the years from 1959 until 1991. They noted that when the ads focused on people fifty years and older, they portrayed them as "capable, important, healthy, and socially active." While the ratio of illustrations of men and women over time approached parity, there were few nonwhites depicted.[22] A look at recent issues of *AARP: The Magazine* reveals that while ads have become more inclusive, the emphasis on successful, active life among older Americans persists. Take, for example, the August–September 2024 issue. The cover featured Kevin Costner, who as an actor and director at age sixty-nine was "doing things his way." It also pointed to how inside, you could read of how you could now solve "8 tricky finance problems" or at fifty you could do what you needed to do to retire at sixty-two. Or you could travel to Las Vegas and participate in "Adventures That Go Beyond the Slots." But if you preferred to remain at home, you could "Stand Up For Yourself!" by fighting "Against A Sitting Disease." When you did, you could take advantage of a Bonus Section that celebrated "Tech Made Easy" by providing "Useful Tips to Simplify Your Life." For women, there was the "Inside Scoop" on how to remain healthy. Inside was chock full of practical advice, such as how to refresh your countertop, how to shop at estate sales, and how to protect yourself against rising costs of insurance.

Similar emphases emerge from a more extensive look at the *AARP Bulletin*. Advertisements filled about 37 percent of its pages—most of them for age-related products—for Walk-In Baths or bath remodels; inexpensive cell phones; a scooter "with anti-tip technology," pictured with an age-appropriate man and below him an asterisk warning you,

"Do not attempt"; insurance policies (some of them offered exclusively to AARP members) for life, dental care, Medicare, and autos; medical alert devices; portable oxygen devices; remedies for liver spots and erectile dysfunction; and electric chairs for getting up stairs. The feature story, covering seven of forty pages, focused on the resurgence of COVID. Shorter articles focused on relevant health issues (memory loss, Alzheimer's), clean energy scams, and technological solutions to problems elders face. More extensive was attention to politics, often with an emphasis on how they affect members: the upcoming presidential election, with a focus on age-relevant pocketbook issues, Medicare, Social Security, and the cost of prescription drugs especially; problems that ensue from congressional reduction of Social Security staffing; and a progress report on the AARP's "national plan for aging—part of our Aging Well in America Initiative."

In addition to long books and magazines such as the AARP's, there are some documentaries, and the striking thing about the relevant ones is the contrast between those that focus on longevity and ones that explore retirement. The former echo researchers and popularizers who envision a future when advances in science and medicine will mean that tens of millions of young Americans will live well past one hundred. In contrast, the latter paint troubling pictures of the lives that people, from young to old, who as seniors will no longer be working for a living, will face or have already faced. *More Life—Decoding the Secret of Aging* offers an exemplary exploration of the prospect of so many people living not just longer but doing so more healthily. Produced by the German government's broadcaster DW Documentary, aka *Deutsche Welle*, and available worldwide in thirty-two languages, it has attracted more than 1.8 million viewers since first offered in May 2022. Several factors make it so compelling. Global in scope, it combines a look at a Blue Zone in Nicoya Costa Rica with scientific and venture capital projects in Hong Kong, the United States, and western Europe. It features talking heads ranging from Nina Khera, a fifteen-year-old American cofounder of Bio-Teen, a start-up that focuses on the science of longevity, to a Costa Rican man aged 103. Recognizing that so many people are living longer and healthily, *More Life* points forward to a world where reaching 120 years (just short, we learn, of the "expiration date" for humans) will be common, with it likely that someone has already been born who will live to 150.

We learn of a famous German painting of 1546 by Lucas Cranach the Elder titled *Fountain of Youth*, which depicts nude elders getting into the water and then emerging at the other side healthy and young. They get dressed and have a sumptuous dinner. The documentary returns to an exploration of what will make this ancient dream come true. Immensely wealthy entrepreneurs are developing advances in biomedical science. Artificial intelligence and genetic experiments will lengthen telomeres artificially, eliminate senescent cells, and regenerate the thymus. On a simpler level, injections, pills, and IV drips are already at work rejuvenating some among us. And though generally optimistic about what healthy habits and genetically based science will make possible, the documentary occasionally expresses caution about medical side effects of scientific advances. More significantly, at the end, the narrator issues a cautious note about interfering with the natural order, because "the development of an anti-aging wonder drug raises issues that threaten the foundations of our natural and social order," given the impact of overpopulation on nature and society. In addition, hinted at but left unexplored is the tension between living a natural life in Costa Rica and the interventions into natural lives driven by investors and scientists. Near the end of the documentary, Anna Gail Glenn, an ex-pat American who has lived on Nicoya, remarks that it worries her when she ponders the "future of biotechnology and changing the composition of our bodies."[23] That is a largely unexplored issue that should bedevil the relationships between those who celebrate Blue Zones and the pursuit of gold and the gold standard of longevity through well-funded science. Unmentioned in *More Life* is that the United States is not currently doing such a great job protecting the lives of seniors, an issue documentaries on retirement explore.

Nomadland: Surviving America in the Twenty-First Century examined this issue in an especially powerful way when it focused, as discussed in the introduction, on down-and-out Americans who travel from place to place living in their vans and searching for work. More prosaic is *The Retirement Gamble*, a *Frontline* documentary that first aired in 2013 and since then has attracted more than seven million viewers. It begins with snapshots of white, middle-class boomers, mostly in their forties and fifties, who face uncertain financial futures, contrasting their reasonably satisfactory current incomes with the small amount of money they had already put aside for the years when they would no longer work for a living. Correspondent Martin Smith highlights the retirement crisis that Americans face. With the change from defined benefit to defined contribution plans and the resulting disappearance of pensions, he reports that risk has shifted from employers to employees. What the "grim" statistics reveal is that too many of those who are still working are dipping into their already-underfunded 401(k)s, a significant proportion of Americans are unable to put aside any savings for their futures, and many of those who are now employed assume they will have to continue working well into their seventies. One well-dressed man, an economist in his early thirties, is unsure whether in retirement he will have to rely on food stamps while Social Security keeps him out of poverty. Uncertainty abounds in a "free for all" world, driven by inflation, risk in the stock and housing markets, and confusing investment options.

Throughout, the center of attention is on traps current employees and future retirees face when deciding how and where to invest, traps set by profit-maximizing financial institutions. On the one hand are mutual funds and powerful investment firms, whose representatives assert that fund managers can outperform the stock market, who are unwilling to acknowledge the importance of having an adviser committed to the responsibility of a fiduciary legally bound to act in the client's best interest and whose representatives oppose efforts by the federal government to protect investors from avaricious financial firms. In contrast stand the film's hero, Jack Bogle of Vanguard, who advocates investing in bundles of stocks with low fees that are passively invested. To underscore the wisdom of Bogle's advice, *The Retirement Gamble* focuses on research on how over long periods of time, Wall Street corporations and Main Street advisers reaped huge financial gains from the more than $10 trillion invested in vehicles that garnered profits from largely opaque fees that significantly eroded what employees had struggled so hard to save for retirement. Thus, the narrator drives home that "saving for retirement remains a bewildering and frightening challenge for millions of Americans." At the end, the producers return to the cast of characters whose fateful experiences the documentary has tracked—some moderately optimistic, others not. The final words come from one man: "I will keep working."[24]

Briefer than documentaries are advertisements on television that reveal how having seniors as customers is big business. As a scholar who is also an inveterate and unpersuadable viewer of daytime television, I have some sense of this. The most common ads, often seasonal, that seem to scream at me are for Medicare Advantage plans. Research by the nonprofit Kaiser Family Foundation reveals the often-deceptive tactics deployed in appeals to sixty-four million eligible citizens. The ads rarely mention the benefits of traditional Medicare or the "potential limitations" of Advantage plans, "such as provider networks or prior authorization requirements." They reference what they call a Medicare hotline rather than the official one. Rarely revealing the quality ratings developed by the federal government's Centers for Medicare and Medicaid Services, they instead hype the extra benefits such as vision, dental, and hearing and the fewer out-of-pocket expenses. Probably in an attempt to market to healthy seniors whose medical expenses will be lower, many of them feature "physically robust seniors engaging in activities such as hiking, yoga, tennis, and even bouncing on a trampoline," instead of seniors with serious disabilities or illnesses. They feature celebrities, most frequently Joe Namath. Now in his early eighties, and someone who from 1965 to 1977 starred in the NFL, he can successfully remind seniors, especially the men among them, of their own glory days.[25]

If ads for Medicare Advantage plans are frequently directed to men, those for A Place for Mom, by its very title, as well as its content, aim at women—often a combination of an elderly female who can no longer live independently and a daughter in charge of finding her "a place for senior living" and a caregiver who will—well—take care of her. My favorite collapses these three roles into two, with a daughter who is also a nurse acknowledging that she is aware that her mom needs to be in a place where a professional who is not her offspring can take care of her. With the cost borne not by the family but by the provider of services, A Place for Mom and its competitors connect family members with advisers who help you explore residential and financial options, including identifying services that will enable a senior family member to age in place. Recognizing that most elderly Americans believe the place for mom or dad is in their homes, these services can also coordinate home health care.[26]

In September 2021, the AARP featured Ken Dychtwald's "Ageism Is Alive and Well in Advertising," which critically discussed advertisements. Citing evidence that Americans over fifty-five control 70 percent of the nation's personal wealth, he warned against depicting them as "cartoonish fuddy-duddies." He described several examples of prejudicial ads, both from 2018. "Dear Young People, Don't Vote" depicted "older people as selfish, uncaring, out-of-touch caricatures who are ruining the future through their lack of concern about the young." The other, "This Is Getting Old," mocked "buffoonish older adults" who had not saved enough for retirement.[27]

Perhaps in response, in late 2022, Tony Coray offered advice on "how to market to seniors" in order to tap into a market that contains many seniors who have "a large amount of disposable income," albeit that in the list of "senior demographics," no one older than seventy-five appears. Keep everything simple and avoid relying too much on technology, since people over sixty-five did not grow up with it. Coray said this even though he mentioned that three out of five seniors own smartphones, over 75 percent have Facebook accounts, and many "actually spend more time online than millennials" and often use YouTube and Pinterest. Since most seniors "see themselves about 5–10 years younger that they are," carefully select appropriate images, as the article itself did. Rather than making a pitch to their children, he advised approaching seniors directly, "without diluting their sense of independence." Instead of relying excessively on words like "the elderly" or "senior citizens," make members of "older generations feel relevant" by not picturing them passively, by emphasizing their wisdom, and by relying of "reasons why" rather than exaggerated hype.[28]

Not surprisingly, the folks at Google or, more precisely, its algorithm realize that retirement and longevity interest me. Very often after dinner, I click on the Google icon on my iPhone and see what I am supposed to be interested in—higher education and politics, for sure, and for some reason, abundant listiness postings, such as "7 More Vibrant Towns in Idaho," and more obscurely, because I once made an inquiry about Helen's hometown, a posting like "Backpacker Joe Spreading God's Love Across America, Stops in Shreveport." But more prominent are stories like ones I espied in early March 2024. First from the *U.S. Sun*, a spin-off of the News Corporation's British tabloid, came Josephine Miller's "Golden Years: We're 65 with Over \$4.1m in Retirement—An Expert Shared Little Known Tax Law That Saves Nearly \$600k When We Withdraw." She told the story of certified financial planner James Conole advising Luke and Shannon how to reduce their future taxes by converting their pretax IRAs into Roth IRAs. Down below were a seemingly unending series of stories that focused on people in their forties, fifties, and sixties who had come to realize how unprepared financially they were for retirement. For example, from the tough-love *Dave Ramsey Show* came the shout-out, "I'm 65 and 'Broke'—A Financial Expert Gave Me Three Goals to 'Get More Radical and Save for Retirement,' but I May Need to Sell My Car." Ramsey told Rick from Boston, "Beans and Rice, Rice and Beans, You Have No Life Until You Radically Change How You Are Living."[29] Google also led me to postings on longevity. Some were human interest stories, like the one in early 2024 on the NBC station in Boston that excitedly featured African American Herlda Senhouse celebrating "Happy 113! Wellesley Woman Believed to Be Oldest MA Resident."[30]

Google also delivered advice about how you too might live so long. It provided a link to an early 2024 article in *Business Insider* in which Gabby Landsverk offered "You Can Boost Your Longevity with 7 Habits That Take 5 Minutes or Less a Day, According to a Doctor." Unlike the time-consuming and expensive fountains of youth advocated by Aubrey de Grey, Elizabeth Blackburn, David A. Sinclair, Nir Barzilai, Andrew J. Steele, and Peter Attia, it offered up the more easily followed Kien Vuu, MD, described as someone who "specializes in antiaging and regenerative medicine." Vuu recommended "making simple, intentional changes to your routine—such as exercise, sleep, and mindfulness"—that could "help improve your well-being in the short term and extend your life without taking up much time." Among his other recommendations were "a simple gratitude practice while you brush your teeth."[31]

Google is just one example of new types of social media that cater to and are used by seniors—prominent among them are Facebook, blogs, podcasts, TED Talks, Instagram, YouTube, and TikTok. As I focused selectively on them, curiously but I suppose not surprisingly, I found that many blogs on both retirement and longevity offered me little that was fresh because they mostly echoed topics more fully available elsewhere.[32] From what I could tell, those that focused on what to do after you no longer worked did not have many followers. And they focused mainly on practical issues more fully covered in popular and readily available how-to books, such as when to begin taking Social Security or enroll in Medicare, how to invest for the long term, whether to invest in annuities, and how to protect yourself from fraud.

Blogs that focus on longevity also had small numbers of followers, normally in the hundreds, and better information is available in the books and related materials of prominent scientists such as Peter Attia. Indeed, *Human Longevity*, listed on one site as the most popular longevity blog, has only 320 followers and mostly follows what Peter Diamandis wrote in *Life Force: How New Breakthroughs in Precision Medicine Can Transform the Quality of Your Life and Those You Love* (2022). Launched in 2013, Human Longevity, Inc., offers to help "you live a healthier, longer life" by relying on "a leading-edge precision health care program to detect and help preempt" life-threatening diseases through a customized "program based on your data, so you can be radically proactive about your health and longevity." Among its recommendations are by-now-familiar ways of optimizing your LDL level, getting better sleep, testing for threats to a long life before they emerge, and expanding your social connections.[33]

Conveniently for me, online I easily found a list titled "The 23 Best TED Talks on Money, Retirement, and Aging to Help You Have a Better Future."[34] It was developed by Kathleen Coxwell, a writer for NewRetirement, "a platform that enables anyone to build a plan that is right for them: their resources, values, goals, and priorities."[35] Some were familiar to me from my previous work on happiness and some from this project, including talks by Dan Buettner and Robert Waldinger. Others focused on practical, psychological, and mental health issues people face as they age into retirement. Two of them struck me as especially interesting, in part because of their contrasting takes.

The first, Jane Fonda's "Life's Third Act," appeared on TEDxWomen in December 2011 and since then has been viewed by almost three million people. This third act was possible, she remarked as she began, in large part because we are living about a third of a century longer than our great-grandparents. This meant that we had to give up the view of our lives as characterized by an arch that began at birth, peaked at midlife, and then declined "into decrepitude." Instead, defying the law of entropy, we should see life's course as a staircase, "the upward ascension of the human spirit, bringing us into wisdom, wholeness, and authenticity." She insisted that older people were happier as they embraced commonalities. For Fonda, the obstacles to well-being in our third acts were genetics, that we could not change, and psychological dynamics, which we could modify by looking back at our lives in ways that gave them "new significance, clarity, and meaning."[36]

Ashton Applewhite's April 2017 TED Talk "Let's End Ageism," which has attracted almost two million views, was a precursor of her book *This Chair Rocks: A Manifesto Against Ageism* (2019), discussed in chapter 4. In a hard-hitting talk, she decried prejudice, stereotyping, and discrimination. In an effort to build a broad-based social movement, she denied the old-young binary and linked ageism to other prejudices, especially homophobia, sexism, and racism. If for Fonda overcoming the trials of longevity were psychological, for Applewhite they were social and economic, with culture and capitalism as the enemies. "You can't make money off satisfaction," she insisted, "but shame and fear create markets, and capitalism always needs new markets. Who says wrinkles are ugly? The multibillion-dollar skin care industry," she responded. She highlighted socioeconomic barriers to successful aging, singling out poverty and inadequate health care. In a rousing, standing-applause-getting finale, Applewhite stated, "Unless we put an end to it, ageism will oppress us all. And that makes it a perfect target for collective action," as she invited her listeners to join her in the fight against ageism. "Let's do it. Let's do it," was the call with which she ended her talk.[37]

Many postings on podcasts, Instagram, TikTok, and YouTube offer little that is fresh or interesting or has attracted many followers. Until I worked on this book, I was a TikTok virgin. But now I can understand its power, not with regard to Chinese surveillance but because of its ability to quickly tell an interesting or sometimes compelling story. Indeed, someone who studied the optimum length of a posting concluded that it was a mere sixteen seconds.[38] There is an abundance of postings that focus on practical issues, many of them cautionary or even dire, but I paid attention to those within the category "retirement life." A hefty portion of them featured people younger than sixty-five, many in their fifties. Nearly all pictured the pleasures of life in retirement. A prominent approach was to go over what a typical day was like. For example, there is a woman, I would say in her fifties, who ended her corporate job. After a "nightmare" beginning when she "floundered around for almost a year," jeanne_retired told her 23,600 followers how she developed a daily pattern—four hours in the morning of waking up, having coffee, and exercising; then, from 10 a.m. to noon, having her "workish time," which might include an hour of corporate consulting; making, editing, and commenting on her TikToks; and working on a novel; in the afternoon, some more "workish time," plus errands and household chores; then dinner with her husband; followed by three hours to relax.[39]

Others focused mainly on pleasure itself. With pictures of her walking on the beach, exercising, and enjoying the company of friends, itsyourjulestime, who has thirty-two thousand followers, answered the question of "what do you want to leave as your legacy," by responding, "living happily ever after."[40] Then there was the common trope that dramatized an event celebrating the transition from employment to retirement. One, titled "Bro Just Started His First Day of Retirement," featured windvin3 performing a joyous forty-one-second dance for his on-site hundreds of friends and colleagues and fifty-five thousand followers who have posted one and a half million likes.[41]

In response to "A Day in the Life of a 62 Year Old Enjoying Retirement," which featured a man brushing his teeth in the morning, walking better now that he has an artificial hip, and watching a hockey game on TV while drinking beer after dinner before going to sleep, Bobleonard70 remarked, "Retirement is the enemy of longevity."[42] And not surprisingly, longevity-themed postings on TikTok featured people, some over one hundred years old, vigorously pursuing life choices familiar to anyone who knows about the scientifically based practices that promise to help people live long lives healthily. A 102-year-old woman under the title "likeminded green" appeared on one with her plan for the next ten years, which centered on a "village for living medicine" of like-minded people.[43] Younger proponents, including scientists featured in "The Longevity Commercial Complex," offer up the familiar recommendations, such as eating and sleeping well, exercising, a full pallet of pills, and a cold bath.[44]

If you want to follow TikTok offerings that focus on the end of life, take a look what Hadley Vlahos, a successful hospice nurse and influencer in her early thirties, has to offer, as reported in her 2023 book *The In-Between: Unforgettable Encounters During Life's Final Moments*. She told stories of her encounters with people on both sides of death's door. "In my experience," she insisted, "people who are happiest at the end of their life are those who have achieved a sense of peace in regard to how they've lived, and who are comfortable in their belief about what comes next." She wrote of "visitations" people have as they approach death, when they "bring with them a sense of calm and peace." Those near life's end "are usually aware of their impending death and at a point where they're reflecting on all the experiences that have, collectively, made a life. Many of these people are also at a point where they're eager to share their most impactful advice. And that's right where I meet them."[45] On TikTok itself, nursehadley, especially with "I'm Not Scared of Dying," drawing on a chapter from her book, movingly explored what death meant to her and to those whom she had comforted as they died.[46]

Then there is what Julie Weed reported on in *The New York Times* in mid-2023 in "As Older TikTok Creators Flourish, Brands Are Signing Them Up." Weed told the stories of several successful senior influencers including Jenny Krupa (aka J-Dog), a ninety-one-year-old with two million followers. With the help of her technologically sophisticated grandson Skylar, she created TikTok posts. One promoted *80 for Brady*, which Paramount Pictures paid her to do. Most influencers of a certain age earn less money than necessary to retire on, perhaps a few hundred dollars to pay for incidentals. A few, like Yamada Davis, have successful offerings. A Japanese American woman and retired software engineer who with the help of her son developed a business centered on *Cooking with Lynja*, she attracted well over a million followers who viewed her offerings four and a half billion times and garnered $50,000 for one video. She died at age sixty-seven on New Year's Day 2024, but that hardly ended the prospect for retired TikTokers. "With its growth continuing," the *New York Times* reporter concluded, "TikTok is likely to keep adding older users, and attracting the sponsored posts that target them." As Mae Karwowski, the founder of Obliviously, a company that connects corporations with senior influencers, remarked, "It's boom time to be an elder content creator."[47]

The TikTok "Retirement House" is the richest lode of relevant social media sites I stumbled on as an example of influencer capitalism that abundantly promotes itself on multiple new media. In 2021, two media-savvy young men living in Los Angeles launched the program on Instagram. Adi Azran, a 2018 graduate of Cal Poly Pomona, where he had majored in marketing management, is head of marketing at Flighthouse Media, a leading TikTok channel. He connected with Brandon Chase, a graduate of Chicago's Columbia College in cinema arts, until then a content creator at Universal Music Group. A January 2023 podcast told of how the posting of the first TikTok video a year before soon attracted several million followers and five hundred million views. From the four hundred or so seniors they saw in virtual auditions, Azran and Chase, then in their late twenties, chose six of them as their cast—three women (Mable, Bubbe, and Rose) and three men (Curtis, Eugene, and Larry) and within each cohort an African American (Rose and Curtis). Apparently they were all at least in their seventies, described for promotional purposes as young people wearing old persons' makeup. Wanting Flighthouse to produce something other than the game shows on TikTok, Azran and Chase developed the brand. They thought of *Jersey Shore* as their model—"stick a bunch of people in a house and watch the drama unfold," Chase remarked. Azran and Chase scripted twenty "really, really raunchy" episodes but, after seeing several, decided to make the series more spontaneous with episodes that highlighted "wholesome, funny content" instead, content that often offered a robust vision of successful aging.[48]

Yet on the podcast, Azran and Chase made clear that each segment was carefully planned, relying as they did on a hook, conflicts, jokes, and resolution to prevent viewers from switching, which Azran said TikTok viewers might do within three seconds. Already on Instagram, YouTube, and TikTok (with 5.7 million followers), crew and cast speculated on the possibility of other outlets Lighthouse might develop in order to enhance the brand: a reality show, streaming, a sketch show, and a senior version of *Saturday Night Live*. An animation feature would get around the issue of what would happen to the show as its cast members aged or died—a prospect that generated laughter among all those on the set as the cast members wondered what it would be like to live in what Eugene called "retirement houses in the sky."

Then there is the issue of why the multiple platforms of "Retirement House" have attracted such large audiences. Aside from its production values, its emphasis on intergenerational cooperation between older performers and younger producers and audience members is a factor, one that resonates with me. The participants honored its evocative power among their followers. Mable remarked "almost immediately we were getting love letters" from younger folks. The six performers were "building a bridge" between generations, as they hit a nerve when they offered new perspectives on aging. From the other generational shore, Azran insisted, "you guys were like a glimmer of hope" who, by "redefining" stereotypes, transformed how people think of getting older. Chase remarked that people of his generation found "inspiration and hope through" the older cast members. Thus, the show promoted a positive view of aging. Young and old recognized the importance of laughter, of which there was plenty on view, as a key to staying young. Someone celebrated "aging but not getting old," and Chase learned that "aging doesn't have to be scary," an idea that the cast members found ludicrous.[49]

Postings about "Retirement House" on TikTok emphasized the theme of cross-generational, fun-loving experiences. A typical example is a minute-long one, apparently sponsored by Joe and Bella, a company that sells "adaptive clothing for seniors and elderly." Accompanying this was the hyped claim that "@retirementhouse is such an amazing group of folks, showing that aging can and should be fun and joyous." Those words came from Steve Aoki, the DJ and electronic music performer at a 3 a.m. show in Las Vegas, "waaay past our bedtime," as one of the seniors said. "He saw us in the crowd and brought us onstage with him!," one of the seniors said, in a way that glossed over what was a carefully arranged production. One by one, we learn of how the stars of "Retirement House" joined in. Aoki "let Mable on the decks and play Taylor Swift with him!" And "he even put headphones on Rose!" while Eugene "did the robot and people loved it." This presentation emphasized a positive view of aging for the benefit of young and old alike, with messages such as "Getting Old Is the Goal. Make Sure to Have Fun Along the Way!" and "You're still 80 and hitting the club with your friends."[50]

There over seven hundred postings for "Retirement House" on Instagram, mostly of its cast having fun. One features the three women in Curaçao. In a video about seven seconds long, Mabel, Rose, and Bubbe stand in a variety of resort scenes as they smile happily and clap rhythmically. They do so to the lyrics of "Magic in the Hamptons," sung by the rapper Lil Yachty, who, born in 1997, was about one-third of the age of the performers. "You know where I go when we're dancing," he sings. "Handshakes in The Hamptons and getting drunk in the mansion with you." Since its posting in September 2023, it has attracted more than four and a half million likes. The three men—Eugene, Curtis, and Larry—

appear in another generation-jumping scene, titled "Three Grandpas on a Bench," even though at least two of them cannot claim that identity. At fifty seconds, it is unusually long for the genre and has attracted fewer likes than the one by the three women, a number under half a million. It opens with the three men sitting on a park bench chewing what they initially think are soft candies. "They taste a little weird," Larry says before asking Eugene where he got them. In his grandson's room, he responds. "The grandson who sells the bongs?" Larry asks urgently. "Oh, shit," Larry and Curtis respond. Curtis performs a Heimlich maneuver on Larry in an attempt to get him to expel the marijuana-laced candy. The strip ends with the three men lying on the grass, high on grass, mouthing wondrous words—in the case of Curtis, "They're no way there's no aliens out there," with Larry saying, "We should start a business," and Eugene responding, "Uber for grandparents."[51]

We end this travelogue from long books to short TikToks with a quote from a posting on Instagram. "Reminder," someone remarked, "the best way to lower our dissatisfaction with life is not to change the world, but to change oneself." To which Henrike Schelper responds, with similar economy, "It's great to focus on what we can control, which is ourselves, rather than trying to change external circumstances beyond our influence," as if we actually had much control over ourselves.[52] Examples abound of how individuals experience aging and death under lonely rather than communal conditions: Sarton's sense of herself as a "solitary" woman as the end of her life approaches; Ephron's end of life in a hospital as opposed to how Gawande's family embraced a rich and century's old ritual; the intensity of the small family circle comprising the world of Roz Chast as her parents approach the end of their lives; the AARP's highly personal advice; the advocacy of retirement plans that benefit corporations at the expense of individuals. To be sure, there are promising alternatives: how the AARP works to strengthen the provisions offered by Social Security, Medicare, and Medicaid; how writers like Applewhite celebrate collective activism, as did Maggie Kuhn and the Gray Panthers; the intergenerational vision offered on TikTok's "Retirement House"; and the ways people living in Blue Zones often rely on each other in dense, albeit small communal setting. Perhaps sometimes the best way to diminish our dissatisfactions with life is not just to change ourselves but to change the world.

Retire On-Screen and Live a Long, Interesting Life

In the early 1990s, my parents were living in a retirement community in Connecticut. Once when I was visiting them, on a bulletin board asking for movies residents would like to see, someone suggested the pornographic classic *Debbie Does Dallas* (1978). When working on this book, my mind has often wandered off to thinking about organizing a film series in such communities, but I doubt if I would follow the suggestion I espied three decades ago. Yet, at least since the 1970s, scores, if not hundreds, of films (and many TV shows) have dramatized major issues that people face in retirement.[1] However, there is one important precursor to these relatively recent treatments, the 1936 movie *Dodsworth*. It relied on Sinclair Lewis's novel of the same name, published in March 1929. Both the novel and the film tell the story of Sam Dodsworth, a man in his early fifties who retires after making a fortune manufacturing automobiles. Seeking new lives, Sam and his wife, Fran, travel to Europe, in a movie directed by William Wyler and starring Walter Huston and Ruth Chatterton. Appropriately enough, as we shall see, aside from acting, they each had another professional passion—Huston as an engineer and Chatterton as an aviator. In most ways, more about liberation than confinement, the on-screen retelling of the story reflected the Roaring Twenties and not the Depression-marked thirties. Yet both novel and film offered treatments of life in retirement, with some of its major themes reverberating in more recent cinematic renditions.

The film's plot, which by and large followed the novel's, had its twists and turns, but its contours were straightforward enough. At age fifty, Sam Dodsworth sold the Revelation Motor Company, which he had built in the midwestern town of Zenith. To us, that may seem like an early retirement age, but remember that in 1929, life expectancy for men was not much older.[2] Now no longer working for a living, he travels to Europe with his wife. Once abroad, they grow apart, as each of them embraces different values and has romantic dalliances, Sam a combination of practical pursuits and an affair with the American divorcée Edith Cortright (Mary Astor), whom he initially meets on the Atlantic crossing and who lives as an expat in Italy; Fran liberation from a bourgeois life in the US Midwest and flings with a series of men—Captain Clyde Lockert (David Niven), whom she meets on the ship but rebuffs when he tries to turn a flirtation into an affair; the wealthy playboy Arnold Iselin (Paul Lukas), who sees "nothing so vulgar" as business; and Baron Kurt Von Obersdorf (Gregory Gaye), whom she hopes to marry, restoring prosperity to his family, described as "poor since the war."

The ways Sam and Fran drift apart reveal their contrasting values and commitments, ones that shape what Sam initially defines as uncertainty in retirement, but Fran chooses liberation abroad over her boring, bourgeois way of life in Middle America. While Fran speaks of her "new life," Sam says that now that he is retired, he will "enjoy life now if it kills [him], and it probably will." Yet his hometown friend Tubby Pearson (Harlan Briggs) insists that men like them should work until they die: "Americans like us can't quit." We soon see Sam's pursuit of the practical, initially as he peers over the ocean liner's railings to spot the first light from England's shore, signaling their arrival, followed by his desire to visit auto factories in Europe and then by his going to historical sites while Fran heads for the hairdresser. Sam describes Fran's friends as "moochers," whose principal contribution to civilization was how to order a sophisticated meal. In contrast to the allure of European sophistication, Sam sees himself as an "ordinary American" whose chief virtues are practicality and ambition.

Sam and Fran face new phases of their lives differently. Fran's prospects turn out to be highly problematic in gendered ways. Sam remarks that Fran is "scared of growing old," and we watch her deal unsuccessfully with aging. Early on, we understand that she cannot embrace the pleasures of being a grandmother. Then, at one point, Edith and Fran engage in a barbed conversation about getting older. "No woman enjoys getting to be thirty-five," Fran tells Edith, who responds by remarking, "When you're my age, you'll look back on thirty-five as a most agreeable time of life." Yet the real crisis comes when Kurt's mother, Baroness Von Obersdorf (Maria Ouspenskaya), who seems preternaturally older than anyone else in the movie, refuses to sanction her son's marriage to Fran, in part because she is not Roman Catholic but more trenchantly because

Fran is too old to produce an heir. Kurt upends Fran's hopes for a new life when he accepts his mother's cruel judgment "of how little happiness there will be for the old wife of a young husband."

In contrast, Sam successfully transitions to a new life driven by his practicality and business acumen. To be sure, he acknowledges that he is getting older, something marked by his wearing glasses that he did not need before. He also jokes that if classical ruins at Paestum are in "excellent preservation," that is more than he is. Near the end of the film, as Sam moves into Edith's villa off the coast of Italy, he reveals his rejuvenating skills when he pridefully gets a boat's motor to work instead of relying on sails, as Edith had hoped. This achievement is, he boasts, something that sets him "raring to go again for the first time" since he sold his business.

The boldness of Sam's entrepreneurial aspirations find expression in the most significant change in *Dodsworth* from print to screen. In the novel, he dreams of developing "a better San Souci Garden," a reference to an artfully designed suburb where residents live without worry, as the French words indicate. This enables him to think of himself in "the tradition of pioneers pushing to the westward, . . . a religious procession, sleeping always in danger, never resting, and opening a new home for a hundred million people." Edith is more supportive of his dreams than is his wife, who mocks his ambitions by remarking, "I do want you to produce something individual and lasting. But an American garden suburb—Phooey."[3]

Several things make possible the ambition Sam expresses seven years later and that Edith fully embraces, "a kind of airline from Moscow to Seattle" that might make him "the first man with his own round the world system." In 1933, Franklin Roosevelt had recognized the Soviet Union, and Dodsworth hopes "those Soviet boys will let" him develop the route. More important were recent advances in aviation. In 1927, Charles Lindbergh had completed his transatlantic flight. Three years later, Frank Whittle invented the jet engine, albeit an innovation not to be deployed commercially for decades. In 1933 and 1935, respectively, the Boeing 247 and the Douglas DC-3 brought technological changes to aircraft that improved their comfort and range. Moreover, surely the film's producers had in mind the launching of Pan American World Airways (Pan Am) in 1927 and Trans World Airways (TWA) in 1930, their names underscoring the importance of Sam's later evocation of a "round the world system."

The film's conclusion underscores the gendered nature of aging. Fran cannot successfully transition to a new life, one marked not by retirement but by failed motherhood and grandmotherhood. Sam faces getting older, but, confirming Tubby's statement that "Americans like us can't quit," retirement is not for him. Productive work turns out to be an antidote to men getting older. On-screen it is unavailable to women, even though in real life, Ruth Chatterton (the flailing and failing Fran on-screen) was a pioneering female aviator precisely at the time when Sam speaks of his own aviation ambitions. Near the film's end, when Sam decides he has to return to Zenith to take care of Fran, Edith says, "you were a young man a moment ago," and now he is all "shriveled." When Sam makes clear that he will abandon Fran before the ship sails to the US from Naples, she wonders what she will do without him. He soon responds by telling her, "You'll have to stop getting younger someday." In return, she plays the aging card when she calls Edith a "washed-out expatriate," to which Sam replies, "love has got to stop someplace short of suicide," as he references one ultimate destination of getting older. Having earlier insisted that when he marries Edith, he is "going back to doing things," in the movie's final seconds, we see Sam, an engineer in his off-screen life, doing real mechanical work as he pilots his boat to her island villa, powered not by sail but by a motor he has earlier mastered.

In important ways, *Dodsworth* provided precedents for many future cinematic treatments of aging and retirement. Like many who followed on-screen, Sam and Fran dip into their bucket list, though with later examples, the destinations are more likely ordinary places in the United States or exotic ones abroad. They associate new lives with travel, even though both redemption and tragedy ensue, as would happen on-screen later on. If stereotypical gender differences suffuse *Dodsworth*, future renditions would offer more nuanced and complicated considerations that move beyond a married couple in one generation to explore a wider range of family dynamics. In the 1920s and 1930s, it was mostly the indigent who ended up in retirement institutions, and if *Dodsworth* as a novel and film is accurate, before World War II well-to-do Americans dreamed of freedom abroad rather than safe confinement at home. At least Sam is happy in retirement. As reflected in films, all that would change later on when, after a lifetime of gainful employment, affluent Americans headed for both the open road and the closed doors of luxurious retirement communities.

Almost four decades separate *Dodsworth* in 1936 and the 1974 film *Harry and Tonto*, the first major post–World War II one in which travel in retirement plays a significant role. A seventy-two-year-old Harry Coombes (Art Carney), retired as a teacher and evicted from his Upper West Side Manhattan apartment, travels across the country, with his cat Tonto, to Los Angeles by car and bus. The film was a commercial success, and Carney won the Academy Award as best actor. We see Harry's life reflected and enhanced by the wide variety of people he encounters. The film critic Roger Ebert wrote at the time that, humorous, charming, and optimistic, this "hasn't been your ordinary road picture, but a sort of farewell voyage by a warm and good old man who is still, at seventy-two, capable of being thankful for the small astonishments offered by life."[4]

In 1957, Jack Kerouac's novel *On the Road* captured the sense of adventure involved in earth-bound travel. Since *Harry and Tonto*, retirement road trips undertaken by singular individuals have appeared frequently on-screen, some notable for their evocative power.[5] Based on actual events, *The Straight Story* (1999) features the World War II vet, widower, and retired farmer Alvin Straight (Richard Farnsworth). At age seventy-two, living on Social Security and unable to get a proper driver's license because of disabilities, he maneuvers a lawn tractor from Iowa to Wisconsin to visit his brother, Lyle (Harry Dean Stanton), who is recovering from a stroke. On the road, he benefits from a series of encounters marked by mutuality before the story culminates in a scene of brotherly reconciliation.

Three years later came *About Schmidt*. Warren Schmidt (Jack Nicholson), recently widowed and retired from his job as an actuary for an Omaha insurance company, faces a series of indignities that mock any sense that this next, unplanned phase of life has any genuine pleasures. After his retirement dinner, his successor rebuffs his offer of help, and Schmidt then finds his work files dispatched into the dustbin of history. Lacking purpose in retirement, he goes on the road, not on a tractor but in his thirty-five-foot Winnebago Adventurer. Nothing but painful events and relationships assault his dignity, something that emphasizes his loneliness and undermines his optimism about being a true adventurer. He discovers an affair that his late wife had with his good friend; painfully engages with his daughter, her fiancé, and her family; and experiences a series of rebuffed romantic relationships.

Yet there are glimmers of a better life. One night, while sitting on the roof of his Winnebago, he interprets the streaking of a meteor across the sky as a sign of reconciliation with his deceased wife. The persistent thread that unconvincingly seems to provide a genuinely satisfying experience comes from Schmidt's epistolary relationship with his Tanzanian foster child, Ndugu Umbo, to whom he pours out his tragedy-laden feelings and experiences—things he can convey to the African boy but not to anyone we see on-screen. At the film's end, Schmidt reads a letter a nun has written about Ndugu because his foster child cannot read or reply to what Schmidt has written or probably even understand it on his own. But the nun does enclose a drawing Ndugu made, of Schmidt and Ndugu holding hands, an image that causes Schmidt to cry. Despite a commanding performance by Nicholson, the film, perhaps unintentionally, strikes me as a critique of the vacuousness of American retirement. As Ebert wrote, the film should provide a lesson to young Americans. "Let it be a lesson to them. If they define their lives only in terms of a good job, a good paycheck and a comfortable suburban existence, they could end up like Schmidt, dead in the water."[6]

Like *The Straight Story* and *About Schmidt*, *Nebraska* (2013) focuses on a man seeking redemption on a road trip. In a film that was a critical and commercial success, the central figure is Woody Grant (Bruce Dern). He has just received a letter, not unlike the ones that so many of us have found in the mail from Publishers Clearing House, that holds out the promise of a million-dollar prize but is actually a scam tempting recipients to purchase magazine subscriptions. Though there is no specific mention of retirement and it is not clear what jobs Woody held earlier on, we see him as an aging alcoholic, emotionally wounded during the Korean War. Like so many other men in the film, he represents problematic and troubled masculinity, especially among middle age and older men. Shot in black and white, *Nebraska* offers bleak pictures of life in mid-America, a theme reversed in its brief ending. The opening scene, of a disheveled, medically compromised, and lonely Woody walking a highway in his hometown of Billings, Montana, on his way to

Lincoln, Nebraska, to collect his million, evokes a lonely world characterized by depressed individuals and communities.

Members of Woody's immediate family do their best to convince him that he is tilting at windmills. His bawdy, irreverent wife, Kate (June Squibb), constantly berates her husband for chasing after gossamer dreams. She continually speaks of putting Woody in a "home," which one son labels as a nursing home, and chastises him for having failed to earn a proper living. Both sons represent the possibility of modern employment: their younger one, David (Will Forte), as a salesman of audio equipment and their older one, Ross (Bob Odenkirk), even more convincingly as a news anchor on a local television station. David is the more empathetically engaged, making clear that his dad both needs to be in a nursing home and would be better served by having something to live for. His dad's quest, he remarks, is not about money. "What's wrong about letting him have his fantasy for a few more days?" he asks as one point.

The film takes us almost nine hundred miles from Billings to Lincoln, where family members, driven by Woody's dream, are going to collect the nonexistent winnings. En route and taking up much of the footage, the Grants return to Woody's hometown of Hawthorne, Nebraska, (in reality Plainville, known as the world's "Klown Kapital"), its fictive version populated by scores of sad, aging men who sit around aimlessly at bars and in homes. "Things are bad for men" in this economy, says Woody's sister-in-law. Word quickly spreads through the town that the prodigal son is a millionaire, despite David's role as the Reality Principle. Settling scores remains the order of the day: for example, for Woody to recover an air compressor that his friend Ed Pegram (Stacy Keach) took from him decades ago and for Ed to recover money he loaned Woody way back when. When local folks ask what Woody will do with his winnings, he replies that he will replace his son's aging Subaru with a new truck, purchase a new air compressor, and leave something for his sons. In a key scene at a local bar, local men mockingly read the scam letter they have stolen from Woody.

Having recovered the promissory letter, Woody and David resume their journey to Lincoln. Arriving at the shabby, modest office whose address is listed on the letter, they encounter a woman who makes clear that they do not have the winning number. Instead, she offers Woody a consolation prize—a hat with "Prize Winner" written on its front. En route back to Billings in a brief end-of-the road sequence, David trades the Subaru for a truck, puts his dad's name on the title, and purchases a new Craftsmen compressor as he fabricates for his dad a story that he had worked out something with prize officials. Going down the streets of Hawthorne en route, David agrees to let his dad drive as he hides on the floor of the passenger side. At last we see Woody's composure and pride restored as he drives the truck past admiring locals, including his old girlfriend, who is now the publisher of the local newspaper.

In these three films—*The Straight Story*, *About Schmidt*, and *Nebraska*—aging in retirement can be a time of remembrance and reconciliation, however troublesome such experiences are. They avoid dealing with the problem that, for many in retirement, the lack of work means there can be little that is meaningful. At their centers are older men problematically facing life after employment. They evoke relationships with others that are complicated—Harry's with Tonto seemingly more satisfying than almost anyone the featured man has with a family member. By and large, elderly men seem ill equipped to deal satisfactorily with the next phase of their lives. Yet hope comes through reconciliation, albeit in many ways evoking a process that is often imperfect. In the middle of *The Straight Story*, Alvin Straight symbolically celebrates the seemingly unbreakable bonds of family, and at the end, he quietly sits with his brother as they silently honor their reconciliation. In *About Schmidt*, Schmidt achieves emotional satisfaction in a dream with his wife and through a geographically and emotionally distant relationship with a young African he will never know. *Nebraska* offers us a picture of intergenerational reconciliation, one marked by a son's generous, albeit fabricated, acts. If not Ebert's version of ending up dead in the water, perhaps we can understand these as stories of men figuratively dead on the road, with retirement as time of remembrance, deeply tinged with sadness about lives unfulfilled.

The Bucket List (2007), a film that helped coin the phrase, offers a very different take on the theme of getting on the road late in life.[7] If the three previous films focus on men traveling in the United States alone or with family members, central to this one is the relationship of two buddies from very different backgrounds playing out their quest at home and around the world. Like the others, familial reconciliation is a central issue but here also involving resolution of the tension between family and friendship. Moreover, with *The Bucket List*, successfully coming to terms with death looms large. Directed by Carl Reiner, it features Jack Nicholson as Edward Perriman Cole and Morgan Freeman as Carter Chambers. Cole is a nihilistic and cynical, four-time-divorced billionaire, and aside from his wealth and power, what is important to him are the enjoyment of the expensive and exotic Indonesian coffee kopi luwak and his lording over his personal assistant, Matthew (Sean Hayes), whom he has humiliated in myriad ways, including by renaming him Thomas. In contrast stands Chambers, an empathetic and deeply learned African American auto mechanic whose family commitments had sidelined him from his hopes of becoming a history professor, though throughout the film, we learn of how extensive and profound is his command of knowledge. If Chambers is at the moment of retirement, Cole at age eighty-one is still working as a corporate tycoon.

The two men meet in a hospital that Cole owns, lying in adjoining beds, where they have realized that their common cancer diagnosis means they do not have long to live. We gradually learn of how different their familial situations are. Cole is alienated from those in his past, including Emily (Jennifer DeFrancisco), his only child. Again in contrast, Chambers is proud of the professional accomplishments of his progeny and supported by his wife, Virginia (Beverly Todd). Throughout much of the story, male friendship rather than family commitments dominates. In the first 40 percent of screen time, the men bond over discussions of what they will do before they die, especially focused on a bucket list Chambers had scribbled on a piece of yellow paper indicating what he would like to do before kicking the bucket. His dreams range from "witness something majestic" to becoming "the first Black president." Cole's are more earthy, both prosaic and risky. "Don't you want to go out with some balls, guns blazing, have a little fun?" he asks, like skydiving and pursuing majesty in the Himalayas.

Insisting Chambers should not be "smothered by pity in grief," Cole uses his more-than-ample financial resources to cross off listed items. Virginia does not want her husband to turn away from familial obligations and states that he "is not for sale." Insisting he "earned some time" for himself, Chambers accepts Cole's offer that the two buddies go off. Traveling by private jet, they skydive, drive souped-up cars on a racetrack, get tattoos (with Cole promising, "No Confederate flag. No Black Jesus"), have a fabulous meal in France, go on an African safari, climb atop the Pyramids, and visit China's Great Wall and India's Taj Mahal. Along the way, they talk to each other of living and dying, as Cole seems to embrace the more encompassing vision Chambers has been pursuing.

Turning points underscore that reconciliation among friends and family members is possible. Chambers evokes ancient wisdom by asking Cole if he has found joy in life and brought joy to others. Cole answers yes to the first but acknowledges the unfinished, regret-filled nature of his relationship with his daughter. "Everyone's afraid to die alone," Chambers remarks, and eventually we see Cole following the message that he left behind before he died, that Cole finally visit his daughter. When he does so, he embraces not only his daughter but also a granddaughter he did not know he had. This provides him with the opportunity to cross one more item off the bucket list, to "kiss the most beautiful girl in the world." Along similar lines, Chambers remarks, "I left a stranger and came back a husband." He lovingly embraces his wife but collapses before their love upon return is consummated. Later, Cole learns that Chambers's cancer has metastasized to the brain. Cole learns from Chambers, a trivia maven with his skills honed watching *Jeopardy!*, that that the coffee he has so savored results from a jungle cat defecating. With the friends laughing robustly, Cole says, "You're shitting me," to which Chambers responds, "the cats beat me to it." Now Chambers can cross off another item, "laugh until I cry." With his cancer temporarily in remission, he delivers a eulogy at his friend's funeral, making clear that he can cross off one more item from the list, "Help a complete stranger for the good." As in some other films, friendship has replaced family in a world where, for some, families are not only smaller but also fractured.

In the final scene, Thomas/Matthew places the bucket list between two cans of Chock Full o'Nuts Coffee filled with the ashes of Cole and Chambers. Earlier on, clouds prevented the two buddies from seeing the mountains in their full majesty, but now Thomas/Matthew can cross off "witness something truly majestic." Although the final scene underscores the importance of friendship across racial and class lines, earlier moments emphasize this this was possible with family reconciliation. In turns out that aging men can fulfill their most robust dreams before they die.

In addition to bucket-list films are those that explore the perils and possibilities of life in a retirement community.[8] I begin with *Mr. Belvedere Rings the Bell* (1951). The final of three Mr. Belvedere films starring Clifton Webb, it both evokes a type of retirement home different from what now reigns and provides an early example of what would later be the common theme of liberation from institutional confinement. A forty-six-year-old Lynn Belvedere (Clifton Webb) earns a living by giving lectures on how to stay young even into your eighties. However, he loses confidence in what he is peddling (and in his own future) when he chances on residents of the Church of John Home for the Aged complaining of ailments that afflict them. He asks the manager of his tours, Emmett (Zero Mostel), who is arranging a twenty-two-city tour, "How does one get into an old age home?" even as he is "beginning to wonder if there's any point" in living to be eighty. Emmett replies that you only get into such a place by living to be eighty years old.

Seeking to study the retirement community, Belvedere goes to see the presiding bishop, who mistakes him for the deceased seventy-seven-year-old Oliver Erwenter. Recognizing Belvedere's "comparative youth," he is nonetheless willing to make an exception but asks, "Why [do] you old codgers keep up the pretense of being young?" Belvedere replies that he appears younger than he is because "clean living and rightful thinking have preserved [his] vigor." Once in residence, Belvedere sees how aging has ravaged the community's residents. They need assistance from nurses, show signs of delusion, and get ready for their naps. Or, as a woman remarks, "the only action" they get is in their stomachs. And the man in charge, the Reverend Charles Watson (Hugh Marlowe), worries about financial difficulties that will lead to budget cuts. We understand that this retirement home is unlike more contemporary, fancy, multi-tiered, and larger ones when we see residents living in dormitory rooms with many beds and everyone (perhaps a dozen or so) eating at a home table headed by the Reverend.

Belvedere enlivens the old-age home. Initially he offers up the bromides like the ones Norman Vincent Peale would provide in his *The Power of Positive Thinking*, published a year after the movie but its assertions already widely abroad in the culture. Live every moment as if it is the last one, he tells fellow residents, adding, "believe you're young, and you'll be young." He also offers residents a special potion (supposedly imported from Tibet but actually a mixture of sugar and alcohol) that he promises will take twenty-five years off everyone's life. If Emmet calls them "old geezers," the placebos actually seem to work, with Belvedere encouraging men to say "dirty words" as we see them chasing after women. Belvedere arranges a church bazaar on the community's grounds to counter the drab conditions under which the residents live. And he fosters a romantic relationship between Reverend Watson, the man in charge, and his assistant, Harriet Trip (Joanne Dru). A reporter's discovery of what has happened initially prompts the residents to return to their drab existence, until Belvedere convinces them that positive thinking can overcome the downside of aging. His confidence in his future restored, Belvedere returns to the lecture circuit, albeit with a hint at the film's end that as a hard-hearted salesman, he is actually cynical about what happened.

Hundreds of thousands of Americans retire abroad, though few of them choose India. The wildly popular and critically successful British film *The Best Exotic Marigold Hotel* (2011) nonetheless captures some of the reasons they do so, as well as the trials and pleasures they experience. Early on, we see Douglas Ainslie (Bill Nighy) and his wife, Jean Ainslie (Penelope Wilton), being shown a place to retire in Britain, where the estate agent points out the "rails on the wall to help [them] get around" and the panic button to push in an emergency. A skeptical Jean remarks, "Thirty years in the civil service and this is all we can afford." Then there is Muriel Donnelly (Maggie Smith), who like many Americans hopes to move abroad, where she can afford medical care, in her case a less expensive hip operation that she can have more quickly than in Britain. Others seek better weather or exotic pleasures—or inexpensive living abroad as a way of recovering from financial reversals at home. Yet above all, the film offers experiences of self-realizations, awakenings, repairs, and reconciliations (in this case for Brits in a postcolonial world) or romantic pleasures of all sorts—gay, straight, marriages breaking up and reconfigured, and relationships across national lines.

The residents soon discover how deceptive is the advertisement for the Best Marigold Hotel, announced with the sign, "For the Elderly and the Beautiful." They had read of a place abroad that is in the "proud tradition of the Raj" within "a luxury development where all the residents are in their golden years." Yet they find that India hardly matches what they were led to expect—dirty quarters, birds freely flying about the property, bedrooms without doors, and telephones that do not work. After all, the proprietor, Sonny Kapoor (Dev Patel), has projected its future in the promotional material, having told his mother (Lillete Dubey) that his dream is to "outsource old age" since there as so many countries that do not like old folks. What ensues is that the hotel is rebuilt along with the guests' own lives, as well the pleasures of a new, exotic place and of reciprocally helpful relationships—often ones across lines colonialism had severed. As we see Norman Cousins (the appropriately named Ronald Pickup) reading the *Karma Sutra*, we hear the narrator, Evelyn Greenslade (Judi Dench), read from a diary: "Like Darwin's finches, we are slowly adapting to our environment. . . . There's no past that we can bring back by longing for it, only a present that re-creates itself."

Even when facing adversity, key players persist. Following the death of a compatriot, someone remarks, "When someone dies you think of your own life, and I don't want to grow older." Investors threaten the hotel's future and Sonny's hope to "build a home for the elderly so wonderful that they will simply refuse to die." Yet hopeful persistence wins. As Greenslade asks rhetorically near the film's ending, "Can we be blamed for feeling that we are too old to change? . . . Everything will be all right in the end, and if it's not all right, then trust me, it's not the end."

As the number of people retiring every year increased, so did the number of US films and TV programs, including an episode in *Seinfeld* about a Florida retirement community, Del Boca Vista. *The Last Laugh* (2019), *Queen Bees* (2021), *80 for Brady* (2023), and Tyler Perry's *Assisted Living* on BET (2020) highlight the gendered and racial dynamics of retirement that involve themes of reconciliation among family members and friends.

The Last Laugh is a buddy movie that underscores the importance of late-in-life liberation from the numbing confinement in a retirement community. The central figures are Al Hart (Chevy Chase), a talent manager who reconnects with his long-ago client Buddy Green (Richard Dreyfus), who had abandoned his career to become a podiatrist. Springing themselves from the retirement community Palm Sunshine, they go on the road, eventually ending up in Manhattan, where Buddy, dying of pancreatic cancer, is a smash success on television. Near the beginning, we listen to a voice-over describing such residences as "paradise," where you can "return to your easy-access bungalow." When the DVD titled *Senior Living* pops out of the TV set, Al crushes it and throws it away. What ensues are abundant cliched critiques of the world they have escaped, among them compulsive watching of Lawrence Welk on the small screen and the obligatory going to the mall and playing canasta. Even more prominent are visual and verbal references to the infirmities of old age: old folks struggling to get around in walkers and wheelchairs; a reference to female inmates as "old and horny," whose male counterparts could satisfy them with the help of Viagra; the necessity to rely on soup for nourishment; ambulances with flashing lights at the community's entrance; and stories about residents dying. Buddy once thought about running a marathon, he quips, but "now, it's standing up for ten minutes." Later on, he tells those in his audience, "You may recognize me from *America's Got Dentures*." When early on Al asks Buddy if it ever bothers him "being around old people," Buddy responds by saying, "We never use the O word" here, before going on to insist that "the politically correct word in 'pre-dead.'"

Yet inevitably the film hits the obligatory high notes. Jeannie (Kate Micucci) supports her grandfather Al, and Buddy reconciles with his son, Charlie (Chris Parnell). Al and Buddy acknowledge the sustaining power of male friendship and meaningful work. In addition, an African American is a key member of the community's chorus. Johnny Sunshine (George Wallace: no, not Mississippi's governor) is one of many African American cast members, more prominent here than in most earlier retirement films and surely in many retirement communities. Early on, he offers the "Doomsday Report" about aging, ill, and dying residents. A prophet of doom early on, near the end we see him laughing as he sits with fellow residents at Palm Sunshine, many with signs of illness and aging, laughing as they watch Buddy in New York capturing audiences with his jokes on a television screen. As the credits roll, Johnny Sunshine proudly celebrates Buddy's performance.

If *The Last Laugh* is about masculine bonding, *Queen Bees* focuses on its feminine equivalent, even as it captures the challenges of residential cliques. Among the subplots are real estate shenanigans that involve (spoiler alert) Helen Wilson (Ellen Burstyn); tensions with her real estate agent daughter, Laura Wilson Crane (Elizabeth Mitchell), that are healed with Helen's grandson Peter Crane (Matthew Barnes) playing a key role; and Helen's romance with a boyfriend (and eventually her husband) Dan Simpson (James Caan). The film opens with Helen in her upscale home, still mourning the loss of her husband, who died three years ago. She calls the retirement community Pine Grove, asking it to stop sending brochures, a copy of which sits on a counter. "I will never be interested in living in your swanky old people's home," she says angrily, while displaying some signs of cognitive loss. What jeopardizes her hopes that she can age in place until she dies is that she often locks herself out of her home, with a culminating incident occurring when she does so, leaving a stove on and causing a fire that so seriously damages her home that she has to move out while reconstruction takes place. She retreats to Pine Grove, temporarily, she hopes.

There she encounters what she resents—compulsive, friendly, welcoming, exclusive social groups and ample facilities and experiences—and that others relish. Among them are art classes, speed dating, bingo, movies, a beauty salon, an indoor pool—and men, not only an age-appropriate one rumored to be a good lover who takes Viagra but also two younger men, a Filipino masseuse, Lito Santos (Alex Mapa), and a hunk of a male exercise instructor, Pablo Leon (Ricky Russert), with whom aging women flirt. Amply in evidence are talks not only of death and illness but also of hearing aids, a residence as a "cell," sagging breasts, and memory problems.

It turns out that work on Helen's damaged home takes longer than expected, delays that make it possible for her to gradually embrace her new life, with her relationships with the Queen Bees playing a central role. They are a group of four women, some of them arrogant ("B stands for 'bitch,'" one outsider remarks) and all of them complicit in arrogantly commandeering an exclusive table where they play bridge. "They're like mean girls but with medical alert bracelets," Helen says to her grandson.

Initially denied membership, Helen joins the group after one of its members dies, remarking that the invitation "felt like an offer from the mob." An African American member, Sally Hanson (Loretta Devine), plays the key role in welcoming Helen. "This isn't high school," Sally nonetheless observes; "it's worse. High school we graduate. Here we die or we fight against it until our last breath." Having joined the club, Helen bonds with Sally, in part to comfort her newfound friend, who is suffering from cancer. Indeed, at one point, they fall asleep on Helen's bed with Sally insisting that a lesbian relationship was not on her "bucket list." As the movie nears its end, reconciliations prevail, including among the Queen Bees. Helen and Dan marry, and they will live not in her now-repaired house but in Pine Grove. And Helen invites her daughter to serve as her maid of honor. "Eighty is the new eighteen," we hear one of the Queen Bees insist.

80 for Brady is a film about a bucket list and women bonding and, in this case, liberation from a retirement community. It stars Tom Brady as himself and four women of a certain age passionately interested in the star quarterback—Lou (Lilly Tomlin), Trish (Jane Fonda), Maura (Rita Moreno), and Betty (Sally Field), all of them around "eighty in people years," though some claim they are younger. Indeed, the resident manager, Tony (Jimmy O. Yang), tells Trish that since the community is for people sixty years and older, she might have to wait a few more years to qualify. With some of the film based on a true story, there is no need here to follow the details of its plot about the four women's crazed determination to see their hero play in Super Bowl LI. For our purposes, several things are notable. The first is that three of Maura's friends liberate her from the Continuing Care Retirement Community Calm Gardens with the help of Mickey (Glynn Turman), her African American suitor, who has shown her how much there is to explore where they both now live—pool aerobics, dancing, game nights, and cooking classes—even though we see a sign reminding residents, "We Take Sleep Seriously." Farther along in the story, Mickey calls Maura to tell her, "Some people have been asking about you under the impression that you've been kidnapped. . . . Some residents here have been eyeing your room." In response, she calls them "vultures" and tells Mickey that "they can have it" since she is moving back to her house because experience with her three friends has awakened her to possibilities of more active life outside Calm Gardens.

Once the game begins, the film explores the parallels between the lives of the four women and Brady's. From the booth where the Patriots' coordinators call plays, Betty, relying on her command of math, advises Brady about a play, as we see him on the field nodding in agreement before he successfully executes the play. Then Lou coaches the quarterback, inspiring him with the parallel between her recovery from chemo and his recovery in this game. All this advice enables Brady to turn the game around and lead the New England Patriots to a triumph over the Atlanta Falcons. In the locker room, Lou connects with Brady, who tells her that her courage inspired him. Later, after Brady has moved to Tampa to play with the Buccaneers, the four women sit on a nearby beach and discuss their futures. When the issue of retirement comes up, the women make clear their critiques. Lou says that Maura does not want to use word because it "sounds so final." Trish chimes in with, "I don't retire. . . . I just change careers, often." Then Betty adds, "Technically I took a sabbatical many years ago, and I just never returned to work." To which Maura adds, "I wasn't asking you girls. I was asking him," as the scene shifts to their hero, who says, "It's a shame to retire, if you feel like you've still got it." Then Maura raises a glass to toast their hero, who had actually recently reversed his decision to stop playing, and she says, "Join the club." This happens even though, poetically, two days before the film's release, Brady announced his retirement from playing professional football.

As we have already seen, reconciliation and retirement come together in many films, at times even more fully.[9] To this writer of a certain age and accumulated life experiences, *On Golden Pond* (1981) is an early and still powerfully evocative exploration of what it means to experience familial reconciliation in a retirement marked by the challenges of aging, dementia included. As evidenced in so many films, reconciliation is Hollywood's solution to the problems of old age. Perhaps this was one reason *On Golden Pond* was wildly successful at both the box office and in the awards competitions, garnering Academy Awards for Henry Fonda and Katherine Hepburn as best actor and best actress and for Ernest Thompson for best adapted screenplay for his drama of the same name.

Ethel Thayer (Hepburn) and her husband, Norman Thayer Jr. (Fonda), return to their summer home on a pond in northern New England. She is younger, more resilient, and healthier than her older, grumpy husband, who suffers from heart problems and cognitive decline as he approaches his eightieth birthday. Images and references to life, death, and everything in between suffuse the film, conveyed in images of animals living on and in the lake, in the couple's lives, and in Norman's reading help-wanted ads in his search for "gainful employment." After they enter the memory-filled house, Norman eyes a framed newspaper with a headlined story of his retirement. Ethel and Norman soon debate the meaning of aging, with her saying, "We're at the far edge of middle aged," and him responding, How can that be if "people don't live to be 150?" followed by his insisting, "You're old, and I'm ancient." When he remarks that when his time comes up, he wants his life ended, his wife responds with, "Your fascination with dying is beginning to frazzle my good humor."

The film's central drama revolves around repairing Norman's troubled relationship with his fictional and real daughter, Chelsea Thayer Wayne (Jane Fonda). Chelsea arrives for what her dad calls his "last birthday party," with her suitor, Bill Ray (Dabney Coleman), and his thirteen-year-old son, Billy (Doug McKeon). Initially the generational problem persists in painful testiness. Over time, after Chelsea and Bill go away on a monthlong trip, the relationship between Norman and Billy provides the bridge over which familial reconciliation becomes palpable. They learn to respect each other, bonding while fishing, doing chores, and facing challenges. "He's like an old lion," Ethel remarks to Billy, "who has to remind himself that he can still roar," and "he's just trying to find his way, just like you." Togetherness reaches its culminating point when their boat crashes at Purgatory Point, following which they help each other survive before Ethel and a friend rescue them. The bonding that Norman and Billy experience soon helps foster the reconciliation between father and daughter, as she proves herself as a diver—a skill Norman had earlier mastered and Billy had recently revealed. At the end, Norman, having recovered from a heart attack, can acknowledge both the satisfaction in his new relationship with his daughter and the pleasures of his continuing one with his wife, underscoring the importance in old age of family commitments.

Similar themes emerge in *In Her Shoes* (2005), in this case where both intergenerational and intragenerational dynamics are especially prominent. The film, which earned reasonable financial and critical responses, features not retirement on an idyllic pond but with scenes of stereotypical aspects of a Continuing Care Retirement Community, especially a high-end one. Like so many others of its ilk, this one is complete with lavish apartments and grounds; residents experiencing a wide range abilities and disabilities; two of the three usual levels, independent living and assisted living; the prominence of an abundant number of cliquish women; discussions of grandchildren; budding romantic relationships between some women and the relatively rare able and willing men; the caring caregivers; and the commonly hidden presence of death, financial difficulties, and illness.[10]

The narratives, in which varieties of women play prominent roles, with men in generally minor or supporting ones, revolve around a plethora of family relationships compromised, as was true in *On Golden Pond*, by poisoned histories. Between two sisters who seem to share little other than a common shoe size—Maggie Feller (Cameron Diaz), a reckless, flirtatious woman who cannot hold a job, and her sister, Rose Feller (Toni Collette), who leaves hers as a lawyer to become a professional dog walker when she discovers that her sister had a fling with Jim Danvers (Richard Burgi), her coworker. Their mother, Caroline, committed suicide because their father, Michael (Ken Howard), had threatened to put her in a mental institution; he then married Sydelle (Candice Azzara), who joins Jews for Jesus, further offending many of those who are committed to Judaism. The sisters' dad, Rose learns when she is trying to steal money from her father, had prevented his daughters from getting birthday cards from their widowed grandmother Ella Hirsch (Shirley MacLaine), who is living in a Florida retirement community.

Ella and her fellow residents in the CCRC play crucial roles on the road to intergenerational reconciliation, which skips over the evil stepmother. It all begins when Maggie, in order to meet her grandmother, moves in with her at her retirement community and asks her for a loan so she can go to New York and become an actor. Ella instead promises to match dollar for dollar any money Maggie earns in her job taking care of residents in assisted living. There she meets a retired English professor (Norman Lloyd). Blind, he asks her to read poems to him, and as a result, we learn that she is dyslexic. Empathetic teacher that he is, the professor helps her overcome what has so far hobbled her, and as a result, she blossoms. When Lloyd helps Maggie tease out a poem about love and loss, we see (and she realizes) that she is quite intelligent. "A-plus, smart girl," the professor says. In addition, following an effort to help an elderly woman, Maggie develops a successful career as personal shopper for residents, with Ella helping her with business arrangements.

Ella also plays a crucial role when, in an attempt at sororal reconciliation, she invites Rose to where she and Maggie live in Florida—an "old folks' home," Maggie calls it; no, Rose responds, a place "for active seniors." In this and other crucial endeavors, including reconciling Rose with her lover, Simon Stein (Mark Feuerstein), a chorus of grannies cajole and conspire to bring people together. The final scene, involving the wedding of Rose and Simon, evokes the theme of familial reconciliation—except for the stepmother, who, at a wedding marked by many references to Judaism and Jewish culture, refuses to follow her husband, who loads his plate with food. In two acts of reconciliation, Michael apologizes to Ella for having kept generations apart and walks Rose down the aisle. Rose marries Simon while wearing Ella's shoes from 1952, a reference to the conflicted role footwear has played earlier in the relationships between Maggie and Rose. More centrally, Maggie, emboldened by how the professor empowered her and moved by the occasion, reads a poem by E. E. Cummings, "i carry your heart with me," also from 1952. Passionately celebrating many unions (between sisters, a newly married couple, and across generations), Maggie's gift moves her sister to tears.

The greatly influential and multiply talented media mogul Tyler Perry broke the mold of on-screen retirement offerings. His TV series *Assisted Living*, broadcast on BET in more than eighty episodes since 2020, follows the drama of a multigenerational African American family's involvement in a retirement home. It tells the story of Jeremy (Na'im Lynn), who, having lost his job, returns to Georgia with his family to assist his grandfather Vinny (J. Anthony Brown), who has purchased a large and decrepit home for the aged. When their efforts stumble, Cora (Tamela Mann) and Mr. Brown (David Mann) arrive and offer both investment funds and business skills, along with their three children, Sandra (Tayler Buck), Phillip (Alex Henderson), and Leah (Courtney Nichole).

Perry also wrote, produced, directed, and acted in a play that takes place in a retirement home, *Madea Gets a Job*. Performed onstage in 2012, it was filmed in Atlanta in June of that year and is now available as a 2013 movie. The action takes place at Easy Rest Retirement Home, a modest, thirty-bed facility, "where better living is an option." It is not at all like the large and fancily lavish and amply staffed places portrayed in other films. With staffing in short supply, the administrators decide to rely on someone required to do community service as part of their sentencing, despite expressing reservation about having a "criminal" in their midst. Early on, Mabel answers the facility's phone, as she calls

East Rest Retirement Home a place "where the people are dying like hell to get out of." That turns out to be Madea, played as Mabel by Perry in drag. The media and popular culture scholar TreaAndrea M. Russworm forgives Perry for portrayals where he "dons a dress and fat suit and masquerades as his signature Black female matriarch, Madea."[11] Or, as another media studies scholar, Miriam J. Petty, observes, Perry offers "deployments of Madea that are sheer play, punning, delight in excess, clowning, riffing."[12] "Loud, opinionated, and unapologetic about her behavior," writes another media scholar, Eric Pierson, "Madea can all too easily be viewed as a stereotype."[13] What strikes me, as an outsider to the world Perry has created and how scholars more knowledgeable than I respond, is the contrast between the often ambivalent scholarly criticism of Perry's work, especially of his portrayal of African American women, and the roaring laughter offered by members of the audience of the filmed version of *Madea Gets a Job*, who I assume are mostly African American and responding with appreciative expressions of recognition.

The problematic situations that Mabel encounters and eventually solves are many—broken hearts and broken relationships, mainly tensions between parents and children. Parents resent that their children have dumped them in a retirement home and then rarely come to visit. Or as Hattie May (played by the wonderfully talented Patrice Lovely) says, her sister "just dropped [her] off": "Dropped me off as if I was nobody."

One subplot commands our attention, the relationship between the community's head, Carla Montgomery (Cheryl Pepsii Riley), and one of the employees she supervises, Allen Murphy (Tony Grant). Early on, Mabel tries to convince Allen, who wants to engage Carla romantically, to give up his Afro wig that, in an effort to make himself more attractive to women, he uses to hide the fact that he is bald. Soon after, Mabel encourages Carla, jilted by a married man she thought was the one for her, to abandon her New Age spiritual journey and return to her Christian church. "God doesn't hook you up with someone who's already hooked up," Mabel tells Carla. Using her commanding skills as a fast-talking adviser, to whom the audience responds with roaring appreciation, Mabel brings Carla and Allen (now with his bald head fully apparent) together by invoking God, Jesus, the church, and genuine relationships—what Russworm characterizes as one of Perry's/Madea's "conservative Christian diatribes."[14] At other moments, Mabel relies on traditional wisdom in her advice to parents, urging them not to let their children rule and to avoid playing favorites and emphasizing the importance of responsibility and learning by experience. "Do not take care of them from cradle to grave," she advises, "but once out of the cradle, let them learn how they will get to the grave."[15] Despite all the differences—with regard to social class, race, and values—*Madea Gets a Job* resembles the other retirement community films in its emphasis on reconciliation, especially in families across generational lines.

Gran Torino (2008) and *A Man Called Otto* (2022) exemplify the theme of reconciliation, albeit across ethnic and in some ways nonfamilial generational ones.[16] The earlier of the two films, which earned tremendous financial rewards and reasonably good critical ones, features yet another curmudgeon of an old man, in this case Clint Eastwood (who also produced and directed the film) as Walt Kowalski. The opening captures Walt, a retired Ford factory worker, at his wife's funeral in a Roman Catholic church, followed by his returning to his home in a neighborhood where Hmong families have replaced working-class white ones. His next-door neighbors are members of the Van Lor family. Early on, Sue Lor (Ahney Her) asks Walt what will happen to the 1972 Gran Torino he has lovingly cared for, a symbol of a bygone era of the United States' once proud but now troubled auto industry. Soon after, her younger brother, Thao Vang Lor (Bee Vang), as part of his unsuccessful initiation into a gang, attempts to steal Walt's prized possession.

Tensions, alienation, and violence suffuse the story. Living alone with his aging Labrador, Walt initially rebuffs the effort of Father Janovich (Christopher Carley), who attempts to fulfill Walt's late wife's wish that the priest console the widowed man. Walt, alienated from his family, suspects that his son covets his Gran Torino and laments that his son is making more money selling Japanese cars that Walt did making them as a union worker in a Ford factory. His son suggests that his father would be better off living in a retirement community than in a problematic neighborhood. Relocated, he would be among folks like him in a place that is "like top-notch resorts," where "they take care of everything." Walt spews racists epithets that I suspect no more recent Hollywood film would deploy. In one of many examples, early in the film, he calls his Hmong neighbors "damned barbarians." At the same time, as producer and director, Eastwood does his best to explore and honor Hmong culture, its communitarian commitments and religious traditions. Yet gangs freely roam the streets. Mexican ones conflict with those from the Hmong community. Members of the Hmong gang-rape Sue Lor, and his compatriots harass and threaten her brother. Walt counterattacks using the guns and skills he developed as a US soldier in the Korean War.

About a quarter of the way through the film, the shift from alienation to reconciliation begins. As would be true in *A Man Called Otto*, the delivery of food from another culture begins the process, in this case when members of the neighboring Hmong family leave food on the steps of Walt's home. Several times, Walt saves Thao Van Lor from attacking gangs. Sue Lor reminds her neighbor that the Hmong fought on the US side in Vietnam. She then invites her neighbor to her home on his birthday. While there, though he calls his hosts "fish heads," he realizes that the shaman, unlike the priest, understands the unhappiness he is facing with the loss of his beloved wife. As Otto will do in a later movie, Walt uses his handyman skills to fix up neighborhood homes, including that of the Lor. Above all, as was true in *On Golden Pond*, it is the relationship of members of the older and younger generations—Walt and Thao Van—that occupies the central position in the coming together of household and cultural traditions. Walt urges Thao Van to "man up" and be "an American," something that apparently involves the deployment of racist epithets. Yet Walt backs up his suggestions with advice about love and work—and the use of his Gran Torino. And as Walt's health problems emerge, he garners care from an Asian American doctor and from Thao Van.

Then the story and its accompanying violence intensify. Members of the Hmong gang attack Walt's home and members of his neighboring family. If Thao Van wants Walt to violently attack the Hmong gang, his mentor has a different idea. Regretting that he killed a North Korean soldier even though he was ready to surrender, in an effort to protect the Lor family, he carefully plans to trap gang members into violence that ends with Walt's death and their arrest by the police. The camera captures Walt lying, Christ-like, on the ground. Before that happens, he reconciles with the priest, as his wife had wanted him to.

A Man Called Otto (2022), which earned reasonably good responses at the box office and from critics, has striking similarities with *Gran Torino*. A grumpy old man lives in a neighborhood that was once mostly a white, working-class one but is now changing with the arrival of immigrants (Mexican, in this case). He has recently retired from a job in a declining industry (steel versus automobiles). Evocative memories of what his late wife wanted him to do help prevent him from total despair, even as, like Walt, he faces medical conditions that will eventually end his life. What sustains both of them are intensifying and reciprocal relationships with people in the neighborhood, including in both cases immigrants who befriend them and boys emerging into adulthood. Their growing commitment to help others, neighbors especially, in practical ways also proves to be crucial in the process of reconciliation.

Incidents early on in *A Man Called Otto* set the stage for the ensuing drama. At the very beginning, in a scene that reveals the protagonist's anger and grumpiness, Otto (Tom Hanks) is buying rope at a hardware store so he can hang himself, foreshadowing one of several failed suicide attempts. Soon after, a scene captures him at a retirement party, where he complains at how badly he has been treated, before someone says, "We all had to adjust after the merger," which led to a severance package and the termination of Otto's employment at age sixty-three. After witnessing the cutting through his face pictured on a cake at the bottom of which is written, "Have Fun!" Otto departs angrily. What ensues are reminders that he represents an older America. Otto wears suits and drives a Chevy with a stick shift. Unable to handle social media, he refers to a "dying America," where "nothing works anymore."

Yet what slowly emerges is evidence of his practicality, compassion, and neighborliness. Three relationships prove critical. Across the street lives Marisol (Mariana Treviño), a woman of Mexican descent whose friendly gestures he initially rebuffs, before he eventually reciprocates in practical Mr. Fixit and transforming ways. Then there is a young man, Malcolm (Mack Bayda), who angers Otto for throwing unwanted advertising circulars into his yard. Eventually Otto mentors Malcolm, having learned that as a schoolteacher, his late wife supported Malcolm when he transitioned to becoming a trans man. Among other acts of gracious kindness is Otto's protecting Reuben (Peter Lawson Jones), his African American friend who suffers from Parkinson's, from a conspiracy by an estranged son and avaricious real estate operatives to force Reuben into a nursing home.

On Golden Pond and *In Her Shoes* highlight coming together within families. In harmony and contrast, *Gran Torino* and *A Man Called Otto* explore reaching out, within neighborhoods, across lines that are both ethnic and generational. Nothing illustrates this better than how both films end with news that Walt and Otto have left the bulk of their estates to those who had reached out to them. Walt gives Tao Van the Silver Star awarded him in Korea and his Gran Torino, on the condition that he keep it in pristine shape; perhaps his beloved Labrador to the Van family; and his home to the Roman Catholic parish. Otto bequeaths to Marisol and her husband the crib he lovingly built when his wife was pregnant, a pregnancy that resulted in a stillbirth and her being disabled. He also leaves them not only his house (which he implores them not to sell to "those real estate bastards"), his savings, and a brand-new truck but also a cat that he had reluctantly cared for. He leaves a car to Malcolm. We learn that Otto has died from a cardiac condition because "his heart, it's too big."

I end this chapter with *Nomadland* (2020), a film that works in parallel ways to Teresa Ghilarducci's how-to book *How to Retire with Enough Money and How to Know What Is Enough* (2015). They both depart from and challenge the often all-too-easy emphasis on the pleasures of or liberation of retirement by using a progressive politics to underscore a more perilous situation. *Nomadland*, like many retirement films, appeared in print before it did on-screen. Yet if with *Dodsworth* there were relatively few major changes from a 1929 novel to a 1936 movie, with *Nomadland* the road to commercial success and three Academy Awards reveals significant differences. They were so significant that Jessica Bruder, who authored the book on which the film was based, on her website uses the word "eponymous" (as in self-named) to describe the book's relationship to film.[17] Her work began with three and a half years of immersive and investigative journalism, the results of which first appeared in her August 2008 cover-story article, "The End of Retirement: When You Can't Afford to Stop Working," in *Harper's Magazine*.[18] Significantly more than was true with the film, this original article and the subsequent book focused on mostly retired nomads (aka "workampers") who labored in many places but especially under dangerous and exacting conditions in Amazon's warehouses under its CamperForce program. Their positions were precarious largely because of the 2008 financial crisis and, over the longer term, stagnant incomes and inadequate pensions and Social Security payments.[19]

"From a distance, many of them could be mistaken for carefree retired RVers," Bruder writes at the outset of *Nomadland*. "In mind-set and appearance, they are largely middle class." As she wrote with the Great Recession very much in mind, Bruder paid attention to abundant data on the economic forces that, for increasing numbers of Americans, meant "the dream of a middle-class life has grown from difficult to impossible." What drove her book were stories of Americans, many of them of retirement age, unable to survive on Social Security because pensions and savings have largely disappeared. Again and again, we encounter people who had once lived middle-class lives provided by apparently secure salaried jobs. Now, she writes, there are so many who live in campers and wander around the nation seeking short-term jobs. "Many said they were 'retired,'" she notes, "even if they anticipated working well into their seventies or eighties." She had long "assumed that most RVers were retirees tootling idly around America, sightseeing and enjoying the relaxation they'd earned after decades of employment." Some are, she admits, but most "were preoccupied with 'work hardening,' an acclimation period of half-day shifts." One couple, the husband an accountant and the wife an interior decorator, she reports, "used to think they would retire to live aboard a sailboat," funded by home equity, but the 2008 real estate crash abruptly ended that dream.[20]

The book's central figure is Linda May, a sixty-four-year-old woman who drove around in her "Squeeze Inn," looking for employment, work that paid little and demanded much in pain and endurance. Like others, Bruder writes, she was "trying to escape an economic paradox: the collision of rising rents and flat wages, . . . with no way to better their lot for the long term and no promise of ever being able to retire." Social Security brought in $525 per month, but when she turned sixty-five, the Medicare deduction would reduce that to $424. She "wondered, not for the first time, how anybody could afford to grow old. Of the many jobs she'd held in her life," Bruder observes, "none had brought even a modicum of lasting financial stability." As Linda acknowledged, she "never managed to get [her]self a pension."[21] Her dream was to build an Earthship—off the grid, made of recycled material, and on inexpensive land.

Bruder's book has two endings. The penultimate one takes place when she is back in Brooklyn. Pondering the nation's future, she wonders, "When do impossible choices start to tear people—a society—

apart?" and "How many people will get crushed by the system?" Then, in an apparently optimistic note, she shifts back to Linda, who is visiting the land where work has begun in preparation for the landing of her Earthship. "Soon the job is done," Bruder reports at the book's ending. "When the excavator departs, Linda walks into the flat, blank space it left behind. This land is ready for her now—one perfect acre, something to build on."[22]

The film appeared three years later than the book. The book's message was how political and economic forces catapulted many Americans (including those who once occupied positions squarely in the middle class) into precarious situations. In contrast, the film is only sporadically and explicitly political, opting as it does for an emphasis on existential crises around issues of grief, anxiety, and relationships. It features Fern (Frances McDormand), who has recently lost her home and job when the US Gypsum mine closed in Empire, Nevada, and, earlier, her husband to cancer. In the book, Bruder describes Empire as "a throwback to the much romanticized heyday of American manufacturing, when factory jobs offered workers a sure footing in the middle class and the chance to raise a family without fear of displacement." It was a place, "like a town suspended in the 1950s, as if the postwar boom had never ended," where cheap rents in a company town and good wages "meant employees could typically cover a month's rent with a day or two of work."[23] On-screen, Empire evokes more personal issues of remembering and mourning.

We follow Fern on the road to so many places, not only wistfully to Empire but also to RV parks where temporary workers gather; to where she gets a job, including in an Amazon warehouse; a national park's campground; Wall Drug in South Dakota; a sugar beet processing facility; the annual Rubber Tramp Rendezvous in Quartzsite, Arizona, which attracts tens of thousands of campers, not all of them Nomads; the houses where her sister and the family of a friend live comfortably; and near the end, back to Empire. In between, much of the footage covers her traveling in her beloved van, named *Vanguard* (not homeless but houseless, she remarks), along roads in the American West. Throughout, she experiences the pleasures of nature, community, friendship, and family. Yet each of them turns out to be problematic. Nature is majestic but also barren, even forbidding. The encampments offer practical self-sufficiency advice and supportive places to live—but for her, only short-lived. Fern benefits from at least three friendships, each of them temporary. One is the book's central figure, Linda May, playing herself, who dreams of settling down on an Earthship she will build in the desert. Then there is Charlene Swankie, also playing herself, who goes off to Alaska after she is given less than a year to live because cancer has spread to her brain. Fern's most sustained relationship is with Dave (David Strathairn), though they never move beyond mutually supportive friendship. As Caitlin Flanagan describes it, perhaps too bleakly, "They have been freed from the sexual energies that define so much of a younger woman's life, long past the age when male sexual energy is a force demanding constant negotiation."[24] Finally, there are two families that offer Fern a settled, bourgeois life: those of her sister and Dave's son. Ultimately, Fern chooses independence over family or community.

Although as a film, *Nomadland* is not centrally about retirement, it nonetheless focuses on what people in the US face when they reach a once normal retirement age, not only illness and death but also the political and economic forces that shape the lives of older people living on the margin. At several points, the political economy of retirement garners attention, highlighting the nation's failed systems of employment, pensions, and Social Security. Work for Amazon in problematically named fulfillment centers highlights the problems with increasing reliance on temp jobs in the service sector. The closure of US Gypsum reminds us of the consequences of the end of union work in mining and manufacturing. When someone in the human resources office at US Gypsum suggests that Fern think of early retirement, she responds by saying, "I don't think I can get by on the benefits." Similarly, Swankie mentions the tough impact of the 2008 economic crisis. She is getting close to sixty-two, she remarks, and Social Security will provide $550 a month, even though she had worked since she was twelve.

These issues come to a head at least twice. One is when Fern visits Dave, who has settled into a secure and comfortable life in the ample home of his son's family. Though Fern enjoys a bounteous dinner reminiscent of a Norman Rockwell repast, a "feast of a family," someone calls it, and the embracing family invites her to stay in their guest house, without saying good-bye, she is on the road again. Fern's rejection of a parallel offer occurs more pointedly when she visits the home where her sister Dot lives. Talk around a BBQ by men in their family turns to the celebration of the benefits of rapacious investing in real estate, something we know was at the heart of the 2008 financial crisis. Fern responds by making clear her principled opposition to persuading people to buy houses they cannot afford, as they rely on using life savings and going into debt. George, a member of her sister's world, responds, "We're not all in a position to chuck everything and hit the road." Dot struggles to place her sister's choices in more favorable light. "What the Nomads are doing," she insists in a way that rings hollow to Fern, is not that different from what pioneers did. Fern is part of an American tradition, she claims. Yet Dot recognizes the virtue of what Fern has done. She knows that her sister cannot opt for the settled and comfortable life by accepting a place in her family's home: "We're not as interesting as the people you meet out there. . . . It's always out there that's more interesting"—interesting maybe but quite imperfect.

Bob Wells, playing himself as a sixty-five-year-old prophet with a Santa Claus beard, offers the most extensive political vision. His father died soon after he retired from a union job at an Alaskan supermarket. Working in the same store, "Bob didn't want his father's fate, but there he was," reported the journalist Stevie Trujillo soon after the film appeared. "As days became decades, he went to a job he hated, worked with people he didn't like, to buy things he didn't want. By his own telling, he was the living embodiment of Thoreau's 'quiet desperation.' He knew he wasn't happy, but it never occurred to him to live differently," until it did.[25]

We hear Fern listening to Wells say, "We not only accept the tyranny of the dollar, the tyranny of the marketplace; we embrace it." He warns, "The *Titanic* is sinking," and "so my goal is to get the lifeboats out and get as many people into the lifeboats as I can." For him and others, the Rubber Tramp Rendezvous is the best lifeboat. "If society was throwing us away and sending us, as the workhorse, out to the pasture, we workhorses had to gather together and take care of each other." At one point, Wells links his analysis to the problematics of retirement. He talks of a guy who worked for corporate America for decades and just before he was ready to retire, human resources notifies him of how precarious his continued employment is. He died ten days later, never able to fulfill dreams of shifting from working for a large organization to enjoying life on his sailboat.

As a film, *Nomad* is a compelling and moving exploration of coming to terms with life's choices in a precarious world and, for our purposes, with the contemporary meaning of the American dream, including in retirement. Relying frequently on a documentary style, it offers appreciative pictures of the natural world and of supportive families, friends, and communities. Although Wells offers the Rubber Tramp Rendezvous as a utopian possibility, the narrative of Fern's life emphasizes the loneliness of the long-distance Nomad.[26] In contrast to so many other films that feature freedom on the road, intense and sustaining connections with friends and family, and even the pleasures retirement brings, here is a story of living in economic wastelands that have upended the lives of people who might have looked forward to something else.

* * *

Films about retirement paint multifaceted and often complicated pictures about retirement and aging in the US, from *Dodsworth* in 1936 to multiple films in the early twenty-first century. With them, the shift is from retirement alone or with family and friends to a plain and financially strapped religious institution to fancy CCRCs with names like Calm Gardens and Palm Sunshine and to struggles in temporary communities on the road. Markers of social class profoundly shape choices, with the outlier *Nomadland* providing a relatively rare example of the choices people make if they do not have well-funded pensions, IRAs, and 401(k)s. And were movies proof of reality, we would conclude that African Americans are beginning to earn their place in upper-middle-class communities, with rare hints of the presence of Asian Americans or Latinos as occupants or employees. Over time, films depict a shift from conditions of retirement as a manly project to something more akin to gender equality, seen in the portrayal of two aging women in the 2015 series *Grace and Frankie*. Discussion of heterosexual relationships dominate more than the presence of LGBTQ folks. Films highlight avoidance of or liberations from the confines of residential communities, with independent living and sustained commitments to meaningful work as alternatives. Despite the frequent references to aging, illness, and death, there is some evidence of increased hope about the prospects of aging in retirement, prospects that include redemption, self-discovery, as well as intergenerational reconciliation. Strikingly, in a world torn by racism as well as striking differences in how socioeconomic groups, nations, and ethnic groups experience aging, so many films deploy fantasies of how we can all get along together. Indeed, with the notable exception of *Nomadland*, the films underscore that, seeking sure bets, Hollywood studios reveal their commitments to happy endings and fulfill moviegoers' hunger for adventure, reconciliation, self-understanding, purpose, and happiness in retirement and a happy ending to life itself, even if life is more complicated and death is inevitable. Above all, it is reconciliation on many levels and in many types, which starts out strong and gathers dominance, that provides optimism about the present and future.

Coda

Historians are better at describing and analyzing the past than predicting the future. Where things now stand provides only imperfect guidance of where they will be in the future. Yet, here goes, because what are the paths forward is a serious issue for tens of millions of aging and aged Americans, as well as their younger friends and family members.

Boomers, born between 1946 and 1964, will continue to shape the experiences of retirement for several decades to come. Some of the oldest Gen Xers, born around 1965, have already begun to retire. The number of Gen Xers is somewhat smaller than boomers, which has implications for the labor market. And they are probably more tech savvy, surely more ethnically diverse, and more likely to have achieved work–life balance. The transformative events of the late 1960s and early 1970s—the civil rights movement, the sexual revolution, the women's movement, and the war in Vietnam—influenced boomers more than Gen Xers, albeit how this shapes the lives of the elderly is far from clear. What is clearer is the impact of macroeconomic forces and changes in public policy. Having entered the work force later than boomers, members of the next generations have benefited less from the increasing values in the housing and stock markets—factors that, along with the shift from defined benefit to defined contributions retirement plans—will probably make their financial situations in retirement less favorable. Ditto uncertainties of the funding of Social Security, Medicare, Medicaid, and relevant initiatives in the sciences and public policies that shape the lives of elders.

In contrast, those who enter the ranks of senior citizens and retirement later than their predecessors are more likely to benefit from medical advances. "The decline of coronary heart disease mortality in the United States and Western Europe is one of the great accomplishments of modern public health and medicine," note the authors of a 2013 paper. "In the United States, the epidemic peaked in the mid-1960s and has now fallen 60% from its zenith."[1] With cancer, the other leading cause of death, the historical trends are significant but less stunning. In 1950, the rate of death from cancer was 193.9 per 100,000, a figure that increased in the next forty years to 216. Since then, due to people smoking less and medical advances in detection and treatment of diseases, the figure has fallen significantly, to 142 in 2022.[2] Thus, those who become elderly later benefit—in both health span and life span—from the advances in detecting and treating heart disease and cancer. Gen Xers and those born even later are also likely to benefit from medical advances for Alzheimer's. First discovered in 1906, the seventh leading cause of death in the US (120,000 annually, compared with 703,000 from heart disease) and the most common kind of dementia, it currently afflicts more than six million Americans. Progress in developing treatments has been slow, and those that are now available are costly, have adverse side effects, and promise only limited help. Nonetheless, those who have not yet achieved the status as elders may well benefit from medical advances that will diminish the impact of Alzheimer's.

I wish I could express optimism about a future in which fewer older Americans suffer from the effects of inequalities of wealth and income. However, given socioeconomic and political forces now in play, it is hard to be hopeful, despite those who envision successful aging. The AARP will continue to thrive by offering its members marketplace perks, even as a robust, inclusive, and sustained political movement by and on behalf of elders does not appear on the horizon. Meaningful gains will be possible if caregivers and care receivers, disproportionately female, come to see their shared obligations. The lack of major advances in public policy affecting elders since the 1970s is likely to persist or worsen. It is possible that more citizens in their seventies and beyond will have to make do by continuing to work. The continuing reversal of free trade may well adversely affect the elderly as consumers. In a similar vein, the decreasing presence of immigrant caregivers, most of them women, is likely to make the lives of elders more difficult. As increasing numbers of people survive into their eighties and beyond, the weakness of provisions of long-term care will become tragically apparent. Long-term and deeply embedded forces will, I assume, continue to make the lives of many African Americans, Latinos, and poor whites not only shorter but also marked by struggles to live decent and safe lives. For these groups, and many others, financial difficulties (especially inadequate funding of retirement, limited opportunities for affordable housing, challenges in obtaining quality health care) and isolation will continue to adversely affect the lives of many among the elderly. Much the same is true of the growing and probably irreversible impact of climate change. Global warming will shape where and how people can live in retirement and continue to threaten their sense of safety—and do so more significantly for those who are less fortunately situated. Intergenerational arrangements, long decreasing in popularity, are more ecological than having seniors relying on cars and living by themselves. As the historian James Chappel has written, Ai-Jen Poo's Caring Across Generations knows "that genuine resolutions to the intertwined problems of aging, climate change, and care will require federal reaction," which, alas, I do not see on the horizon.[3]

In contrast, perhaps those who embrace the promise of longevity—not just a longer life span but a more robust health span—will have their vision validated, with millions living longer and heathier lives. Skeptical me, I foresee what may turn out to be more realistic possibilities. Maybe some of the progress made in the lives of African American and disabled seniors will continue. Advances in technologies, including media ones, may enhance the lives of those who are fortunate enough to live long lives healthily. The same may be true of improvements in intergenerational relationships, both familial and contingent, as well as stronger and more effective activist organizations that act with and for the elderly. The future, dear reader, who is younger than I am, is yours.

ACKNOWLEDGMENTS

Retired from teaching college students but not from researching and writing books, I benefited greatly from the engagement of colleagues, family members, and friends, some whom I have known for decades, some who responded to questions from a stranger, and two whose identities remain unknown—and all of them younger, I assume, that this aging historian.

I have benefited from the reactions of those who read what I had written. In response to "A Short History of Longevity," Dan Jacobs prodded me to think ever more subtly about the work of Erik H. Erikson and more generally about how authors have written about the stages of life. Susan Matt also looked at a version of this chapter with her usual acuity and interest. John Demos offered a probing and richly suggestive reading of this chapter and more generally remained a vitally important interlocutor on a range of issues that my work raised. When she read early versions of the introduction and the chapter on how-to books, Cori Field responded with the insights and knowledge she has developed in her own pathbreaking work on the history of aging. Steve Katz exemplified the kindness of strangers when he followed up on my initial inquiry by engaging in sustained, probing, and immensely helpful email exchanges that helped me expand and deepen my understanding about the field of aging studies. Jay Olshansky shared his wisdom and work in ways that deepened my knowledge of discussions of fountains of youthful aging. Lynn Dumenil, with her usual engagement and editorial skills, read a number of chapters in ways that helped improve them greatly. William Graebner responded to the entire manuscript—and as a pioneer in the field of the history of retirement, he did so with precision, command of the field, and extensive suggestions about how to clarify, extend, and sharpen my findings. Gary Cross and Flannery Burke, who read the entire manuscript, made wonderfully useful suggestions on how to improve it.

So many friends, family members, and colleagues, I believe all of them younger than I am, offered me leads and suggestions that helped me move the project along in ways that strengthened and clarified what I was writing. The long list includes Carl Abbott, David Abel, Don Brenneis, Flannery Burke, Alan Castel, Kathleen Dalton, Florri Darwin, Micaela di Leonardo, Susan Douglas, Lynn Dumenil, Lucie Fielding, Teresa Ghilarducci, Carole K. Holahan, David Hollinger, Ben Horowitz, Sarah Horowitz, Leon Kass, Jim Kovac, Susan Lewinnek, Fred Lynch, Justine McGovern, Marla Miller, Alicia Munnell, Joe Newhouse, Meg Newhouse, Nell Painter, Miriam Petty, Carol Rigolot, Tony Rotundo, Marc Schulz, Carl Smith, Jane Smith, Philippe Sommer, Bruce Vladeck, Anna Whitcomb, Steve Whitfield, Alona Wilson, and Abby Wolf.

In a series of sustained, deeply moving conversations, Arthur Barsky and John Demos served as essential interlocutors as we engaged in extensive and wonderfully helpful discussions about the science, personal experiences, and cultures of aging.

Absolutely essential to my work are the librarians and collections of the Harvard College Library; the Pasadena, California, Public Library; and the Cambridge Public Library, which included books from the regional Minuteman Library Network.

Even in retirement, Smith College continues to support my scholarly work.

More or less by happenstance, courtesy of Gary Cross, this book found a resting place at NYU Press and the transformative stewardship of Clara Platter. From the very first, she supported the book's publication and from then on was always there with encouragement, wisdom, and skillful editorial work. She commissioned two readings—both of which were extraordinarily knowledgeable and supportive. Yet they appropriately pressed me to deepen my engagement with scholarship that I already knew of and now encountered for the first time. At NYU Press, others helped, including Brianna Jean, Andrew Katz, and Valerie Zaborski.

Finally, I am grateful to the love of my life, Helen L. Horowitz. First, last, and always.

PREFACE

1 Daniel Horowitz, *Betty Friedan and the Making of "The Feminine Mystique": The American Left, the Cold War, and Modern Feminism* (University of Massachusetts Press, 1988), 236–37.

2 Jerry Svendsen quoted in Judith Ann Trolander, *From Sun Cities to the Villages: A History of Active, Adult, Age-Restricted Communities* (University Press of Florida, 2011), 1.

3 Reader #1 for NYU Press.

4 Reader #2 for NYU Press.

5 Stephen Katz to author, January 29, 2005.

6 Jerrold Hirsch, letter to editor, *New Yorker*, October 30, 2023, 5.

7 Editorial Board, "Can Americans Age Gracefully?," *New York Times*, September 10, 2023.

8 Susan Matt to author, January 15, 2024; John Demos to author, September 10, 2023; John Demos, "Old Age in Early New England," *American Journal of Sociology* 84 (1978): S248.

9 Catherine Porter, "Fight over Retirement in France Is a Question of Identity," *New York Times*, March 7, 2023.

10 Michelle Pannor Silver, *Retirement and Its Discontents: Why We Won't Stop Working, Even If We Can* (Columbia University Press, 2018), 17–18.

INTRODUCTION

1 Mireille Silcoff, "Senior Year: Television Celebrated Older People—but Only for Seeming like Sexy Ones," *New York Times Magazine*, October 29, 2023, 11–14.

2 Silcoff, "Senior Year."

3 David Marchese, "Hadley Vlahos Wants Us to Try to Make Peace with Death, Not to Extend Life," *New York Times Magazine*, October 29, 2023.

4 Corrine T. Field and Nicholas L. Syrett, introduction to *Age in America: The Colonial Era to the Present*, ed. Field and Syrett (New York University Press, 2015), 1.

5 This chronology relies on David Hackett Fischer, *Growing Old in America* (Oxford University Press, 1977). For a somewhat different take, see W. Andrew Achenbaum, *Old Age in the New Land: The American Experience Since 1790* (Johns Hopkins University Press, 1978). Katherine Ann Otis, "Everything Old Is New Again: A Social and Cultural History of Life on the Retirement Frontier,

1950–2000" (PhD diss., University of North Carolina at Chapel Hill, 2008), provides an up-to-date and comprehensive survey of the literature on retirement; in addition, she offers an exceedingly suggestive discussion of life in retirement, one that focuses on Southern Florida and advances our understanding of a number of issues including sexuality, politics from below, intergenerational relations, advice literature, on-the-ground community organizing, and life among Jewish elders.

6 In *This Chair Rocks: A Manifesto Against Ageism* (Celadon, 2016), 10, Ashton Applewhite announces her preference for "olders," as "the only unobjectionable term used to describe older people," a "clear and value neutral" word that "emphasizes that age is a continuum." In *Maggie Kuhn on Aging*, ed. Dieter Hessel (Westminster Press, 1977), 14, Maggie Kuhn notes her preference for "the elders, the experienced ones; we are maturing, growing adults responsible for the survival of our society." Throughout *Golden Years: How Americans Invented and Reinvented Old Age* (Basic Books, 2024), James Chappel charts the changing use of such terms: see, for example, 11 and 178.

7 Daniel R. George and Peter J. Whitehouse's *American Dementia: Brain Health in an Unhealthy Society* (Johns Hopkins University Press, 2021) explores the biological and social dimensions of memory loss.

8 W. Andrew Achenbaum, "Delineating Old Age: From Functional Status to Bureaucratic Criteria," in Field and Syrett, *Age in America*, 301.

9 Teresa Ghilarducci, *How to Retire with Enough Money and How to Know What Is Enough* (Workman 2015), 1–2, 5, 9, 15.

10 Among the scholarship on retirement and longevity on which I have drawn when necessary and to varying degrees are Achenbaum, *Old Age in the New Land*; Achenbaum, "Delineating Old Age"; W. Andrew Achenbaum, *Crossing Frontiers: Gerontology Emerges as a Science* (Cambridge University Press, 1995); Howard P. Chudacoff, *How Old Are You? Age Consciousness in American Culture* (Princeton University Press, 1989); Joseph F. Coughlin, *The Longevity Economy: Unlocking the World's Fastest-Growing, Most Misunderstood Market* (Public Affairs, 2017); John Demos, "Old Age in Early New England," in *Past, Present, and Personal: The Family and the Life Course in American History* (Oxford University Press, 1986), 139–85; Field and Syrett, *Age in America*; Fischer, *Growing Old in America*; William Graebner, *A History of Retirement: The Meaning and Function of an American Institution, 1885–1978* (Yale University Press, 1980); William Graebner, "Age and Retirement: Major Issues in the American Experience," in Field and Syrett, *Age in America*, 187–208; Carole Haber and Brian Gratton, *Old Age and the Search for Security: An American Social History* (Indiana University Press, 1984); Steven Mintz, *The Prime of Life: A History of Modern Adulthood* (Harvard University Press, 2015); David VanTassel and Peter N. Stearns, eds., *Old Age in a Bureaucratic Society: The Elderly, the Experts, and the State in American History* (Greenwood, 1986). Since 1976, *The Handbook of Aging*, which eventually became a series of *Handbooks of Aging*, has served as indispensable introductions to the field.

11 Statista, "Life Expectancy (From Birth) in the United States, from 1860 to 2020," accessed December 13, 2024, www.statista.com.

12 Lauren Medina, Shannon Sabo, and Jonathan Vespa, *Living Longer: Historical and Projected Life Expectancy in the United States, 1960 to 2060* (US Census Bureau, 2020), www.census.gov; Jonathan Rauch, "The Longevity Revolution," *The Atlantic*, January 2025, 86.

13 Graebner, *History of Retirement*, 215.

14 Erin Blakemore, "Poorhouses Were Designed to Punish People for Their Poverty," *History: This Day in History*, January 30, 2018, www.history.com.

15 Robert L. Clark, Lee A. Craig, and Jack W. Wilson, *A History of Public Sector Pensions in the United States* (University of Pennsylvania Press, 2003), 1–5.

16 Brian Gratton, *Urban Elders: Family, Work, and Welfare Among Boston's Aged, 1890–1950* (Temple University Press, 1986), 10, 179.

17 Chappel, *Golden Years*, 3–4.

18 For a chronicle of these political and economic gains, see Chappel, *Golden Years*, especially the introduction and chapters 2, 3, 6, and 9.

19 The following discussion of two paths forward relies on Chappel, *Golden Years*, 21–62. In addition, as I revised, I found especially useful his focus on public policy, sexuality, older Americans who are disabled and queer, women as caregivers and recipients of care, media, and generational dynamics.

20 Mary Frances Berry, *My Face Is Black Is True: Callie House and the Struggle for Ex-Slave Reparations* (Knopf, 2005).

21 Chappel, *Golden Years*, 33–34.

22 Quoted in Chappel, *Golden Years*, 39.

23 Chappel, *Golden Years*, 21, 23, 39, 51. On FDR's connections with the Fraternal Order of Eagles and support for its approach, see Chappel, *Golden Years*, 47. Federal legislation helped drive the poverty rate for people over sixty-five from about 30 percent in the mid-1960s to 10.9 percent in 2022: the statistic comes from Rauch, "Longevity Revolution," 85.

24 Graebner, *History of Retirement*, 230–31, 242–62, 270.

25 John D. Landis and Kirk McClure, "Rethinking Federal Housing Policy," *Journal of the American Planning Association* 76 (2010): 319–48.

26 Theresa Andrasfay and Noreen Goldman, "Reductions in 2020 US Life Expectancy Due to COVID-19 and the Disproportionate Impact on the Black and Latino Populations," *PNAS* 118, no. 5 (2021): e201476118.

27 Andrasfay and Goldman, "Reductions in 2020 US Life Expectancy."

28 Keith R. Knapp, Douglas M. Olson, Katie Smith Sloan, and Mark Parkinson, "The Senior Living Field: Background, History, and Its Current and Future State," in *The Health Services Executive (HSE™): Tools for Leading Long-Term Care and Senior Living Organizations*, ed. Keith R. Knapp and Douglas M. Olson (Springer, 2020), 7.

29 Statista, "Annual Growth of Real GDP in the United States of America from 1930 to 2022," accessed December 13, 2024, www.statista.com.

30 Stephen Katz, "Precarious Life, Human Development and the Life Course: Critical Intersections," in *Precarity and Aging: Understanding Insecurity and Risk in Later Life*, ed. Amanda Grenier, Chris Phillipson, and Richard A. Settersten Jr. (Policy Press, 2020), explores some of the key issues connecting precarity and aging.

31 Reed Abelson and Jordan Rau, "Facing Financial Ruin as Costs Soar for Elder Care," *New York Times*, November 14, 2023.

32 Robert H. Binstock, "From Compassionate Ageism to Intergenerational Conflict?," *Gerontologist* 50 (October 2010): 575–77.

33 Alan Schmadtke, "Average Retirement Savings by Age," InCharge, December 12, 2023, www.incharge.org.

34 Pension Rights Center, "Income of Today's Older Adults," accessed December 13, 2024, https://pensionrights.org. On the change from defined benefit to defined contribution, see Jacob S. Hacker, *The Great Risk Shift: The New Economic Insecurity and the Decline of the American Dream*, rev. ed. (Oxford University Press, 2008), 109–35.

35 Jessica Bruder, "The End of Retirement: When You Can't Afford to Stop Working," *Harper's Magazine*, August 2014.

36 Miriam Jordan, "Retirement Without a Net: The Plight of America's Aging Farmworkers," *New York Times*, December 5, 2023.

37 Goldman Sachs Retirement and Investment Services, *Retirement Survey & Insights Report 2022: Navigating the Financial Vortex* (2022), www.gsam.com.

38 C. Eugene Steurle and Glenn Kramon, "The U.S. Needs Older Americans to Work More and Take Less," *New York Times*, October 28, 2023.

39 Paula Span, "The Income Gap Jeopardizing Retirement for Millions," *New York Times*, January 6, 2024.

40 Editorial Board, "Can Americans Age Gracefully?" See also Bernhard Warner, "Who Wants to Live Forever?," *New York Times*, January 21, 2023. For similar discussions, see "The Wisdom Issue," *Boston Globe*, September 22, 2024.

41 Sarah Lamb, preface to *Successful Aging as a Contemporary Obsession*, ed. Lamb (Rutgers University Press, 2017), xi–xiv (quote on xii); Sarah Lamb, Jessica Robbins-Ruszkowski, and Anna I. Corwin, "Successful Aging as a Twenty-First Century Obsession," in Lamb, *Successful Aging*, 1–23. For an example of a celebration of successful aging, this one by a neuroscientist, see Daniel J. Levitin, *Successful Aging: A Neurologist Explores Power and Potential of Our Lives* (Dutton, 2020).

42 Stephen Katz, *Disciplining Old Age: The Formation of Gerontological Knowledge* (University of Virginia Press, 1996); Meredith Minkler and Carroll L. Estes, eds., *Critical Gerontology: Perspectives from Political and Moral Economy* (Baywood, 1999).

CHAPTER 1. HERE'S HOW TO RETIRE AND LIVE A LONG AND HAPPY LIFE

1 Among the lists I am relying on are Most Recommended Books, "Thirteen Best Retirement Planning Books of All Time," accessed December 6, 2023, www.mostrecommendedbooks.com, which relies on the most systematic method of selection; Good Reads, "Retirement Books," accessed December 6, 2023, www.

goodreads.com; and Retirement Wisdom, "Best Books on Retirement," accessed December 6, 2023, www.retirementwisdom.com. Chappel, *Golden Years*, 220–23, discusses three additional approaches: to elder sexuality, in Dr. Ruth and Paula B. Doress-Worters, *Ourselves, Growing Older: Women Aging with Knowledge and Power* (Simon and Schuster, 1987); to "successful aging," in John W. Rowe, *Successful Aging* (Pantheon, 1998); and to self-care, in James F. Fries and Donald M. Vickery, *Take Care of Yourself: A Consumer's Guide to Medical Care* (Addison-Wesley, 1976). Roger Rosenblatt, *Rules for Aging: A Wry and Witty Guide to Life* (Harcourt, 2000), wonderfully breaks the mold of advice books. For another study of retirement and advice literature, see Katherine Ann Otis, "Everything Old Is New Again: A Social and Cultural History of Life on the Retirement Frontier, 1950–2000" (PhD diss., University of North Carolina at Chapel Hill, 2008).

2 Graebner, "Age and Retirement," 194.

3 Amber Christ and Tracey Gronniger, *Older Women and Poverty: Special Report* (Justice in Aging, 2018), www.justiceinaging.org.

4 Harriet Edleson, *12 Ways to Retire on Less: Planning an Affordable Future* (Rowman and Littlefield, 2021), which in turn relies on the Federal Reserve Board's Survey of Consumer Finances. On delaying retirement, see Alicia Haydock Munnell, *Working Longer: The Solution to the Retirement Income Challenge* (Brookings Institution Press, 2008).

5 Joseph F. Coughlin, "Old Age Is Made Up," *Financial Advisor*, November 1, 2019.

6 Jane Bryant Quinn, *How to Make Your Money Last: The Indispensable Retirement Guide*, 2nd ed. (Simon and Schuster, 2020).

7 Quinn, *Money Last*, xviii, 1, 2, 3, 23, 386.

8 Suze Orman, *The Ultimate Retirement Guide for 50+: Winning Strategies to Make Your Money Last a Lifetime* (Hay House, 2020) 5, 294, 296.

9 Ernie J. Zelinski, *How to Retire Happy, Wild, and Free: Retirement Wisdom That You Won't Get from Your Financial Advisor* (Visions International, 2017), 1, 4, 228.

10 Zelinski, *Retire Happy*, 231.

11 Steve Lopez, *Independence Day: What I Learned About Retirement from Some Who've Done It and Some Who Never Will* (HarperCollins, 2022), relies on a series of stories and interviews about his decision to retire.

12 Fritz Gilbert, *Keys to a Successful Retirement: Staying Happy, Active, and Productive in Your Retirement Years* (Rockridge, 2020), 1–2.

13 Gilbert, *Keys*, 19, 113.

14 Patrice Jenkins, *What Will I Do All Day? Wisdom to Get You Over Retirement and On with Living!* (n.p., 2011), 96.

15 Edleson, *12 Ways to Retire on Less*, back cover of hardback, 6, 28.

16 Chris Hogan, *Retire Inspired: It's Not an Age, It's a Financial Number* (Ramsey, 2016).

17 Ramsey Solutions, "We Get Excited About Mondays," accessed December 6, 2024, www.ramseysolutions.com.

18 Dave Ramsey, *The Total Money Make Over: A Proven Plan for Financial Fitness* (Nelson, 2013), xvii–xviii.

19 Thelma Reese and Barbara M. Fleisher, *The New Senior Man: Exploring New Horizons, New Opportunities* (Rowman and Littlefield, 2017), dust jacket, 2, 5.

20 Anne C. Coon and Judith Ann Feuerherm, *Thriving in Retirement: Lessons from Baby Boomer Women* (Praeger, 2017), 131, 144.

21 Barbara M. Fleisher and Thelma Reese, *The New Senior Woman: Reinventing the Years Beyond Mid-Life* (Rowman and Littlefield, 2013), 1, 9–10, 221.

22 Carol Levine, *Navigating Your Later Years for Dummies* (Wiley, 2018), 254–82 (quote on 255). Mick Peterson, Bill Lyons, Robert Reeves, and Jessay Martin, *The Old Gays' Guide to the Good Life: By the Old Gays of TikTok* (HarperCollins, 2023), 180–87, 203–12, discusses getting older and experiencing the approach of death.

23 Nancy Collamer, *Second-Act Careers: 50+ Ways to Profit from Your Passions During Semi-Retirement* (Ten Speed, 2013), dust jacket, 255.

24 Collamer, *Second-Act Careers*, 2, 188, 250.

25 Teresa Ghilarducci, *Work, Retire, Repeat: The Uncertainty of Retirement in the New Economy* (University of Chicago Press, 2024).

26 Transamerica Institute, *Emerging from the COVID-19 Pandemic: A Compendium About U.S. Workers' Retirement Outlook* (2022), 11, 16, 17, www.transamericainstitute.org.

27 Transamerica Institute, *Emerging from the COVID-19 Pandemic*.

28 Transamerica Institute, *Emerging from the COVID-19 Pandemic*, 290.

29 Transamerica Institute, *Emerging from the COVID-19 Pandemic*, 302–51 (quote on 303). Distinctive African American perspectives on aging may help explain why many remain optimistic despite comparatively less auspicious financial situations. See Frederick C. Knight, *Black Elders: The Meaning of Age in American Slavery and Freedom* (University of Pennsylvania Press, 2024); and Leslie J. Pollard, *Complaint to the Lord: Perspectives on the African American Elderly* (Associated University Presses, 1996).

30 Mitch Anthony, *The New Retirementality: Planning Your Life and Living Your Dreams . . . at Any Age You Want*, 4th ed. (Wiley, 2014), dust jacket, xii.

31 Robin Ryan, *Retirement Reinvention: May Your Next Act Be Your Best Act* (Penguin, 2018), xi.

32 Robin Ryan, home page, accessed December 6, 2024, https://robinryan.com.

33 Ryan, *Retirement Reinvention*, xii.

34 David C. Borchard, with Patricia A. Donohue, *The Joy of Retirement: Finding Happiness, Freedom, and the Life You've Always Wanted* (American Management Association, 2008), v–xi.

35 Kenneth S. Shultz, with Megan Kaye and Mike Annesley, *Happy Retirement: The Psychology of Reinvention* (DK, 2015), 76.

36 Richard N. Bolles and John E. Nelson, *What Color Is Your Parachute? For Retirement: Planning a Prosperous, Healthy, and Happy Future*, 2nd ed. (Ten Speed, 2010), 190–91.

37 See, for example, Rob Berger, *Retire Before Mom and Dad: The Simple Numbers Behind a Lifetime of Financial Freedom* (Glenbrook, 2019), 6.

38 Richard Siegel and Rabbi Laura Geller, *Getting Good at Getting Older* (Behrman House, 2019).

39 Ken Dychtwald and Daniel J. Kadlec, *A New Purpose: Redefining Money, Family, Work, Retirement, and Success* (HarperCollins, 2009), 4.

40 David Ramsey, foreword to Hogan, *Retire Inspired*, xi.

41 Gilbert, *Successful Retirement*, 138.

42 Zelinski, *Retire Happy*, 4.

43 Jeri Sedlar and Rick Miners, *Don't Retire, Rewire! 5 Steps to Fulfilling Work That Fuels Your Passion, Suits Your Personality, and Fills Your Pocket*, 3rd ed. (Penguin Random House, 2018), dust jacket, 235–36, 245.

44 Thelma Reese and B. J. Kittredge, *How Seniors Are Saving the World: Retirement Activism to the Rescue!* (Rowman and Littlefield, 2020), x, xv, 55, 101, 132–33.

45 Pew Research Center, "Working After Retirement: The Gap Between Expectations and Reality," accessed December 6, 2024, www.pewresearch.org.

46 See Chris Farrell, *Purpose and a Paycheck: Finding Meaning, Money, and Happiness in the Second Half of Life* (HarperCollins, 2019).

47 Sedlar and Miners, *Don't Retire*, xiv.

48 Ryan, *Retirement Reinvention*, 7.

49 Hyrum W. Smith, *Purposeful Retirement: How to Bring Happiness and Meaning to Your Retirement* (Mango, 2019), 192.

50 See, for example, Sedlar and Miners, *Don't Retire*, 224–26.

51 Farrell, *Purpose and a Paycheck*, 182.

52 Bolles and Nelson, *What Color Is Your Parachute?*, ix, xii.

53 Customer reviews on *How to Retire Happy, Wild, and Free*, by Ernie J. Zelinski, Amazon, accessed October 4, 2024 (no longer available), www.amazon.com.

54 Paul Higgs and Chris Gilleard, *Rethinking Old Age: Theorising the Fourth Stage* (Palgrave, 2015), vii, viii.

55 Borchard, *Joy of Retirement*, 228–31.

56 Alan D. Castel, *Better with Age: The Psychology of Successful Aging* (Oxford University Press, 2019), is an example of a book by a serious scholar that relies on research but also can be read as an advice book, and a highly optimistic one at that.

57 Michelle Pannor Silver, *Retirement and Its Discontents: Why We Won't Stop Working, Even If We Can* (Columbia University Press, 2018), ix–x, xiii.

58 Silver, *Retirement and Its Discontents*, x, 18–19, 158–59, 191–92.

59 Silver, *Retirement and Its Discontents*, 15–17, 57–58.

60 Ghilarducci, *How to Retire with Enough Money*, 96, 100, 108–110. For the plan, see her *When I'm Sixty-Four: The Plot Against Pensions and the Plan to Save Them* (Princeton University Press, 2017).

CHAPTER 2. A SHORT HISTORY OF LONGEVITY

1 Richard Sandomir, "Louise Levy, Who Was Studied for Her Very Long Life, Is Dead at 112," *New York Times*, July 27, 2023.

2 Lucian Boia, *Forever Young: A Cultural History*, trans. Trista Selous (Reaktion, 2004), offers a worldwide and long history of ideas about longevity, focusing on three strategies: that of traditional religion, which relies on the notion that there is something after life; the idea that though the individual passes, the community endures; and the belief that if it is not possible to promote unending longevity, then at least people might live much longer and healthier lives.

3 At many points, I draw on Lawrence J. Friedman's magisterial *Identity's Architect: A Biography of Erik H. Erikson* (Scribner, 1999). Kathleen Woodward, *Aging and Its Discontents: Freud and Other Fictions* (Indiana University Press, 1991), offers a critique of Freudianism. David Gutmann, *Reclaimed Powers: Men and Women in Later Life* (Basic Books, 1987), provides a rich gender-focused analysis of aging that draws on cross-cultural studies, depth psychology, and sociology.

4 On Erik Erikson's focus on the life cycle, see Friedman, *Identity's Architect*, 215–41. In *Enjoy Old Age: A Program of Self-Management* (Norton, 1983), B. F. Skinner (then seventy-nine) and Margaret E. Vaughan (a much younger psychologist) offered a jaunty discussion of behaviors that represented what the title suggested—from remaining in touch with the past to having a good day.

5 Erik H. Erikson, *Childhood and Society* (1950), 35th anniversary ed. (Norton, 1985), 247–74. The most relevant section of the earlier edition—Erik H. Erikson, *Childhood and Society* (Norton, 1950), 231–33—is not substantially different from the later one, 268–69.

6 For the feminist criticism of Erikson, see Friedman, *Identity's Architect*, 423–26.

7 Erikson, *Childhood and Society* (1985), 268–69. Later in the essay, Erikson briefly focused on "what old age can be," when trust develops "into the most mature *faith* that a person can muster in his cultural setting and historical period." Erikson, *Childhood and Society* (1985), 172.

8 Erik H. Erikson, *Identity: Youth and Crisis* (Norton, 1968), 139–41.

9 Friedman, *Identity's Architect*, 227.

10 Erik H. Erikson "Reflections on Dr. Borg's Life Cycle," *Daedalus* 105 (Spring 1976): 23.

11 Daniel Jacobs, "Imaging Erikson," *American Imago* 82 (Spring 2025): 88.

12 Friedman, *Identity's Architect*, 443.

13 Letters from Erikson to Ellen Katz, October 15, 1976, and to Harry Weinstein, May 25, 1976, quoted in Friedman, *Identity's Architect*, 443–44.

14 Daniel Benveniste to Robert Jay Lifton, July 24, 1991, quoted in Friedman, *Identity's Architect*, 467.

15 Erik H. Erikson, *The Life Cycle Completed: A Review* (Norton, 1982). On these years, see Friedman, *Identity's Architect*, 437–81. Among the other late treatments of these issues is Erikson "Reflections on Dr. Borg's Life Cycle," 1–28.

16 Erikson, *Life Cycle Completed*, 61–64.

17 Erikson, *Life Cycle Completed*, 32–33, 61–66.

18 Erik H. Erikson, Joan M. Erikson, and Helen Q. Kivnick, *Vital Involvement in Old Age* (Norton, 1986). Friedman, *Identity's Architect*, 461–62, makes clear that

Erik contributed little, if anything, to his book, despite his name appearing as an author. The one exception is a section titled "The Life Cycle," 327–33. On Kivnick, see Debra J. Sheets, Michael A. Smyer, and Linda D. Davis, "The Legacy of Helen Q. Kivnick," *The Gerontologist* 61 (April 2021): 397–400.

19 Erikson et al., *Vital Involvement*, 296–99, 302, 310, 314–15.

20 Erikson et al., *Vital Involvement*, 301, 304, 391, 331.

21 Erikson et al., *Vital Involvement*, 334.

22 Erik H. Erikson, *The Life Cycle Completed: Extended Version with New Chapters on the Ninth Stage of Development by Joan M. Erikson* (Norton, 1997), in which the new contributions appear in "Preface to the Extended Version" (1–9) and "The Ninth Stage" (105–29).

23 J. Erikson, "Preface to the Extended Version," 4.

24 J. Erikson, "The Ninth Stage," 105–6, 112–14.

25 J. Erikson, "Old Age and Community," 115–21.

26 J. Erikson, "Gerotranscendence," 124–29.

27 On the impact of World War I, see Carole K. Holahan and Robert B. Sears, in association with Lee J. Cronbach, *The Gifted Group in Later Maturity* (Stanford University Press, 1995), 1.

28 Lewis M. Terman, "Editor's Preface," in *The Early Mental Traits of Three Hundred Geniuses*, by Catharine Morris Cox (Stanford University Press, 1926), v.

29 Cox, *Early Mental Traits*; Holahan and Sears, *Gifted Group in Later Maturity*; Howard S. Friedman and Leslie R. Martin, *The Longevity Project: Surprising Discoveries for Health and Long Life from the Landmark Eight-Decade Study* (Penguin, 2011). For an interview of Friedman and Martin, see Veronique Greenwood, "The Longevity Project: Decades of Data Reveal Pathways to Long Life," *The Atlantic*, March 10, 2011. For evaluations of Terman's work in light of criticism of him for less than fully acceptable scientific methods, to say nothing of a racist and sexist focus on eugenics, see Russell T. Warne, "An Evaluation (and Vindication?) of Lewis Terman: What the Father of Gifted Education Can Teach the 21st Century," *Gifted Child Quarterly* 63 (January 2019): 3–21; Mitchell Leslie, "The Vexing Legacy of Lewis Terman," *Stanford Magazine*, July–August 2020; Joel N. Shurkin, *Terman's Kids: The Groundbreaking Study of How the Gifted Grew Up* (Little, Brown, 1992). On Terman's life, see Henry L. Minton, *Lewis M. Terman: Pioneer in Psychological Testing* (New York University Press, 1988). Shurkin, *Terman's Kids*, does not track the cohort beyond adulthood and into old age.

30 Holahan and Sears, *Gifted Group*, 1, 3. Note that on page 272, the authors say that the group had attained "an average age of 67."

31 Holahan and Sears, *Gifted Group*, 80, 267, 268, 269. For the discussion of retirement, see 64–81 and 113–20, with the quote on 80.

32 Holahan and Sears, *Gifted Group*, 269–70. For their discussion of how gender affected lives and aging, see 272–75.

33 Ernest R. Hilgard and Albert H. Hastorf, foreword to *Gifted Group*, ix; Holahan and Sears, *Gifted Group*, 276.

34 Friedman and Martin, *Longevity Project*, 34, 39, 48.

35 Friedman and Martin, *Longevity Project*, 6, 7, 167–68, 182, 204.

36 Friedman and Martin, *Longevity Project*, 214.

37 Friedman and Martin, *Longevity Project*, 206, 217, 219.

38 Friedman and Martin, *Longevity Project*, 142–44, 206.

39 iResearchNet: Psychology, "Berkeley/Oakland Longitudinal Studies," accessed December 11, 2024, https://psychology.iresearchnet.com.

40 Among the exceptions as articles are C. J. Jones and W. Meredith, "Developmental Paths of Psychological Health from Early Adolescence to Late Adulthood," *Psychology and Aging* 15 (June 2000): 351–60; Paul Wink, Lucia Ciciolla, Michele Dillon, and Allison Tracy, "Religiousness, Spiritual Seeking, and Personality: Findings from a Longitudinal Study," *Journal of Personality* 75 (October 2007): 1051–70, which focuses on late adulthood; and Constance Jones, Norman Livson, and Harvey Peskin, "Longitudinal Hierarchical Linear Modeling Analyses of California Psychological Inventory Data from Age 33 to 75: An Examination of Stability and Change in Adult Personality," *Journal of Personality Assessment* 80 (June 2003): 294–308. For some work that follows members of this cohort past their late seventies, see Jack Block, in collaboration with Norma Haan, *Lives Through Time* (Bancroft, 1971); Glen Elder, *Children of the Great Depression* (1974), 25th ed. (Westview, 1999); John Clausen, *American Lives: Looking Back at the Children of the Great Depression* (Free Press, 1993), which contains a section titled "The Later Years: Looking Forward and Looking Back" (487–516); and Dorothy H. Eichhorn, John A. Clausen, Norma Haan, Marjorie P. Honzik, and Paul H. Mussen, eds., *Past and Present in Middle Life* (Academic Press, 1981).

41 Erikson et al., *Vital Involvement*, 21, 28, 30.

42 Erikson et al., *Vital Involvement*, 54–238.

43 Erikson et al., *Vital Involvement*, 56, 73, 104.

44 Sheldon Glueck and Eleanor Glueck, *Unravelling Juvenile Delinquency* (Harvard University Press, 1950), 14, 30. This chapter does not include a discussion of every longitudinal study; among others are one that focuses on nurses (Susan E. Hankinson, Graham A. Colditz, JoAnn E. Manson, and Frank E. Speizer, *Healthy Women, Healthy Lives: A Guide to Preventing Disease from the Landmark Nurses' Health Study* [Simon and Schuster, 2011]) and one that focuses on nuns (Jennnifer Nalewicki, "Extreme Longevity: The Secret to Living Longer May Be Hiding with Nuns . . . and Jellyfish," *Live Science*, March 30, 2023, www.livescience.com).

45 Among the books on the study are Earnest Albert Hooton, *"Young Man, You Are Normal": Findings from a Study of Students* (G. P. Putman, 1945); Clark Wright Heath, *What People Are: A Study of Normal Young Men* (Harvard University Press, 1945); George E. Valliant, *Adaptation to Life* (Little, Brown, 1977); George E. Valliant, *Aging Well: Surprising Guideposts to a Happier Life from the Landmark Harvard Study of Adult Development* (Little, Brown, 2002); George E. Valliant, *Triumphs of Experience: The Men of the Harvard Grant Study* (Harvard University Press, 2012). Vaillant, *Triumphs*, 3–7, provides information on studies other than

the ones discussed here, including American ones begun after World War II and some in western Europe.

46 Heath, *What People Are*, vii, 3, 5.

47 If Vaillant in *Aging Well* paid a reasonable amount of attention to Terman's studies, Holahan and Sears in *The Gifted Group in Later Maturity* referred to the Harvard study minimally.

48 Vaillant, *Adaptation to Life*, 3–5, 12, 30–31. Hooton, *"Young Man, You Are Normal,"* makes clear that early on, normality was the focus of the study.

49 Vaillant, *Adaptation to Life*, 29, 33, 326, 350, 367–68.

50 Vaillant, *Adaptation to Life*, 44, 233–34.

51 Vaillant, *Aging Well*, 40, 43.

52 Vaillant, *Aging Well*, 3, 5, 13, 304.

53 Vaillant, *Aging Well*, 215–46 (quotes on 220, 229, 236, 248, 257).

54 Vaillant, *Aging Well*, 12, 45, 49, 159.

55 Vaillant, *Triumphs*, 221, 223.

56 Robert Waldinger, "What Makes a Good Life? Lessons from the Longest Study on Happiness," TEDx Talk, November 2015, www.ted.com; and Robert Waldinger and Marc Schulz, *The Good Life: Lessons from the World's Longest Scientific Study of Happiness* (Simon and Schuster, 2023), 129.

57 See also Sam Harris, "The Long Game: A Conversation with Robert Waldinger," *Making Sense* (podcast), January 1, 2023, www.samharris.org; Emine Samer, "Forget Regret! How to Have a Happy Life—According to the World's Leading Expert," *The Guardian*, February 6, 2023, www.theguardian.com; Liz Mineo, "Harvard Study, Almost 80 Years Old, Has Proved That Embracing Community Helps Us Live Longer and Be Happier," *Harvard Gazette*, April 4, 2017.

58 Waldinger and Schulz, *Good Life*, 49–50.

59 Harris, "Long Game."

60 Waldinger and Schulz, *Good Life*, 18.

61 On the experiment testing the power of talking to a stranger, see Waldinger, "What Makes a Good Life?"

62 Waldinger and Schulz, *Good Life*, 149–50.

63 Waldinger and Schulz, *Good Life*, 1, 10, 23; Waldinger, "What Makes a Good Life?"

64 Waldinger and Schulz, *Good Life*, 10, 22, 92.

65 Waldinger and Schulz, *Good Life*, 78–80, on their more limited discussion of life after sixty-six.

66 Waldinger and Schulz, *Good Life*, 57–58, 89, 98, 281.

67 "Interactive Workbook: The Good Life by Robert Waldinger and Marc Schulz: Lessons from the World's Longest Scientific Study of Happiness," Amazon, accessed December 11, 2024, www.amazon.com.

68 Waldinger and Schulz, *Good Life*, 22, 25. To be sure, at some moments, they do discuss the lives of African Americans but not Latinos (45–46). Note that in "What Makes a Good Life?," Waldinger remarks that people could "connect around shared interests" such as in a gardening club or political causes.

CHAPTER 3. THE LONGEVITY COMMERCIAL COMPLEX

1 In determining which books I would focus on, I relied on best-sellers lists from Amazon, Goodreads, Google's list of "Top Longevity Books," Chat GPT3, and Chat GPT4. For important introductions to the field that do not offer advice, see the three-volume James E. Birren, ed., *The Handbooks of Aging*, 4th ed. (Academic, 1996); and Harry R. Moody and Jennifer R. Sasser, *Aging: Concepts and Controversies*, 10th ed. (Sage, 2020). Stephen G. Post and Robert H. Binstock, eds., *The Fountain of Youth: Cultural, Scientific, and Ethical Perspectives on A Biomedical Goal* (Oxford University Press, 2004), remains a useful introduction to many important issues in the field of longevity. The immensely popular magazine *Longevity* spreads the word to people eager for uplifting advice. Rina Knoeff, "Old as Methuselah? Supercentenarians, Narrative Wisdom and the Importance of History for Health," University of Groningen, June 30, 2023, www.rug.nl, is the most recent historical exploration of prolongevity.

2 Aubrey de Grey, with Michael Rae, *Ending Aging: The Rejuvenation Breakthroughs That Could Reverse Human Aging in Our Lifetime* (St. Martin's, 2007); Elizabeth Blackburn and Elissa Epel, *The Telomere Effect: A Revolutionary Approach to Living Younger, Healthier, Longer* (Grand Central, 2017); David A. Sinclair, with Matthew D. LaPlante, *Lifespan: Why We Age—and Why We Don't Have To* (Atria, 2019); Nir Barzilai and Toni Robino, *Age Later: Health Span, Life Span, and the New Science of Longevity* (St. Martin's, 2020); Andrew J. Steele, *Ageless: The New Science of Getting Older Without Getting Old* (Doubleday, 2020); Peter Attia, with Bill Gifford, *Outlive: The Science and Art of Longevity* (Random House, 2023).

3 G. Stanley Hall, *Senescence: The Last Half of Life* (Appleton, 1922), is an earlier and somewhat parallel book. He told readers of what regimens they might follow to live a longer, healthy life. Among them were not only watching what they ate and how they slept and exercised but also whether to accept other nostrums including cold or warm baths; "thyroid extract and perhaps Brown-Sequard's testicular juices"; Metchnikoff's tablets, an early version of probiotic pills; "rubbing or self-massage on rising and retiring"; and how cereals from Kellogg's Battle Creek would foster proper bowel movements (Hall, *Senescence*, viii, xvi, xxii).

4 Methuselah Foundation, "Making 90 the New 50 by 2020," accessed December 11, 2024, www.mfoundation.org.

5 SENS Research Foundation, "Joining Forces on a Shared Mission," accessed December 11, 2024, www.sens.org.

6 Annalee Armstrong, "Anti-Aging Foundation SENS Fires de Grey After Allegations He Interfered with Investigation into His Conduct," *FIERCE Biotech*, August 23, 2021, www.fiercebiotech.com.

7 AgeX Therapeutics Relations, home page, accessed December 12, 2024, https://investors.agexinc.com.

8 Macmillan, "*Ending Aging*," accessed December 12, 2024, https://us.macmillan.com.

9 Huber Warner, Julie Anderson, Steven Austad, et al., "Science Facts and the SENS Agenda," *EMBO Reports*, November 1, 2005, www.embopress.org.

10   William Bains, "Steam Engine Time: A Review of 'Ending Aging' by Aubrey de Grey," *Bioscience Hypotheses* 1 (2008): 281.

11   Timothy D. Lundeen, comment on *Ending Aging*, Amazon, September 14, 2007, www.amazon.com.

12   H.H., comment on *Ending Aging*, Amazon, August 26, 2012, www.amazon.com.

13   National Human Genome Research Institute, "Telomere," accessed December 2024, www.genome.gov.

14   Nicholas Roznovsky, "Epel Selected as 'Influencer in Aging,' Will Be Honored by Alliance for Aging Research in September," UCSF Department of Psychiatry and Behavioral Sciences, April 21, 2017, https://psychiatry.ucsf.edu.

15   Steve, comment on *The Telomere Effect*, Amazon, February 1, 2017, www.amazon.com.

16   Amazon page for *The Stress Prescription*, accessed December 12, 2024, www.amazon.com.

17   Tally Health, "Live Healthier, Longer," accessed December 24, 2024, https://tally-health.com.

18   David Agus, "The Geneticist Who Is Making Age Reversal Real," *Time*, April 23, 2014.

19   David Sinclair, quoted in Jennifer Couzin, "Aging Research's Family Feud," *Science*, February 27, 2004, 1279.

20   Antonio Regaldo, "How Scientists Want to Make You Young Again," *MIT Technology Review*, October 25, 2022.

21   Headline for Antonio Regalado, "Meet Altos Labs, Silicon Valley's Latest Wild Bet on Living Forever," *MIT Technology Review*, September 4, 2021.

22   "95% scientific jargon" quote: Amazon customer, comment on *Lifespan*, Amazon, August 29, 2023, www.amazon.com. The other two quotes are also from Amazon customers' comments on *Lifespan*, accessed December 12, 2024 (no longer available).

23   Toni Robino's LinkedIn page, accessed December 12, 2024, www.linkedin.com.

24   Nir Barzilai, quoted in Claudia Dreifus, "A Conversation with Nir Barzilai; It's Not the Yogurt: Looking for Longevity Genes," *New York Times*, February 24, 2004.

25   M. Reza Jabal, comment on *Age Later*, Amazon, November 22, 2021, www.amazon.com; VeryFitOma, comment on *Age Later*, Amazon, April 25, 2021, www.amazon.com.

26   Andrew Steele's *Ageless* website, accessed December 12, 2024, https://andrewsteele.co.uk.

27   Scienceogram UK, "Making Sense of Science Spending," accessed December 12, 2024, https://scienceogram.org.

28   Jeff L., comment on *Ageless*, Amazon, May 10, 2022, www.amazon.com; Rob Knepper, comment on *Ageless*, Amazon, April 25, 2022, www.amazon.com.

29   Amazon page for *Ageless*, accessed December 24, 2024, www.amazon.com.

30   Ted Anton, *The Longevity Seekers: Science, Business, and the Fountain of Youth* (University of Chicago Press, 2013), offers dramatic stories about the search for scientific fountains of youth from 1980 to 2013. Among others, he focuses on the work of Barzilai and Sinclair.

31 Sinclair, *Lifespan*, 158.

32 Barzilai, *Age Later*, 44, 156.

33 Steele, *Ageless*, 52, 107.

34 De Grey, *Ending Aging*, 133.

35 Blackburn and Epel, *Telomere Effect*, 6, 13.

36 Sinclair, *Lifespan*, xxii, 147–48, 218.

37 Steele, *Ageless*, 14, 144–45.

38 Steele, *Ageless*, 27.

39 Blackburn and Epel, *Telomere Effect*, 116.

40 Steele, *Ageless*, 10, 12, 17, 311. On how problematic is the evidence for the stories of people who lived well past one hundred, see Saul Newman, "Sorry, No Secret to Life Is Going to Make You Live to 110," *New York Times*, January 20, 2025.

41 Barzilai, *Age Later*, 6, 9, 100, 171.

42 Sinclair, *Lifespan*, 219, 261, 265; Steele, *Ageless*, 12; de Grey, *Ending Aging*, 11. In *Age Later*, 173, Barzilai more fully acknowledges barriers to a utopian future.

43 Sinclair, *Lifespan*, 214, 217.

44 Anne Case and Angus Deacon, *Deaths of Despair and the Future of Capitalism* (Princeton University Press, 2020).

45 For their recommendations, see Barzilai, *Age Later*, 187–243; de Grey, *Ending Aging*, 311–39; Steele, *Ageless*, 246–69; Sinclair, *Lifespan*, 262–93.

46 De Grey, *Ending Aging*, 312, 325, 335, 336, 338, 339.

47 Blackburn and Epel, *Telomere Effect*, 67, 100, 136, 235–36, 321 (with the quotes on 7, 53, 71, 268, 271); Barzilai, *Age Later*, 235, 236.

48 Blackburn and Epel, *Telomere Effect*, 325.

49 Eight years before, Gifford had published *Spring Chicken: Stay Young Forever (or Die Trying)* (Grand Central, 2015).

50 Podcast Mentions, "Peter Attia Bio: A Deep Dive into the Life and Achievements of the Longevity Expert," accessed December 12, 2024, https://podcastmentions. com. I am also relying on biographical information found at Attia's website, https://peterattiamd.com (accessed December 12, 2024). For a critical assessment of NuSi, from which Attia resigned at the end of 2015, see Stephan J. Guyenet, "The Science of Body Weight and Health," Stephan J. Guyenet's website, accessed December 12, 2024, www.stephanguyenet.com.

51 Attia, *Outlive*, 41–42, 48, 49, 377–78, 407; The Bridge to Recovery, "About Us," accessed December 12, 2024, www.thebridgetorecovery.com.

52 Attia, *Outlive*, 9–10, 17.

53 "Death Is Inevitable but Aging Is Not with Dr. David Sinclair," episode 71 of *The Dr. Hyman Show* (podcast), September 11, 2019, https://podcasts.apple.com.

54 Mark Hyman, *Young Forever: The Secrets to Living Your Longest, Healthiest Life* (Little Brown, 2023), xii–xiv, 3, 167, 283.

55 Hyman, *Forever Young*, xvii.

56 Hyman, *Forever Young*, xx, 14, 15, 31, 249. See Hyman, *Forever Young*, 167–276, for his more than ample presentation of his recommendations.

57 Hyman, *Forever Young*, 155, 170, 171.

58 Hyman, *Forever Young*, 283–84. The response of readers on Amazon to *Young Forever*, although not as abundant as those for Sinclair, are similar in approval range to those for the five authors discussed earlier. Amazon, comments on *Young Forever*, accessed October 26, 2024, www.amazon.com. Endorsements for the book came not only from Epel, Sinclair, Buettner, and Robbins but also from Google founder Eric Schmidt: Hyman, *Forever Young*, i–iii.

59 Grossman Wellness Center, home page, accessed December 12, 2024, www.grossmanwellness.com.

60 Ray Kurzweil and Terry Grossman, *Fantastic Voyage: Live Long Enough to Live Forever* (Rodale, 2004), 3–4, 357, 365.

61 Samuel Johnson, comment on *Fantastic Voyage*, Amazon, October 12, 2008, www.amazon.com; wtx, comment on *Fantastic Voyage*, Amazon, July 23, 2016, www.amazon.com; William, comment on *Fantastic Voyage*, Amazon, February 20, 2005, www.amazon.com.

62 Tony Robbins and Peter H. Diamandis, with Robert Hariri, *Life Force: How New Breakthroughs in Precision Medicine Can Transform the Quality of Your Life and Those You Love* (Simon and Schuster, 2022), dust jacket.

63 Robbins and Diamandis, *Life Force*, iv, x, 5, 19, 38.

64 Robbins and Diamandis, *Life Force*, 348, 370–89, 580, 596, 595, 605, 619.

65 "Experience Explosive Growth," Tony Robbins's website, accessed February 11, 2025, www.tonyrobbins.com.

66 Héctor García and Francesc Miralles, *Ikigai: The Japanese Secret to a Long and Happy Life*, trans. Heather Cleary (Penguin, 2016), 2, 4.

67 García and Miralles, *Ikigai*, 10–11, 165–66, 172–73, 176, 185.

68 Dan Buettner, "On Assignment—The Secret of Longevity," *National Geographic*, November 2005. For information, see websites of the Buettner and Blue Zones, accessed December 12, 2024: www.danbuettner.com and www.bluezones.com. These websites contain little in the way of biographical information, so I am relying on Wikipedia, "Dan Buettner," accessed December 12, 2024, https://en.wikipedia.org.

69 Dan Buettner, *The Blue Zones: 9 Lessons for Living Longer from the People Who've Lived the Longest*, 2nd ed. (National Geographic, 2012). The only significant difference from the first edition, Dan Buettner, *The Blue Zone: Lessons for Living Longer from People Who've Lived the Longest* (National Geographic, 2008), is the addition of a five-page final chapter titled "Reflecting on the Lessons," 299–303. For critiques of the data on which Blue Zones rely, see Dana G. Smith, "Do People in 'Blue Zones' Actually Live Longer?," *New York Times*, October 24. 2004.

70 Smith, "Do People in 'Blue Zones.'"

71 Buettner, *9 Lessons*, 3.

72 S. Jay Olshansky, Leonard Hayflick, and Bruce A. Carnes, "Position Statement on Human Aging," *Journals of Gerontology, Series A* 57 (August 1, 2002): B295.

73 Buettner, *9 Lessons*, xxi, xxiii, 4.

74 Thomas A. Perls, in Buettner, *9 Lessons*, 20.

75 Buettner, *9 Lessons*, xxi, 62–63, 118–19, 165, 223, 259, 264–98.

76 Adventist Health, "Locations," accessed December 12, 2024, www.adventisthealth.org.

77 Buettner, *9 Lessons*, 301.

78 See, for example, the website for Immunocologie products, https://immunocologie.com (accessed December 12, 2024).

79 Jessica Hamzelou, "The Quest to Legitimize Longevity Medicine," *MIT Technology Review*, March 18, 2024.

80 Graham Walker, "A Skeptic's Review of Peter Attila's *Outlive*," LinkedIn, January 13, 2024, www.linkedin.com.

81 "Platinum Partnerships," Tony Robbins's website, accessed December 12, 2024, www.tonyrobbins.com.

82 Grossman Wellness Center, "How Can We Help?," accessed December 12, 2024, www.grossmanwellness.com. The UltraWellness Center in Lenox, Massachusetts, is somewhat more readily transparent on costs: UltraWellness Center, "Pricing," accessed December 12, 2024, www.ultrawellnesscenter.com.

83 David Sinclair, "David Sinclair Explains What an Aging Population Means for Economies Around the World," World Economic Forum, Davos Agenda, January 18, 2022, www.weforum.org; David Sinclair, quoted in Alvin Powell, "Longevity and Anti-Aging Research: 'Prime Time for an Impact on the Globe,'" *Harvard Gazette*, March 8, 2019.

84 Robert H. Binstock, "The Search for Prolongevity: A Contentious Pursuit," in *The Fountain of Youth: Cultural, Scientific, and Ethical Perspectives on a Biomedical Goal*, ed. Stephen G. Post and Robert H. Binstock (Oxford University Press, 2004), 17.

85 A4M Medicine Redefined, home page, December 12, 2024, www.a4m.com.

86 Binstock, "Search for Prolongevity," 18, including the quote.

87 This discussion of the conflicts between two warring camps as of 2004 relies on Binstock, "Search for Prolongevity," 17–32.

88 S. Jay Olshansky, Leonard Hayflick, and Bruce A. Carnes, "No Truth to the Fountain of Youth," *Scientific American* 286 (June 2002): 92–95 (quotes on 92–93). Michela Cozza, Kirsten L. Ellison, and Stephen Katz, "Hacking Age," *Sociology Compass*, August 29, 2022, https://doi.org/10.1111/soc4.13034, explores important issues in scientific interventions in the lives of the aging. Stephen Katz, "Precarious Life, Human Development and the Life Course: Critical Intersections," in Grenier et al., *Precarity and Aging*, provides another critique of the optimistic longevity claims.

89 February 12, 2002, news about A4M, quoted in Binstock, "Search for Prolongevity," 25.

90 A4M 2002 response, quoted in Binstock, "Search for Prolongevity," 25.

91 Valerie Reitman, "A Rift in Business, Science of Aging," *Los Angeles Times*, January 12, 2004.

92 S. Jay Olshansky, Bradley Willcox, Lloyd Demetrius, and Hiram Beltrán Sánchez, "Implausibility of Radical Life Extension in Humans," *Nature Aging*, October 7,

2024. The story of this finding was front-page news in *The New York Times*: Dana G. Smith, "Study of Life Spans Suggests Humans May Be at Their Peak," *New York Times*, October 9, 2024.

93 On this focus on health span, based on the proposition that extended life span is likely to be costly to society and debilitating to individuals, see S. Jay Olshansky, "From Life Span to Health Span: Declaring 'Victory' in the Pursuit of Human Longevity," *Cold Spring Harbor Perspectives in Medicine* 12, no. 12 (2022): a041480, https://doi.org/10.1101/cshperspect.a041480; and James L. Kirkland, S. Jay Olshansky, and George M. Martin, eds., *Aging: Geroscience as the New Public Health Frontier*, 2nd ed. (Cold Spring Harbor Laboratory Press, 2024).

94 S. Jay Olshansky, telephone conversation with author, June 27, 2024.

95 S. Jay Olshansky, "Don't Fall for the Cult of Immortality," *BBC News*, December 3, 2004, http://news.bbc.co.uk.

96 This comes from R. John Davenport, "And the Loser Is . . . : Silver Fleece Awards 'Honor' Antiaging Quackery (Questionable Therapies)," *Science of Aging Knowledge Environment*, February 20, 2002, https://doi.org/10.1126/sageke.2002.7nw21.

97 Andrew J. Scott, *The Longevity Imperative: How to Build a Healthier and More Productive Society to Support Our Longer Life* (Basic, 2024).

98 Scott, *Longevity Imperative*, 49, 120.

99 Scott, *Longevity Imperative*, 3, 5, 13, 55.

100 Scott, *Longevity Imperative*, 14.

101 Binstock, "Search for Prolongevity," 28–32, explores this issue, as articulated especially by Leon Kass and Daniel Calhoun.

102 Leon R. Kass, "L'Chaim and Its Limits: Why Not Immortality?," *First Things* 13 (May 2001): 17.

103 Susan Jacoby, *Never Say Die: The Myth and Marketing of the New Old Age* (Pantheon, 2011), 255.

104 Kass, "L'Chaim and Its Limits," 20, 21, 24.

105 Dhruv Khullar, "No Time to Die: When Does the Quest for a Healthy Life Become Unhealthy?," *New Yorker*, April 22–29, 2024, and Ezekiel Emanuel quoted in same. Christopher Beam, "The Meme King of Longevity Now Wants to Sell You Olive Oil," *New York Times*, January 12, 2024, reports on the work of Bryan Johnson, a Silicon Valley longevity guru whose followers go on "Don't Die Meet-Ups" and whose work has drawn skeptical responses, including from Nil Barzilai and Andrew Steele. In "Key to Longevity Is Boring," *New York Times*, July 14, 2024, Brad Stulberg makes the case for relying on diet, exercise, meaningful relations (and no cigarettes and limited alcohol), instead of "a complicated and often contradictory menu of 'biohacks' . . . and 'protocols.'"

106 Stephen Katz, introduction to *Cultural Aging: Life Course, Lifestyle, and Senior Worlds*, ed. Katz (Broadview, 2005), 17, 32. Again, I am indebted to Lamb et al., "Successful Aging." Chappel, *Golden Years*, 220–23, discusses key moments in the history of the promotion of successful aging, including the 1998 publication of John W. Rowe's *Successful Aging*. Jacoby, *Never Say Die*, 8–9, casts an appropriately

skeptical eye on the search for miraculous solutions and instead calls for more attention to the socioeconomic challenges that so many elders, women especially, contend with.

107 Joe Kloc, "Gilgamesh, Ponce and the Quest to Live Forever," *New York Times,* January 19, 2025.

CHAPTER 4. AGING ORGANIZATIONS

1 Chappel, *Golden Years,* 10–14. The aging organizations under consideration hardly exhaust the field. Such a list would also include *Retirement Management Journal, Contemporary Long-Term Care,* and *Retirement Community Business,* and among many organizations are the American Senior Housing Association, the HCIA Health Care Industry Association, the American Senior Housing Association, and Senior Living Industries.

2 Bernice l. Neugarten, "The Rise of the Young-Old," *New York Times,* January 18, 1975. Achenbaum, *Crossing Frontiers,* 100–108, explores the context at the University of Chicago that shaped the work of Neugarten. Chappel, *Golden Years,* 255, discusses the emergence of the notion of the frail elderly from the mid-1970s on.

3 Bernice L. Neugarten, Joan W. Moore, and John C. Lowe, "Age Norms, Age Constraints, and Adult Socialization," *American Journal of Sociology* 70 (1965): 710, 714, 716–17.

4 Bernice L. Neugarten, "Age Groups in American Society and the Rise of the Young-Old," *Annals of the American Academy of Political and Social Science* 415 (September 1974): 187–95, reprinted in *The Meaning of Age: Selected Papers on Bernice A. Neugarten,* ed. Dail A. Neugarten (University of Chicago Press, 1996), with the quote on 36.

5 Henry A. Fairlie, "Talking 'bout My Generation," *New Republic* 199 (March 28, 1988): 19–21; Robert N. Butler, "Living Longer, Contributing Longer," *JAMA Network,* October 22, 1997.

6 Katz, introduction to *Cultural Aging,* 16.

7 Bernice L. Neugarten, "New Perspectives on Aging and Social Policy," in Dail A. Neugarten, ed., *Meaning of Age,* 374–75, from The Leon and Josephine Winkelman Lecture delivered at the University of Michigan on January 25, 1982. In "The Prescience and Influence of Bernice Neugarten," in D. Neugarten, *Meaning of Age,* Robert H. Binstock remarks that by the very late 1980s, "the themes of age divisiveness and intergenerational equity had been adopted by the media, academics, and elite sectors of American society as routine perspectives for describing many social policy issues" (337).

8 Bernice L. Neugarten and Dail A. Neugarten, "Age in the Aging Society," *Daedalus* 115 (Winter 1986): 33, 35, 37, 38, 42.

9 Susan J. Douglas, *In Our Prime: How Older Women Are Reinventing the Road Ahead* (Norton, 2020), 47–48. More precisely, it would be accurate to see the Gray Panthers as the first large and sustained organization for and by older people; for an important precedent, see Berry, *My Face Is Black Is True.*

10 Maggie Kuhn, with Christina Long and Laura Quinn, *No Stone Unturned: The Life and Times of Maggie Kuhn* (Ballantine, 1991), 127, 128, including quote from John MacKay on 127. I assume the words are those of Kuhn, however much shaped by Long and Quinn. The documentary *Maggie Growls: All About Maggie Kuhn and the Gray Panthers*, produced and directed by Barbara Attie and Janet Goldwater and aired on PBS in 2003, on which I have also relied, provides some information not available in *No Stone Unturned*. See Gray Panthers, "Maggie Growls: All About Maggie Kuhn and the Gray Panthers," YouTube, April 1, 2023, www.youtube.com/watch?v=pBT5ZdBJaBA.

11 Kuhn, *No Stone Unturned*, 129.

12 My discussion of Maggie Kuhn and the Gray Panthers relies on Kuhn, *No Stone Unturned*; and Roger Sanjek, *Gray Panthers* (University of Pennsylvania Press, 2009). Sanjek's book is an extraordinarily well-researched work of scholarship by an anthropologist who is both a participant on the local level and a skilled observer on the local and national ones. Throughout, I have relied heavily on what he accomplished. There is relatively little scholarship on Kuhn, but a good place to begin is Carroll Estes and Elena Portacolone, "Maggie Kuhn: Social Theorist of Radical Gerontology," *International Journal of Sociology and Social Policy* 29 (2009): 15–26. Among the most recent scholarship on the Gray Panthers is Amanda Ciafone, "The Gray Panthers Are Watching: Gray Women's Media Activism in the 1970s and 80s," *Feminist Media Studies* 21 (2019): 265–80.

13 Kuhn, *No Stone Unturned*, 128–30, 134.

14 Reuben Gums, June 1, 1982, interview, quoted in Sanjek, *Gray Panthers*, 22.

15 Unnamed woman, quoted in Kuhn, *No Stone Unturned*, 139.

16 Maggie Kuhn to William Scranton, December 17, 1970, quoted in Sanjek, *Gray Panthers*, 23. Here and elsewhere, Sanjek was drawing on the Maggie Kuhn Papers at the Presbyterian Historical Society in Philadelphia.

17 Maggie Kuhn, mimeographed "Gray Panther History," ca. March 1972, quoted in Sanjek, *Gray Panthers*, 23.

18 Kuhn, *No Stone Unturned*, 135.

19 On nomenclature, see her interview at the Women's Center of Florida Junior College, ca. 1983: FSCJ LLC, "Worth Quoting: Maggie Kuhn—Age: Image and Attitudes," YouTube, January 2, 2019, www.youtube.com/watch?v=ddEDOLSaGeE.

20 Kuhn, *No Stone Unturned*, 138.

21 Kuhn, *No Stone Unturned*, 150.

22 Maggie Kuhn, in *Maggie Kuhn on Aging*, ed. Dieter Hessel (Westminster, 1977), 15.

23 Kuhn, unidentified source, 1972, quoted in Sanjek, *Gray Panthers*, xxi.

24 Kuhn, *No Stone Unturned*, 153–54.

25 Kuhn, *Maggie Kuhn on Aging*, 122.

26 Kuhn, *No Stone Unturned*, 154–55. In her discussion of disengagement theory, Kuhn cited Carroll L. Estes, *The Aging Enterprise: A Critical Examination of Social Policies and Services for the Aged* (Jossey-Bass, 1979).

27 Ethel Shanas and George L. Maddox, "Health, Health Resources, and the Utilization of Care," in *Handbook of Aging and the Social Sciences*, ed. Robert H. Binstock and Ethel Shanas, 2nd ed. (Van Nostrand Reinhold, 1985), 696.

28 Kuhn, *No Stone Unturned*, 141–42, including the quote from Frank Heinz; Eleanor Blau, "Gray Panthers About to Liberate Aged," *New York Times*, May 21, 1972. Elaine Cumming and William E. Henry, *Growing Old: The Process of Disengagement* (Basic Books, 1961), is the foundational text, one that relied on a study of several hundred people between fifty and ninety. For a critique of its approach, see Katz, *Disciplining Old Age*, 121–23.

29 Sanjek, *Gray Panthers*, 236. In assessing the history and contributions of the Gray Panthers, I am relying on Sanjek, *Gray Panthers*, especially his final chapter, "The Gray Panther Legacy," 227–52; and Chappel, *Golden Years*, 161–65.

30 Betty Friedan, *The Fountain of Age* (Simon and Schuster, 1993), 634.

31 Friedan, *Fountain of Age*, 24, 71–72, 451, 471, 632.

32 Friedan, *Fountain of Age*, 381. Long before Friedan called retirement communities "playpens," Maggie Kuhn did so: Kuhn, *Maggie Kuhn on Aging*, 43.

33 Friedan, *Fountain of Age*, 383, citing Kent A. McClelland, "Self-Conception and Life Satisfaction: Integrating Aged Subculture and Activity Theory," *Journal of Gerontology* 37 (1982): 723–32.

34 Friedan, *Fountain of Age*, 385–86.

35 Friedan, *Fountain of Age*, 386–87, presumably relying on Morton A. Lieberman, "Institutionalization of the Aged: Effects on Behavior," *Journal of Gerontology* 24 (July 1969): 330–40.

36 Friedan, *Fountain of Age*, 382.

37 Ruth E. Ray, "The Personal as Political: The Legacy of Betty Friedan," in *Age Matters: Realigning Feminist Thinking*, ed. Toni M. Calasanti and Kathleen F. Slevin (Routledge, 2006), 37.

38 Ray, "Personal as Political," 24, 37, 39.

39 Toni M. Calasanti and Kathleen F. Slevin, "Introduction: Age Matters," in Calasanti and Slevin, *Age Matters*, 1.

40 Margaret Morganroth Gullette, *Ending Ageism; or, How Not to Shoot Old People* (Rutgers University Press, 2017), 203. For another exploration of the connections between gender and aging, see Margaret Cruikshank, *Learning to Be Old: Gender, Culture, and Aging*, 2nd ed. (Rowman and Littlefield, 2009).

41 Applewhite, *This Chair Rocks*, 8, 9, 11.

42 Applewhite, *This Chair Rocks*, 14–15, 16, 17–18, 61. Among the people involved in the effort to fight for progressive social and political changes for olders are Bill McKibben, who in 2022 founded Third Act, and Teresa Ghilarducci, who in *Work, Retire, Repeat*, 163–96, urgently advocated for better jobs and pensions and called for a Gray New Deal.

43 National Domestic Workers Alliance, home page, accessed December 20, 2024, www.domesticworkers.org.

44 Ai-Jen Poo and Ariane Conrad, *The Age of Dignity: Preparing for the Elder Boom in a Changing America* (New Press, 2015).

45 Chappel, *Golden Years*, 121–43, chronicles the efforts led by Jacquelyne Jackson, who focused on challenges African American elders faced.

46 Bernice Neugarten, "The End of Gerontology?," *Center on Aging* (Buehler Center on Aging, McGaw Medical Center of Northwestern University) 10 (Spring 1994).

47 Scott H. Podolsky, "Metchnikoff and the Microbiome," *The Lancet* 380 (November 24, 2012): 1810–11. Achenbaum, *Crossing Frontiers*, is an indispensable source on the history of gerontology, including the GSA, university centers, and the National Institute on Aging.

48 E. V. Cowdry, *Problems of Aging: Biological and Medical Aspects* (Williams and Wilkins, 1938).

49 GSA, "GSA History," accessed December 26, 2024, www.geron.org. For a more general history of gerontology, see Patsy R. Smith, "A Historical Perspective in Aging and Gerontology," in *The Collective Spirit of Aging Across Cultures*, ed. Halaevalu F. Ofahengaue Vakalahi, Gaynell M. Simpton, and Nancy Giunta (Springer, 2014), 7–27. The GSA is hardly the only relevant organization; others include the American Geriatric Society, the American Federation for Aging Research, the American Society on Aging, the National Council on Aging, the National Hispanic Council on Aging, and the American Aging Association. Katz, *Disciplining Old Age*, 111, notes the existence of 375 aging-related journals.

50 Katz, introduction to *Cultural Aging*, 12. Achenbaum, *Crossing Frontiers*, 125–56, is a rare example of commanding research on the history of GSA.

51 Katz, *Disciplining Old Age*, 79–80, 104–34 (quote on 114); see also Stephen Katz and Bryan Green, "The Government of Detail: The Case of Social Policy on Aging," in Katz, *Cultural Aging*, 53–69; and Stephen Katz, "Critical Gerontological Theory: Intellectual Fieldwork and the Nomadic Life of Ideas," in Katz, *Cultural Aging*, 85–100.

52 Minkler and Estes, *Critical Gerontology*.

53 This summary relies heavily on Minkler and Estes, *Critical Gerontology* (with the quote from Meredith Minkler and Carroll L. Estes, "Concluding Note," 376); and Katz, *Disciplining Old Age*, especially 6, 8–9. For a sustained, cogent, and comprehensive critique of optimism about aging, one that includes a critique of an emphasis of ageism, see Jacoby, *Never Say Die*.

54 Maggie Kuhn, quoted in Friedan, *Fountain of Age*, 634.

55 In my discussion of the AARP, I am relying heavily on Christine L. Day, *AARP: America's Largest Interest Group and Its Impact* (Praeger, 2017), especially 1–30. There are at least two other books on the organization: Charles R. Morris, *The AARP: America's Most Powerful Lobby and the Clash of Generations* (Random House, 1996) and Frederick R. Lynch, *One Nation Under AARP: The Fight over Medicare, Social Security, and America's Future* (University of California Press, 2011).

56 Chappel, *Golden Years*, 178.

57 Ethel Percy Andrus, "The Aged and Retired," in *Who Is My Neighbor?*, ed. Esther Pike (Seabury, 1960), 122.

58 Chappel, *Golden Years*, 179, 193, 195.

59 Chappel, *Golden Years*, 179.

60 On the political headwinds, see Day, *AARP*, 14–25; and in a more detailed way, Lynch, *One Nation Under AARP*.

61 For the AARP's Experience Corps, which focuses on volunteerism, see AARP, "2024 Experience Corps National Meeting," accessed December 13, 2024, www.aarp.org.

62 Sanjek, *Gray Panthers*, 152, provides the date when they met.

63 Friedan, *Fountain of Age*, 16.

64 Robert N. Butler, "Age-ism: Another Form of Bigotry," *The Gerontologist* 9 (Winter 1969): 243–46; Chappel, *Golden Years*, 187.

65 Robert N. Butler, *Why Survive? Being Old in America* (Harper and Row, 1975), 204.

66 For a detailed history, see NIA, "History," accessed November 8, 2024, www.nia.nih.gov. See also Joseph T. Freeman, "Some Notes on the History of the National Institute on Aging," *The Gerontologist* 20 (October 1980): 610–14.

67 In discussions the NIA, I am drawing on NIA, "NIA's Strategic Directions for Research," accessed December 13, 2024, www.nia.nih.gov.

68 Carroll L. Estes and Elizabeth A. Binney, "The Biomedicalization of Aging: Dangers and Dilemmas," *The Gerontologist* 29 (October 1989): 587, 588.

69 Estes and Binney, "Biomedicalization of Aging," 594, 595.

70 Estes and Binney, "Biomedicalization of Aging," 594, 595.

71 Kuhn, *No Stone Unturned*, 155–56; Estes, *Aging Enterprise*, x.

72 Here I am relying on the center's website: Center for Retirement Research, home page, accessed February 23, 2024, https://crr.bc.edu.

73 Alicia H. Munnell, "Do We Have a Retirement Crisis?," Center for Retirement Research, July 15, 2024, https://crr.bc.edu.

74 Jeff Sommer, "The Social Security Fix Nobody Wants to Talk About," *New York Times*, May 31, 2024.

75 Stanford Center on Longevity, "Century-Long Lives Are Here: We're Not Ready," accessed December 13, 2024, https://longevity.stanford.edu.

76 Laura L. Carstensen, *A Long Bright Future: Happiness, Health, and Financial Security in an Age of Increased Longevity* (Broadway, 2011), 253–83 (quote on 253).

77 Carstensen, *Long Bright Future*, 6, 10, 11, 12.

78 For the history of the center and school, I am relying on website for the Leonard Davis School of Gerontology, accessed June 17, 2025, https://gero.usc.edu; and Achenbaum, *Crossing Frontiers*, 109–13.

79 Leonard Davis School of Gerontology, home page.

80 Ken Dychtwald, "Remembering Maggie Kuhn: Gray Panthers Founder on the 5 Myths of Aging," *Huffington Post*, May 31, 2012, www.huffpost.com.

81 Age Wave, "About Age Wave," accessed December 13, 2024, https://agewave.com.

82 See Ken Dychtwald, with Joe Flower, *Age Wave: The Challenges and Opportunities of an Aging America* (Tarcher, 1989), quote on 269; Dychtwald, *Age Power: How the 21st Century Will Be Ruled by the New Old* (Tarcher, 1999); and Dychtwald, with Robert Morison, *What Retirees Want: a Holistic View of Life's Third Age* (Wiley, 2022). For a list of books on how to market to seniors published from 1989 to 1999, see Katz, *Cultural Aging*, 195. On Dychtwald, see Chappel, *Golden Years*, 212–23. See also the writings of Marc Freedman, including *How to Live Forever: The Enduring Power of Connecting the Generations* (PublicAffairs, 2018), *Encore: Finding Work That Matters in the Second Half of Life* (Hachette, 2007), and *Prime Time: How Baby Boomers Will Revolutionize Retirement and Transform America* (PublicAffairs, 1999).

83 MIT AgeLab, "About Us," accessed February 13, 2024, https://agelab.mit.edu.

84 Coughlin, *Longevity Economy*, 6, 64, 239.

85 Coughlin, *Longevity Economy*, 19, 20, 119, 171, 194, 209, 298.

86 Chappel, *Golden Years*, 191.

CHAPTER 5. HOUSING SENIORS

1 See Chappel, *Golden Years*, 93–120, 251–66, for discussions of housing for seniors in the late twentieth and early twenty-first centuries.

2 I have had to piece together the early history of where seniors lived. A decent place to begin is Jeff Hoyt, "200+ Years of Senior Living History," SeniorLiving.org, December 6, 2023, www.seniorliving.org. Not until after 1870 did more than 25 percent of Americans live in urban areas. Carole Haber, *Beyond Sixty-Five: The Dilemma of Old Age in America's Past* (Cambridge University Press, 1983), explores the processes by which the way experts defined senescence resulted in some of the elderly coming to be segregated and institutionalized. There are some important essays on senior housing in Van Tassel and Stearns, *Old Age in a Bureaucratic Society*. For a discussion of relatively rare scholarly explorations of elder housing, see Stephen Katz, "Eleven Spaces of Age: Snowbirds, and the Gerontology of Aging: The Elderscapes of Charlotte County, Florida," in Katz, *Cultural Aging*, 202–29. There is relatively little scholarship on today's unhoused elderly; one exception is Ellis Jourdan Hews, "'There Are No Bathrooms Available': How Older Adults Experiencing Homelessness Manage Their Daily Activities" (master's thesis, Portland State University, 2021).

3 Thompson, Connecticut, "History of 19th Century American Poorhouses," accessed December 12, 2024, www.thompsonct.org. See also Bruce Vladeck, *Unloving Care: The Nursing Home Tragedy* (Basic, 1980), 33–35. In *The Next Shift: The Fall of Industry and the Rise of Health Care in Rust Belt America* (Harvard University Press, 2021), 220–43, Gabriel Winant explores the impact of deindustrialization and aging on institutions that care for aging Americans and on the women who care for elders. Margaret Morganroth Gullette, *American Eldercide: How It Happened, How to Prevent It* (University of Chicago Press, 2024), examines the devastating impact COVID-19 had on residents of nursing homes.

4 Hoyt, "200+ Years."

5 Masonic Care Community New York, "About the Masonic Care Community in Utica, NY," accessed December 12, 2024, https://masonichomeny.org.

6 Henry Rogers Seager, *Social Insurance: A Program of Social Reform* (Macmillan, 1910), 117.

7 I am relying here on Hoyt, "200+ Years."

8 Haber and Gratton, *Old Age and the Search for Security*, 175.

9 On the transformative power of Social Security, see Haber and Gratton, *Old Age and the Search for Security*, 181–85.

10 B. Vladeck, *Unloving Care*, 4; for the larger context, see 30–70.

11 Joint Center for Housing Studies of Harvard University, *Housing America's Older Adults 2023* (2023), 4. For a wonderfully nuanced discussion of the importance of where seniors live, see Joyce Weil, *Why Place Matters: Place and Place Attachments for Older Adults* (Routledge, 2024).

12 I find figures on how many seniors live in public housing hard to come by, but one recent estimate is that 53 percent of the 1.13 million people residing in public housing are disabled and/or are living in a household headed by someone sixty-two or older. Slightly less than half of the adults involved are capable of working: Mica O'Brien and Susan J. Popkin, "Our Aging Public Housing Puts Older Americans at Risk," Urban Institute, January 30, 2020, www.urban.org.

13 A useful starting place is National Institute on Aging, "Aging in Place: Growing Older at Home," October 12, 2023, www.nia.nih.gov. Chappel, *Golden Years*, 104–11, focuses on the some of the services that helped make aging in place possible.

14 Since 2004, Kendal Corporation, the Quaker operator of CCRCs, has offered Kendal at Home.

15 Recent scholarly articles on which I have drawn explore almost forty years of research on NORCs: Jiaxuan E, Bo Xia, Connie Susilawati, Quing Chen, and Xuechun Wang, "An Overview of Naturally Occurring Retirement Communities (NORCs) for Ageing in Place," *Buildings* 12 (April 2022): 519, https://doi.org/10.3390/buildings12050519; Simone Parniak, "Naturally Occurring Retirement Communities: Scoping Review," *Journal of Medical Internet Research: Aging* 5, no. 2 (2022): e34577, https://doi.org/10.2196/34577.

16 Michael Hunt and Gail Gunter-Hunt, "Naturally Occurring Retirement Communities," *Journal of Housing for the Elderly* 3 (December 1986): 3.

17 AARP, *Understanding Senior Housing for the 1990s: Survey of Consumer Preferences, Concerns, and Needs* (1992); John Buntin, "Seniors and the City," *Governing*, March 24, 2010, www.governing.com.

18 Buntin, "Seniors and the City."

19 Older Americans Act of 1965, Pub. L. 89-73, 79 Stat. 218, as amended through Pub. L. 116-131 (2020).

20 National Opinion Research Center, University of Chicago, "Equity and Aging in the Community," April 22, 2022, https://apnorc.org.

21 Congregate housing and cohousing are two types of residential arrangements, but they are not necessarily NORCs.

22 Much rarer than urban NORCs are rural ones: see Michael E. Hunt, Linda J. Marshall, and John L. Merrill, "Rural Areas That Affect Older Migrants," *Journal of Architectural and Planning Research* 19 (Spring 2002): 44–56; Stacey Grant-Savela, "Active Living Among Older Residents of a Rural Naturally Occurring Retirement Community," *Journal of Applied Gerontology* 29 (October 2010): 531–53.

23 Carrie Graham and Shannon Guzman, "The Village Model: Current Trends, Challenges, and Opportunities," AARP Public Policy Institute, October 2022, www.aarp.org. For information on the Village to Village Network, see Village to Village Network, "Village Movement," accessed December 12, 2024, https://vtvnetwork.clubexpress.com. In *Insights on Developing Research Capacity for Healthy Aging with Villages*, a 2024 report by RAND, Alina I. Palimaru, Allyson D. Gittens, Nilofer Chollampat, and Regina A. Shih explore the prospects for healthy aging in these communities.

24 Beacon Village, "Welcome to Beacon Hill Village," accessed December 12, 2024, www.beaconhillvillage.org. See also an organization that serves Cambridge, Massachusetts, and adjoining towns: Cambridge Neighbors, https://cambridgeneighbors.org (accessed December 12, 2024).

25 Fredda Vladeck, *A Good Place to Grow Old: New York's Model for NORC Social Service Programs* (United Hospital Fund, 2004), 3–4, https://media.uhfnyc.org. Among other senior projects are the AFL-CIO's Four Freedom House in Miami and a cottage community developed by the Fraternal Order of Elks.

26 This draws on Jiaxuan et al., "Overview," 523–24.

27 F. Vladeck, *Good Place*, 1, 4–6.

28 F. Vladeck, *Good Place*, 14.

29 For another well-documented case, this one in Los Angeles, see Susan Enguidanos, John Pynoos, Maria Siciliano, Lauren Diepenbrock, and Susan Alexman, "Integrating Community Servies Within a NORC: The Park LaBrea Experience," *Cityscape: A Journal of Policy Development and Research* 12 (July 2010): 29–45. Like the Penn South project and others in New York, Jewish communal agencies supported the development of this one in Los Angeles.

30 F. Vladeck, *Good Place*, 1–4.

31 F. Vladeck, *Good Place*, 5–6.

32 F. Vladeck, *Good Place*, 4, 6–7, 9–10.

33 F. Vladeck, *Good Place*, 18–19.

34 Judith Ann Trolander, in *From Sun Cities to the Villages: A History of Active, Adult, Age-Restricted Communities* (University Press of Florida, 2011), 280, writes that in 2000, six hundred thousand seniors occupied trailer courts, and my guess is that half of those were in age-restricted ones.

35 On 55+ trailer parks, see Kendall Jennings, "Why Do RV Parks Have Age Restrictions?," *Camper Report*, June 20, 2022, https://camperreport.com; Trolander, *From Sun Cities*, 23–27; and Andrew Hurley, *Diners, Bowling Alleys and Trailer Parks:*

Chasing the American Dream in the Postwar Consumer Culture (Basic Books, 2001), 258–65.

36 The information comes from Sun Communities, "Friendly Village of La Habra," accessed January 26, 2024, www.suncommunities.com.

37 Weil, *Why Place Matters*, 16–17, discusses these opposites.

38 Sallie McBrien, "55 and Older Communities Rules and Regulation Guide: What Is a 55+ Community?," *Your At Home Team* (blog), January 31, 2022, www.yourathometeam.com. There is an abundant literature on 55+ communities. The two most comprehensive ones are Trolander, *From Sun Cities*; and Andrew D. Blechman, *Leisureville: Adventures in a World Without Children* (Grove, 2008). Calvin Trillin's "Wake Up and Live," *New Yorker*, April 4, 1964, was among the earliest reports. See also Frances Fitzgerald, *Cities on a Hill: A Journey Through Contemporary American Cultures* (Simon and Schuster, 1986), 203–45; Flannery Burke, "From Senior Citizen to Sun Citian: Aging and Race in Neoliberal Retirement," *Journal of Arizona History* 61 (Autumn–Winter 2020): 589–613; and, on Sun City, John M. Findlay, *Magic Lands: Western Cityscapes and American Culture After 1940* (University of California Press, 1992), 160–213; and Blechman, *Leisureville*.

39 Jonathan Rauch, "The Longevity Revolution," *The Atlantic*, January 2025, 84. Webb took pride in and never expressed regret that during World War II he had built the Poston War Relocation Center, which imprisoned Japanese Americans. Youngstown's founder, Benjamin Schleifer, also developed Circle City nearby, a retirement community modeled on a kibbutz and affiliated with the socialist Jewish Workingmen's Circle: Blechman, *Leisureville*, 30, mentions this as a failed enterprise.

40 Trolander, *From Sun Cities*, 5, 112–23, 289.

41 Trillin, "Wake Up and Live," 169. For another criticism, see Kuhn, *Maggie Kuhn on Aging*, 44: "a façade of congeniality, but . . . little real evidence of community."

42 Trillin, "Wake Up and Live," 172.

43 Trolander, *From Sun Cities*, 136–48, 241–49; for the trend toward greater diversity in the new century, see 224–26. For the most trenchant and recent critical assessment of 55+ communities, see Burke, "From Senior Citizen."

44 Trolander, *From Sun Cities*, 176–87, offers a useful summary of its development and characteristics.

45 The Villages, home page, accessed February 1, 2024, www.thevillages.com. For another 55+ community, see the Jimmy Buffett–inspired Latitude Margaritaville: Latitude Margaritaville, home page, accessed February 14, 2024, www.latitude-margaritaville.com; and the subject of a March 28, 2022, *New Yorker* article, "Retirement the Margaritaville Way," by Nick Paumgarten.

46 These statistics are from the first years of the twenty-first century and can be found in US Census Bureau, "QuickFacts: The Villages CDP, Florida," accessed February 2, 2024, www.census.gov.

47 The Villages, "Dream a Little *Dream*," brochure, n.d., 31, 34, 49.

48 In this discussion, I draw on The Villages, home page, accessed December 12, 2024, www.thevillages.com. Jacoby, *Never Say Die*, 286, offers a critique of the search for retirement in a sunny (literally and figuratively) community.

49 Hugh Bartling, "Tourism as Everyday Life: An Inquiry into The Villages, Florida," *Tourism Geographies* 8 (November 2006): 380.

50 Amanda M. Brian, "The Faux History of The Villages, Florida," *Southern Cultures* 20 (Winter 2014): 60.

51 Deane Simpson, "Small-Town Metropolitanism and 'The Middle of Nowhere,'" *Architectural Design* 86 (July 2016): 89, 91.

52 Sarah Fishleder, Lawrence Schonfeld, Jaime Corvin, Susan Tyler, and Carla VandeWeerd, "Drinking Behavior Among Older Adults in a Planned Retirement Community: Results from The Villages Survey," *Geriatric Psychiatry* 31 (May 2016): 536–43; Abdallah Kinero, Kabhabhela Bukuru, Enock Mwambeleko, Thobias Sando, and Priyanka Alluri, "Modeling Injury Severity of Crashes Involving Golf Carts: A Case Study of The Villages, Florida," *Traffic Injury Prevention* 25 (January 2004): 165–72. For a study carried out before the growth and proliferation of retirement community options, see the less-than-optimistic *Last Home for the Aged* (Jossey Bass, 1976), by Sheldon Tobin and Morton Lieberman.

53 Benedict Brook, "Dark Side of Paradise: 'Sinister' Cracks Show in Perfect Suburb," *New Zealand Herald*, February 5, 2022, www.nzherald.co., accessed December 12, 2024.

54 Jean Baudrillard, "The Procession of Simulacra," in *Simulacra and Simulation*, trans. Sheila Faria Glaser (University of Michigan Press, 1994), 1.

55 Ryan Grim, "The Villages Vendetta: How a Grassroots Revolt in the Iconic Retirement Community Ended with a 72-Year-Old Political Prisoner," *The Intercept*, February 5, 2023, https://theintercept.com.

56 Michael D. Shear, "Trump Retweets Racist Video Showing Supporter Yelling 'White Power,'" *New York Times*, June 28, 2020.

57 Michelle Cottle, "The 'Disney' for Boomers Puts Hedonism on Full Display," *New York Times*, March 3, 2022; Hannah Critchfield, "Why Is The Villages Known as 'the STD Capital of America?,'" *Tampa Bay Times*, August 12, 2022.

58 Lance Oppenheim, dir., *Some Kind of Heaven* (2020).

59 Although not exactly a CCRC, the nonprofit The Cambridge Homes has a storied history that goes back to 1887: Senior Living Residences, "Welcome to the Cambridge Homes," accessed December 16, 2024, www.seniorlivingresidences.com.

60 Among other sources, this discussion relies on John W. Milford, Diane L. Griffeath, and Darlene Yee-Melichar, "Continuing Care Retirement Communities," in *Long-Term Care Administration and Management: Effective Practices and Quality Programs in Eldercare*, ed. Darlene Yee-Melichar, Cristina M. Flores, Edwin P. Cabigao (Springer 2014), 91–103; and Benjamin W. Pearce, *Senior Living Communities: Operations Management and Marketing for Assisted Living, Congregate, and Continuing Care Retirement Communities* (Johns Hopkins University Press, 1998); a third edition appeared in May 2024. Conferences are another

source of information for those who manage senior communities: for a listing, see Susan Saldibar, "2022 Top Senior Living Conferences," *Senior Living Foresight*, February 3, 2022, www.seniorlivingforesight.net.

61 On the studies that highlight the benefits of CCRC living, see Milford et al., "Continuing Care Retirement Communities," 102. Entering "continuing care retirement community" in Google Scholar leads to scholarly articles, many of which focus on what is involved in the initial decision to move, the later decision to shift to levels within the community, factors that affect well-being, and the importance of social connections and activities.

62 Amie Clark, "Life on a College or University Campus—An Alternative Retirement Destination," TheSeniorList, February 5, 2024, www.theseniorlist.com.

63 Materials on Lasell Village in author's possession.

64 Weil, *Why Place Matters*, 15–16.

65 Pearce, *Senior Living Communities*, 79, 107.

66 Pearce, *Senior Living Communities*, 41, 108, 211.

67 Weil, *Why Place Matters*, 18.

68 Pearce, *Senior Living Communities*, 79–82.

69 Paula Span, "Conflict Is Common in Elder-Care Settings," *New York Times*, June 11, 2024.

70 Clary Estes, "Historic High Rates of STI's Among Older Americans," *Forbes*, February 26, 2020.

71 Brookdale Senior Living, "Welcome to Brookdale," accessed February 12, 2004, www.brookdale.com. For information on one of the United States' largest owners of senior communities, see Argentum Lument, "2021 Largest Providers Report," accessed February 13, 2024, www.argentum.org.

72 Pearce, *Senior Living Communities*, 210–11, 214.

73 Erving Goffman, *Asylums: Essays on the Social Situation of Mental Patients and Other Inmates* (Doubleday, 1961); Chappel, *Golden Years*, 119.

74 Jacqueline S. Weinstock and Lynne A. Bond, "Defining and Promoting Quality of Life at a Continuing Care Retirement Community: A Case Study," *Senior Housing & Care Journal* 26 (2018): 61–73 (quotes on 66–72).

75 This marketing strategy underscores the avoidance of the challenges faced by many elders in their "fourth age," an issue explored in Paul Higgs and Chris Gilleard, *Personhood, Identity, and Care in Advanced Old Age* (Policy, 2016).

76 Here and in the following paragraphs, I am relying on promotional material from the following CCRCs: in the Boston area, Lasell Village, Brookhaven, Newbury Court, and Waterstone; in Charlottesville, Virginia, The Colonnades and Westminster Canterbury; and in Pasadena, California, Villa Gardens and Monte Cedro.

77 Áegis Living, "Where to Begin," accessed January 31, 2024, www.aegisliving.com. Although not entirely apparent, I suspect that Chinese Americans are the principal group targeted for such communities. On how another Asian American group experienced longevity, see Ken Chih-Yan Sun, *Time and Migration: How Long-Term Taiwanese Migrants Negotiate Later Life* (Cornell University Press, 2021).

78 Jessica Portner, "In Los Angeles; Senior Communities, Promotoras Offers Health Guidance in Spanish," *California Health Report*, June 30, 2017, www.calhealthreport.org.

79 AssistedLiving.org, "Assisted Living for Spanish and Latinx Seniors," April 18, 2023, www.assistedliving.org. "The Ballad of Sunset Hall" (1992) and the film *Sunset Story* (2003) capture a very different kind of retirement community, this one in Los Angeles that houses seniors long committed to progressive social movements: "The Ballad of Sunset Hall," accessed December 24, 2024, https://archive.org.

80 Maureen Stanley, "LGBTQ Retirement Communities and Cities in the US," SeniorLiving.org, September 6, 2024, www.seniorliving.org.

81 Jasmine Browley, "These Are the Best Places for Black People to Retire," *Essence*, May 26, 2023, www.essence.com. See also, "Top 12 Retirement Cities for African Americans," UrbanAreas.net, ca. 2021, https://urbanareas.net. For information on how African Americans have faced discrimination in securing places in nursing homes and assisted living, see Paying for Senior Care, "Assisted Living for African American Seniors," accessed February 1, 2024, www.payingforseniorcare.com.

82 Sue Matthews Petrovski, *Shelved: A Memoir of Aging in America* (Purdue University Press, 2018), 2, 6, 62, 78.

83 Petrovski, *Shelved*, 6, 75–76, 83, 119–20.

84 Joint Center for Housing Studies of Harvard University, *Housing America's Older Adults 2023*, 4.

85 Joint Center for Housing Studies of Harvard University, *Housing America's Older Adults 2023*, 4–23 (quote on 14). Among other summaries of recent trends, in terms of both demography and public policy, see Keith R. Knapp, Douglas M. Olson, Katie Smith Sloan, and Mark Parkinson, "The Senior Living Field: Background, History, and Its Current and Future State," in Keith R. Knapp and Douglas M. Olson, eds., *The Health Services Executive (HSE™): Tools for Leading Long-Term Care and Senior Living Organizations* (Springer 2020), 3–17 and recent articles listed on https://www.nia.nih.gov.

86 Chappel, *Golden Years*, 254.

87 On these arrangements, see Chappel, *Golden Years*, 268–79.

CHAPTER 6. FROM LONG BOOKS TO BRIEF TIKTOKS

1 Relevant founding dates are often somewhat elusive, but among the recent ones, the following chronology is reasonable: Google 1996; blogs 1998; podcasts 2004; TED Talks 2006; Twitter 2006; TikTok 2017. Fritz Gilbert, *Keys to a Successful Retirement: Staying Happy, Active, and Productive in Your Retirement Years* (Rockridge, 2020), 115–25, offers lists of resources, including websites, blogs, books, and podcasts.

2 Arthur Brooks, *From Strength to Strength: Finding Success, Happiness, and Deep Purpose in the Second Half of Life* (Penguin, 2022), xiv, 21, 29, 41, 45.

3 Nell Painter, *Old in Art School: A Memoir of Starting Over* (Counterpoint, 2018). Meredith Marah, *The New Old Me: My Late-Life Reinvention* (Blue Rider, 2017), is

one of the many other memoirs on starting over. See this one by Painter's mother: Dona L. Irvin, *I Hope I Look That Good When I'm That Old: An Older African American Woman Speaks to All* (Writers Club, 2002).

4 Painter, *Old in Art School*, 4–5, 10–13, 79. For an example of her experience of racism at RISD, see Painter, *Old in Art School*, 170.

5 See, for examples, her 2006 takes on Kara Walker and her 2007 version of Max Beckmann's *Self-Portrait*: Painter, *Old in Art School*, 69, 94, 214–15.

6 Painter, *Old in Art School*, 102–3, 275–76.

7 May Sarton, *At Eighty-Two: A Journal* (Norton, 1996), 11.

8 Sarton, *At Eighty-Two*, 15, 17, 85.

9 Sarton, *At Eighty-Two*, 27, 72.

10 Sarton, *At Eighty-Two*, 139, 143, 252.

11 Sarton, *At Eighty-Two*, 337, 345.

12 Nora Ephron, *I Remember Nothing and Other Reflections* (Knopf, 2010), 5–6.

13 Ephron, *I Remember Nothing*, 127–31.

14 Janet Maslin, "I Feel Bad About My Memory," *New York Times*, November 4, 2010.

15 Jacob Bernstein, "Nora Ephron's Final Act," *New York Times Magazine*, March 6, 2013.

16 Atul Gawande, *Being Mortal: Medicine and What Matters in the End* (Holt, 2014), 8–9, 77, 127.

17 Gawande, *Being Mortal*, 261.

18 Bernstein, "Nora Ephron's Final Act."

19 Elizabeth Marshall Thomas, *Growing Old: Notes on Aging with Something like Grace* (HarperOne, 2020), 1, 77–78, 133–34, 198. Among other books on aging that deserve more attention than I offer here are Louise Aronson's compassionate and nuanced *Elderhood: Redefining Aging, Transforming Medicine, Reimagining Life* (Bloomsbury, 2019); Sherwin R. Nuland, *How We Die: Reflections on Life's Final Chapter* (Random House, 1994); Lee Gutkind, *My Last Eight Thousand Days: An American Male in His Seventies* (University of Georgia Press, 2020); and Marietta Pritchard, *The Way to Go: Portrait of a Residential Hospice* (Impress, 2010).

20 Roz Chast, *Can't We Talk About Something More Pleasant? A Memoir* (Bloomsbury, 2014), 3–4, 95, 121, 128, 136, 183.

21 Jeff Elkins, "*Modern Maturity* Magazine Disrupts Stereotypes About Aging," ca. 2009, www.aarp.org.

22 Scott D. Roberts and Nan Zhou, "The 50 and Older Characters in the Advertisements of *Modern Maturity*: Growing Older, Getting Better?," *Journal of Applied Gerontology* 16 (June 1997): 208–20.

23 DW Documentary, "More Life—Decoding the Secret of Aging," YouTube, May 28, 2022, www.youtube.com/watch?v=y-5VLHcTDSQ&t=29sm.

24 Frontline PBS, "The Retirement Gamble," YouTube, September 21, 2021, www.youtube.com/watch?v=lkOQNPIsO-Q.

25 Kaiser Family Foundation, "KFF Research Shows That Medicare Open Enrollment TV Ads Are Dominated by Medicare Advantage Plans Featuring Celebri-

ties, Active and Fit Seniors, and Promises of Savings and Extra Benefits Without Fundamental Plan Information," news release, September 20, 2023, www.kff.org.

26 A Place for Mom, "In-Home Care Options for Elderly Parents," accessed January 11, 2024, www.aplaceformom.com.

27 Ken Dychtwald, "Ageism Is Alive and Well in Advertising," accessed September 8, 2021, www.aarp.org.

28 Tony Coray, "How to Market to Seniors," SheerED, accessed November 16, 2022, www.sheerid.com.

29 This strand of stories began with Josephine Miller, "Golden Years: We're 65 with Over $4.1 in Retirement—An Expert Shared Little Known Tax Law That Saves Nearly $600k When We Withdraw," *U.S. Sun*, March 6, 2024, www.the-sun.com.

30 "Happy 113! Wellesley woman believed to be oldest MA resident celebrates birthday," https://www.youtube.com/watch?v=rV_OMUFT6E0, accessed December 7, 2024.

31 Gabby Landsverk, "You Can Boost Your Longevity with 7 Habits That Take 5 Minutes or Less a Day, According to a Doctor," *Business Insider*, January 23, 2024, www.businessinsider.com.

32 Postings on X, formerly known as Twitter, partly but not solely because they are so short that they do not provide much information; with both retirement and longevity, they offer data more fully available elsewhere. Moreover, there are fewer than fifteen hundred members of the "Longevity Community" (https://twitter.com/i/communities/1509918311932383237, accessed December 7, 2024). Much of what appears there is advocacy of testing and supplements that can prolong live. What is offered about retirement is even less helpful, in part because it captures any use of the word, including news of a famous person going into or coming out of retirement.

33 Feedly, "Human Longevity," accessed December 7, 2024, https://feedly.com/i/subscription/feed%2Fhttp%3A%2F%2Fwww.humanlongevity.com%2Ffeed%2F.

34 Kathleen Coxwell, "The 23 Best Ted Talks on Money, Retirement, and Aging to Help You Have a Beter Future," Pinterest, accessed December 7, 2024, https://kr.pinterest.com/pin/195836283795823197/.

35 Allie Phan, "Boldin—The First Truly People-Inspired Financial Planning Platform," Boldin, January 9, 2025, www.boldin.com.

36 Jane Fonda, "Life's Third Act," TED Talk, December 2011, www.ted.com.

37 Ashton Applewhite, "Let's End Ageism," TED Talk, April 2017, www.ted.com.

38 Dan Slee, "Clipped: I Watched the 100 Best TikTok Videos to Find the Optimum Length of a Clip," Dan Slee's website, January 21, 2020, https://danslee.co.uk.

39 jeanne_retired, "Finding Structure in Retirement," TikTok, July 29, 2023, www.tiktok.com/@jdawgretires/video/7261198885102669098?lang=en&q=retirement%20life&t=1711806808233.

40 itsyourjulestime, "You're your Julestime," TikTok, March 13, 2023, www.tiktok.com/@cheekyblondejules/video/7210198747891076398?lang=en&q=retirement%20life&t=1711806808233.

41 windvin3, "Bro Just Started His First Day of Retirement," TikTok, December 12, 2023, www.tiktok.com/@windvin3/video/7311715473484221739?lang=en&q=retire ment%20life&t=1711806808233.

42 Bobleonard70, comment on "A day in the life of a 62 year old enjoying retirement," TikTok, accessed December 12, 2023 (no longer available), www.tiktok. com/@richretires/video/7180554449499295018?lang=en&q=retirement%20 life&t=1711806808233.

43 mindbodygreen, "I'm 102 and I have a 10 year plan," TikTok, June 22, 2023, www.tiktok.com/@mindbodygreen/video/7247588701419621678?lang=en&q=longev ity%20research&t=1711817617057.

44 "The Longevity Commercial Complex," TikTok, accessed December 7, 2024 (no longer available), www.tiktok.com.

45 Hadley Vlahos, *The In-Between: Unforgettable Encounters During Life's Final Moments* (Ballantine, 2023), 249–51. Christopher Kerr, MD, has a 2015 TEDxBuffalo that has attracted over five million views: TEDx Talks, "I See Dead People: Dreams and Visions of the Dying," YouTube, December 2, 2015, www.youtube. com/watch?v=rbnBe-vXGQM?; and featured in Phoebe Zerwick, "What Deathbed Visions Teach Us About the Living," *New York Times*, March 12, 2024.

46 nursehadley, "I'm Not Scared of Dying," March 27, 2024, www.tiktok.com/@ nursehadley/video/7351036531659902239?lang=en.

47 Julie Weed, "As Older TikTok Creators Flourish, Brands Are Signing Them Up," *New York Times*, June 3, 2023.

48 "Seniors Reveal the Secret Team Behind Retirement House, Addition [*sic*: audition?] Process and & How It All Started," YouTube, n.d. (no longer available), www.youtube.com/watch?v=BUVnwBjmy8s&list=PLSB5jna2x48ne8gO5Gn1kTE Q9rEizgPoG&index=4.

49 "Seniors Reveal the Secret Team."

50 hellojoeandbella, "Getting Old Is the Goal. Make Sure to Have Fun Along the Way," TikTok, April 3, 2024, www.tiktok.com/@hellojoeandbella/video/735364126 8125109546?q=retirementhouse&t=1712162427366.

51 These can be found on "Retirementhouse," Instagram, accessed December 7, 2024, www.instagram.com/retirementhouse.

52 Henrike Schelper posting, Instagram, accessed December 7, 2024, www.insta gram.com/arthurcbrooks/p/C5HaXgfKTTS/.

CHAPTER 7. RETIRE ON-SCREEN AND LIVE A LONG, INTERESTING LIFE

1 There is some scholarship on retirement films, including two special issues of *Journal of British Cinema and Television*: "Gender, Ageing and Sexuality in British Cinema after Thatcher," vol. 13 (October 2016); and "Screening Old Age," vol. 14, no. 2 (April 2017). Chappel, *Golden Years*, offers extensive and compelling discussions of the television series *The Golden Girls* (201–27), with an emphasis on women's health and sexuality; some other television shows (167–69); and some films that I have not focused on (150–51, 169–71).

2   Berkeley Demography, "Life Expectancy in the USA, 1900–1998," accessed December 10, 2024, https://u.demog.berkeley.edu.

3   Sinclair Lewis, *Dodsworth* (Harcourt, Brace, 1929), 263, 264, 352.

4   Roger Ebert, review of *Harry and Tonto*, January 1, 1974, RogerEbert.com, www.rogerebert.com.

5   See, as another example, *Lost in America* (1985).

6   Robert Ebert, review of *About Schmidt*, December 20, 2002, RogerEbert.com, www.rogerebert.com.

7   *The Leisure Seeker* (2017) is an on-the-road film about a retired couple who travel and cross off the one item on their bucket list—Ernest Hemingway's Key West home—before her cancer and his Alzheimer's would make that quest impossible. There are some parallels between road and bucket list movies and buddy flicks. See, for example, *Grumpy Old Men* (2017) and the four seasons of *The Kominsky Method* (2018–21), which, if not specifically about retirement, nonetheless profoundly explores aging.

8   *Cocoon* (1985), not available for viewing, focuses on aliens from another planet who help rejuvenate residents of a retirement community: for a discussion, see Chappel, *Golden Years*, 211. Among the many other treatments are the Spanish animated *Wrinkles* (2011); the British *The Quartet* (2012); the Israeli *The Farewell Party* (2014); the television series *The Cool Kids* (2018–19); the British *Remember Me* (2021); and the French *Maison de retraite* (2022).

9   Aside from some other films under consideration, such as *Nebraska*, among other treatments of intergenerational relationships are the movie *The Lion in Winter* (1968) and two TV series, *Me and My Grandma* (2017) and *A Man on the Inside* (2024). Among the other films that focus, among other themes, on reconciliation and rebirth are *Unforgiven* (1992), *Away from Her* (2006), *Amour* (2012), *Still Mine* (2012), *The Hundred-Year-Old Man Who Climbed Out the Window and Disappeared* (2013), *Birdman* (2014), *Still Alice* (2014), *Up* (2019), *Ford v. Ferrari* (2019), and *Jerry and Marge Go Large* (2022).

10 The film was based on Jennifer Weiner's novel *In Her Shoes* (Atria Books, 2002).

11 TreaAndrea M. Russworm, introduction to *From Madea to Media Mogul: Theorizing Tyler Perry*, ed. TreaAndrea M. Russworm, Samantha N. Sheppard, and Karen M. Bowdre (University Press of Mississippi, 2016), xiv.

12 Miriam J. Petty, epilogue to Russworm et al., *From Madea to Media Mogul*, 235.

13 Eric Pierson, foreword to Russworm et al., *From Madea to Media Mogul*, vii.

14 Russworm, introduction to *From Madea to Media Mogul*, v.

15 Tyler Perry's *Madea Gets a Job* (2013), YouTube, accessed December 10, 2024, www.youtube.com/watch?v=b5OlFmy_U7k.

16 There is extensive discussion about the treatment of Hmong peoples in *Gran Torino*, and among the best place to start is Louisa Schein, "Hmong Actors Making History Part 2: Met the Gran Torino Family," *Hmong Today*, October 4, 2008, https://web.archive.org.

17 "Bio," Jessica Bruder's website, accessed December 10, 2024, www.jessicabruder.com/bio.

18 Jessica Bruder, "The End of Retirement," *Harper's Monthly*, August 2008.

19 Jessica Bruder, *Nomadland: Surviving America in the Twenty-First Century* (Norton, 2017). Neither the film nor the movie adequately reflected the significant number of African Americans and Latinos who work in Amazon warehouses; in the book (*Nomadland*, 179–80), Bruder does discuss why so few nomads are African American.

20 Bruder, *Nomadland*, xiii, 7, 47, 54, 56.

21 Bruder, *Nomadland*, 7, 30.

22 Bruder, *Nomadland*, 247–48, 251.

23 Bruder, *Nomadland*, 39–40.

24 Caitlin Flanagan, "The Anti-Consumption Weirdos of *Nomadland*," *The Atlantic* May 5, 2021.

25 Stevie Trujillo, "Off-Road, Off-Grid: The Wandering Nomads Wandering America's Backcountry," *The Guardian*, February 4, 2021.

26 Among the most important analyses of the film, few, if any, of them focus significantly on the issue of retirement. See, for example, Arabella Cai, "'No, I'm Not Homeless. I'm Just Houseless': A Breakdown of *Nomadland*," NYU Comm Club, April 30, 2022, www.nyucommclub.com; Colin Grant, "On the Road Again: From Covered Wagons to Camper Vans: Twenty-First-Century Nomads in the US," *Times Literary Supplement*, February 26, 2021.

CODA

1 David S. Jones and Jeremy A Greene. "The Decline and Rise of Coronary Heart Disease: Understanding Public Health Catastrophism." *American Journal of Public Health* 103 (2013): 1207.

2 Statista, "Deaths by Cancer in the U.S. from 1950 to 2022," accessed December 10, 2024, www.statista.com.

3 Chappel, *Golden Year*, 293; for Chappel's guardedly optimistic discussion of the future for elders, see 279–96.

INDEX

DANIEL HOROWITZ is the Mary Huggins Gamble Foundation Chair and Professor of American Studies Emeritus at Smith College. Among his publications are *The Morality of Spending: Attitudes Toward the Consumer Society in America, 1875–1940*, selected by Choice as one of the outstanding academic books of 1985; *The Anxieties of Affluence: Critiques of American Consumer Culture, 1939–1979*, selected by Choice as one of the outstanding books of 2004 and winner of the Eugene M. Kayden Prize for the best book published in the humanities in 2004 by a university press; *Consuming Pleasures: Intellectuals and Popular Culture in the Postwar World*; *Reality TV's Shark Tank and the American Dream in Uncertain Times*; *American Dreams, American Nightmares: Culture and Crisis in Residential Real Estate from the Great Recession to the COVID-19 Pandemic*; and *Bear with Me: A Cultural History of Famous Bears in America*. Among the honors he has received are fellowships from the John Simon Guggenheim Memorial Foundation, two from the National Endowment for the Humanities, and one from the National Humanities Center, and an appointment as Honorary Visiting Fellow at the Schlesinger Library, Radcliffe College, Harvard University. As he writes this, he lives with his wife, the historian Helen Lefkowitz Horowitz, in Cambridge, Massachusetts. They are the parents of two children—Ben, a computer scientist in the Bay Area, and Sarah, a professor of history at Washington and Lee University.